GHOSTHUNTING
KENTUCKY

AMERICA'S
HAUNTED ROAD TRIP

Titles in the *America's Haunted Road Trip* Series:

GHOSTHUNTING
KENTUCKY

PATTI STARR

CLERISY PRESS

Published by Clerisy Press
Distributed by Publishers Group West
Printed in the United States of America
First edition 2010

Library of Congress Cataloging-in-Publication Data

Starr, Patti Acord.
  Ghosthunting Kentucky / by Patti Starr.
  p. cm.

  ISBN-13: 978-1-57860-352-7 (pbk.); ISBN-10: 1-57860-352-8 (pbk.)
  ISBN 978-1-57860-413-5 (ebook); ISBN 978-1-57860-590-3 (hardcover)

  1. Ghost—Kentucky. 2. Ghosts—Research—Methodology. I. Title.

  BF1472.U6S7325 2010
  133.109769—dc22
                                        2010020568

Editor: John Kachuba
Cover design: Scott McGrew
The photos in *Ghosthunting Kentucky* appear courtesy of: Buffalo Trace Distillery, pp. 21, 25; Jailer's Inn, p. 55; Lock and Key Café, p. 68; S.H.O.C.K./Jennifer Kirkland, p. 135; Nancy E. Moss, p. 154; Todd Matthews, p. 163; Tom Halstead, p. 187 and back cover; Misti Dawn Covey, p. 199; Coal Miners' Museum, p. 208; Toshimi Jenkins, p. 230. All other photos appear courtesy of the author.

Clerisy Press
An imprint of AdventureKEEN
306 Greenup Street
Covington, KY 41101
www.clerisypress.com

TABLE OF CONTENTS

EAST

Welcome to America's Haunted Road Trip

DO YOU BELIEVE IN GHOSTS?

If you are like 52 percent of Americans (according to a recent Harris Poll), you *do* believe that ghosts walk among us. Perhaps you have heard your name called in a dark and empty house. It could be that you have awoken to the sound of footsteps outside your bedroom door, only to find no one there. It is possible that you saw your grandmother sitting in her favorite rocker chair, the same grandmother who had passed away several years before. Maybe you took a photo of a crumbling, deserted farmhouse and discovered strange mists and orbs in the photo, anomalies that were not visible to your naked eye.

If you have experienced similar paranormal events, then you know that ghosts exist. Even if you have not yet experienced these things, you are curious about the paranormal world, the spirit realm. If you weren't, you would not now be reading this Preface to the latest book in the *America's Haunted Road Trip* series from Clerisy Press.

Over the last several years, I have investigated haunted locations across the country and with each new site, I found myself becoming more fascinated with ghosts. What are they? How do they manifest themselves? Why are they here? These are just a few of the questions I have been asking. No doubt, you have been asking the same questions.

The books in the *America's Haunted Road Trip* series can help you find the answers to your questions about ghosts. We've gathered together some of America's top ghost writers (no pun intended) and researchers and asked them to write about their states' favorite haunts. Each location that they write about is open to the public so that you can visit them for yourself and try out your ghosthunting skills. In addition to telling you about their often hair-raising adventures, the writers have included maps and travel directions so that you can take your own haunted road trip.

If you're planning on traveling through the hills and "hollers" of Kentucky, then Patti Starr's *Ghosthunting Kentucky* is just the guide you need for a paranormal tour of the Bluegrass State. While Kentucky is noted for its Thoroughbred racehorses and bourbon, spirits of another sort abound. Patti, a professional ghosthunter and founder of Ghost Chasers International, has been hot on their trail for many years. Ride shotgun with Patti as she seeks out pioneer ghosts at the old Boone Tavern in Berea and tries to communicate with spirits at the infamous Waverly Hills Sanitarium in Louisville. Stay close by her side as she searches for Civil War ghosts at the Perryville Battlefield and at nearby Maple Hill Manor, which was pressed into service as a field hospital for the Perryville wounded. Tag along with Patti to Bobby Mackey's Music World in Wilder as she tries to coax the boot-scootin' ghost of Johanna to make an appearance. Patti has visited all these spine-tingling haunted sites and plenty more. So, hang on tight; *Ghosthunting Kentucky* is a scary ride.

But once you've finished reading this book, don't unbuckle your seatbelt. There are still forty-nine states left for your haunted road trip! See you on the road!

John Kachuba
Editor, America's Haunted Road Trip

Central

Bardstown, Nelson County
Jailer's Inn Bed-and-Breakfast
The Old Talbott Tavern

Berea, Madison County
Boone Tavern

Berry, Harrison County
Mullins Log Cabin

Bloomfield, Nelson County
Springhill Winery Bed-and-Breakfast

Cynthiana, Harrison County
Rohs Opera House

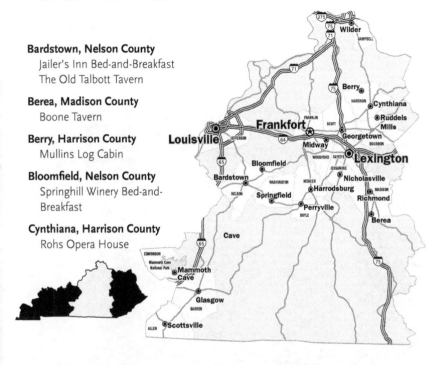

Frankfort, Franklin County
Buffalo Trace Distillery

Georgetown, Scott County
Lock and Key Cafe
Tent Girl, Georgetown Cemetery

Glasgow, Barron County
Hall Place Bed-and-Breakfast

Harrodsburg, Mercer County
Mud Meeting House and Cemetery

Lexington, Fayette County
Kentucky Theatre
Mansion at Griffin Gate Resort

Louisville, Jefferson County
Waverly Hills Sanatorium

Mammoth Cave, Edmonson County
Mammoth Cave National Park

Midway, Woodford County
Thoroughbred Community Theater

Nicholasville, Jessamine County
Planters Row Golf Course Clubhouse

Perryville, Boyle County
Perryville Battlefield State Historic Site

Richmond, Madison County
White Hall Historic House

Ruddells Mills, Bourbon County
Colville Covered Bridge

Scottsville, Allen County
The Haunted Hospital

Springfield, Washington County
Maple Hill Manor Bed-and-Breakfast

Wilder, Campbell County
Bobby Mackey's Music World

CHAPTER 1

Bobby Mackey's Music World
WILDER, CAMPBELL COUNTY

ONE OF THE MOST FREQUENTLY ASKED questions I get about ghosthunting in Kentucky is, "Have you ever investigated Bobby Mackey's place in Wilder, Kentucky?" Of all the sites that I have investigated, none can compare to the history of death, murder, and human sacrifice that is recorded at this locale. Over the years Bobby Mackey's Music World has become known as one of the most sinister and haunted spots in America. Its reputation for being inhabited by tormented entities derived from the bizarre history that surrounds the area. For about 120 years, this place has evolved from owner to owner with a history that includes murders, suicides, demonic rituals, and slaughtered animals.

I called one of my ghosthunter graduates, Susan Rushing, who lives within a few miles of Wilder, to ask her if she could help me get into Bobby Mackey's place for a ghost investigation and to interview some of the employees. Susan, a devoted ghost-hunter herself, graciously offered to make arrangements but held me hostage to my promise that she would be able to join us on the ghost investigation. She has a knack for accomplishing anything once she sets her mind to it. Susan, with her wit and charm, had no problems securing an appointment for our team to investigate this haunted Mecca.

We also invited Cynthia Spicer, another one of my gradu-ates, to go with us on the investigation. Even though Cynthia is a single mom raising two little girls, she still found time to work a ghosthunt. The three of us—Cynthia, Chuck, and I—headed out early in the day to meet Susan in Wilder before heading out for Bobby's by 3:00 P.M. We came close to canceling our trip to Wilder. A few days before we were scheduled to leave, Kentucky was hit by one of the most destructive ice storms since 2003. The roads were cleared, but the walkways and parking lots were still heavily covered in ice and snow. When we arrived in Wilder and got out of the car we had to hold on to each other for sta-bility as we started on the icy path to the front door of Bobby Mackey's. Before we had gotten too far, Bobby Mackey's PR/mar-keting manager, R.J., joined us. He was bundled in his thick, red coat, black hat, and plaid scarf in an attempt to ward off the bitter cold. He was worried that one of us might fall, so after a quick picture-taking session in front of our car, we headed for the inside of the building. R.J. loved the vanity license plate on our car, which sported the word "Ghosts," and made sure to get a picture of it for their Web site.

As I entered the main doors of the famous honky-tonk, I felt the energy crawl up my back and shoulders, as if I was being greeted by invisible creatures of the unknown. I later explained that eerie feeling to another one of my graduates, J.C. Harris, and he told me about the time he did an investigation at Mackey's a few months before me. He also had the same creepy feeling, which prompted him to raise his camera for quick snapshots of the entrance straight ahead. He captured an interesting mist accompanied by a faint purple spirit orb as he walked down the foyer.

Before continuing into the building, I looked to the right and saw a warning sign on the wall that stated the place was haunted, and, by entering at your own risk, the club would not be responsible if you were attacked by unseen forces. I thought it was a great marketing gimmick, but R.J. told me that someone tried to sue Bobby because they claimed they had been attacked by a ghost. The case was dismissed, but the management thought it would be best to warn others about the possible dangers.

R.J. shared with us some of the history of Mackey's as we proceeded into the belly of this haunted icon. Since the 1800s the building has sheltered many personalities, and some of them were not so good. R.J. said that for over forty years the building served as an animal slaughterhouse where the blood of the animals would drain into a well under the basement that flowed out to the nearby Licking River. Some people believed that satanic worshippers performed sacrificial rites on the property.

Several different clubs and lounges have occupied the space. After the slaughterhouse closed, it was not until the 1930s that another company opened for business. During the years that clubs and bars were in operation, there were numerous fights, attacks, and killings that surrounded the Primrose Country Club, the Latin Quarters, the Blue Grass Inn, and the Hard Rock Café. It was Bobby's intention to change all of that by bringing in a better type of entertainment when he opened Bobby Mackey's Music World in 1978.

R.J. told us that Bobby gave up the chance to record songs in Nashville to put all his time and money into his new country music bar. Bobby was already a well-known country singer in Kentucky with several popular albums to his credit and was looking forward to having his own place to perform.

As I was standing near the dimly lit bar listening to R.J. recount the past, I noticed a rather husky fellow wearing a dark hoody. He walked over to join us. He was Matt Coates, the building supervisor, but he sure looked more like a bouncer to me. I thought to myself, if there were any ghosts or demons haunting this place surely they would think twice before taking him on. I turned back to R.J. to ask him more questions, and he assured me that I would probably get a better account of the hauntings by talking to Matt. He had been with Bobby Mackey for five years and was there during most of the ghost investigations that had been performed at the club. I figured now was the best time to grab my digital audio recorder to chronicle his accounts of suspicious ghostly activity.

"So, Matt," I asked, "tell me about what you have witnessed here at Bobby Mackey's." Without hesitating Matt said, "One night while I was standing over by the mechanical bull, I saw a man sitting at one of the tables across the other side of the room. I started to walk over to see who he was and noticed that he was dressed like someone from the 1800s. As I approached him, he stood up, and even though it was dark, I could see that he had a mustache. He then turned and walked to the back door where he vanished." "What did you do next?" I said. "I packed up my tools and went home." "Did you ever see him again?" "Yes," Matt admitted, "but I guess I've gotten used to him, and I don't pay him any mind anymore."

I asked him if he had any idea of who the man might be, and he said he might be Scott Jackson or Alonzo Walling. He told me the story of these two dental students from Cincinnati who were part of an occult group called the Seven Hooded Ghost Men in the late 1800s. They would secretly meet in the abandoned slaughterhouse and perform rituals where they would sacrifice animals and mentally retarded children. They also killed Scott's girlfriend, Pearl Bryan, who was five months pregnant at the time, and after severing her head, they threw it down the well during a satanic ritual. They were both tried and found guilty of her murder and were hanged for this heinous crime. I gestured to my team, who were checking out the mechanical bull area for possible evidence, to go into the basement. We would proceed with the interview there.

The basement was huge, with many rooms to choose from, but our interest was in the room that contained the foreboding well. This supposed portal led into the depths of hell, where so many body parts had been banished during satanic rituals. Susan and Cynthia stopped immediately as we entered the room. I was already in the room when I heard Susan remark, "Wow!" I spun around to see what was the matter. Both women said they saw a thick mist, almost like a veil, before them, surrounding the room. Matt said that he, too, had seen this same phenomena many times, although at this particular time neither he nor I saw it. After Susan and Cynthia stepped into the room to join Matt and me, the mist vanished.

Matt pointed out a small room off to the side that he called the jail room. He said it was the room where the occultists put the children before they sacrificed them and threw them down the well. I went into the room and the others claimed that they saw a spirit orb fly around my head. Could this be a spirit from one of the children that had been thrown into the jail room?

Then Matt guided us over to an open doorway on the other side of the room, where stairs proceeded up to nowhere. I thought how bizarre that the stairs just led up to a plastered wall. It's possible that during Prohibition, bootleggers may have used the stairs to bring liquor up to the bar. They probably brought it up from the river so no one would catch them smuggling the illegal booze. There could have been a door leading to the outside that had been closed off in later years.

I saw that in one corner of the room the floor had been ripped up and the gruesome well opening was exposed. There was a barricade of wooden slats built in front of the well so no one would accidentally fall in. I asked Matt who ripped up the floor, and as he lifted his leg to brace himself on the barricade he answered, "Carl had a dream that Johanna came to him and pointed at the floor. She told him that if he would rip up the floor in the basement, he would find the well and her diary there."

"Who are Carl and Johanna?" I asked. Matt said that Carl Lawson was a maintenance man who'd been employed at Bobby's for a long time. He lived in an apartment above the club. He started seeing shadows and hearing disembodied voices shortly after he came to work there. It wasn't long until he started seeing a full-body apparition of a woman. Later, he claimed that he had conversations with her and that he thought the ghost's name was Johanna. She was a young woman who committed suicide after her boyfriend was murdered. She found out that her father, owner of the Latin Quarters, arranged to have her boyfriend, Robert Randall, killed so that they couldn't be together. She had met Robert Randall while he was a singer at the club and had fallen in love with him. Her father begged her to forget him, but she was bound and determined to marry him. Her father took things into his own hands and, with his mafia connection, had one of his gangsters kill him. After Johanna took her own life, they found her body in the basement in the same room that housed the well. She was five months pregnant.

I was struck by the coincidences: two women whose deaths were connected to the site of Mackey's nightclub and both were five months pregnant at the time of their deaths. Later on, during

my interview with Bobby, I found another interesting coincidence. Johanna's boyfriend's name was Robert Randall, and
Bobby Mackey's full name is Robert Randall Mackey. Bobby has
even written a song titled "Johanna" as a tribute to her life there.

I asked Matt if Bobby and his wife, Janet, had ever experienced any of the paranormal commotion, and he shared another
story with me about Janet. Shortly after they purchased the place,
Janet, who was pregnant at the time, went upstairs to clean the
apartment. She stopped in the middle of her work because she
thought she heard voices in the apartment. At first she couldn't
make out what they were saying. When she resumed her work,
they started talking again. Again, Janet stopped what she was
doing. The voices grew louder and spoke more clearly, and as
she listened, she understood them saying, "Get out of here." She
became very upset and started to leave the apartment. All of a
sudden, she felt invisible hands take a hold of her, preventing her
from leaving. She struggled and pulled away from the control-
ling force and ran for the stairs. Reaching for the railing, Janet
started down the stairs, but the enraged ghost pushed her. She
lost her footing and fell down the stairs. As she lay on her back
at the bottom of the stairs, she looked up to see a figure looking
down at her and then it walked away. The fall pushed Janet into
premature labor. The doctor was able to stop the labor, and her
healthy baby was born closer to the delivery date. Even though
Janet had experienced other strange happenings, such as doors
opening on their own, lights flickering with static sounds, and a
ladder that walked toward her, being pushed down the stairs was
enough for her. She vowed never to return to the place. However,
she did return to Bobby Mackey's Music World two years later to
help bartend on Friday and Saturday nights. She would clean up
quickly and leave as soon as her shift was over—and she would
never stay in the building alone.

We wrapped up our investigation, and two days later I called
Bobby Mackey to get his take on all the ghosts at his place. He

was every bit a gentleman and so kind to answer my questions. He told me right up front that he did not believe in ghosts. He assured me that nothing out of the ordinary had ever happened to him, even though Janet did have some incredible experiences. I asked him how he felt about having the same name as Johanna's boyfriend. He said that it was a strange coincidence, but nothing more than that.

Unlike Bobby, Janet felt that Johanna was the one who pushed her, since Janet was also pregnant—here again, another coincidence. Janet also married a man with the name Robert Randall, the same name as Johanna's boyfriend. The ghost might have believed that Janet's husband, Bobby, was her boyfriend reincarnated. Janet admitted to Bobby that she thought that Johanna attacked her because of jealousy towards her. A couple of days after talking to Bobby, I called R.J. to get a few more details for my story. He told me that Janet had passed away only the day before. I was truly shocked and asked if she had been sick. He explained that Janet had suffered with COPD (Chronic Obstructive Pulmonary Disease) for some time but had it under control with medication. She had gone to her daughter's house to baby-sit her grandchildren while her daughter and son-in-law went out on a Valentine's Day date. When they returned, they asked Janet if she was going to bed, and she replied that she wanted to stay up and watch TV for a while. The following morning they found Janet slumped over on the couch as if she had fallen asleep while watching TV. When they tried to wake her, they realized that she had passed away some time during the night. "At least Janet was able to spend her last hours with her grandchildren, whom she loved and adored with all her heart," R.J. said.

I dedicate this chapter to this loving and devoted woman, Janet Mackey, who was loved by all who knew her. Janet Mackey had been married to Bobby for forty-two years and was only a couple of days short of her sixty-first birthday.

CHAPTER 2

Boone Tavern
BEREA, MADISON COUNTY

WHEN I FIRST MOVED to Bardstown, Kentucky, in 1995, I met a talented and unique young lady of twelve, Shoshana Gross. I was a member of the Bardstown Community Theater(BCT), and Shoshana's mom, Tova, was also a member there. Once Shoshana and I met, we became instant friends. Occasionally I would arrange to spend time with her on weekends. She was extremely talented, with her musical skills of writing songs and playing the guitar, which kept me entertained on our weekends together. Shoshana is quite the success now as she lives with her husband in Scotland.

One day Shoshana called me to let me know that she had decided to go to Berea College, located in Berea, Kentucky. I was not familiar with the college until Shoshana shared with me the history. The college was founded about 150 years ago by Reverend John Gregg Fee. He was a strong believer in equality by providing interracial and co-educational advantages for students in the Appalachian area. The town literally developed around the college.

"How will you be able to afford to go there?" I asked. Shoshana replied, "This is the beauty of it. Berea offers a tuition-free education. The money is provided by donations and other monetary means. Because of my good grades and high scores, I qualify to go there." I congratulated her, and she said, "I have some more great news. There is an old hotel there called Boone Tavern that is supposed to be haunted." Okay, now she really had my attention. I asked her, "What do you know about it?" "When I got into town I read about it in a brochure I picked up at the hotel. The Boone Tavern was built in 1909 to provide guests with lodging and meals while they were visiting the president of Berea College. As the number of visitors grew, so did the tavern, and it has been offering lodging ever since. During my short stay in Berea, I did hear stories from the students and locals that the tavern was haunted but didn't have time to listen to all the stories. I knew I had to call you so you could check it out," Shoshona replied.

Shortly after getting this lead, I did just as Shoshana had suggested and made arrangements to conduct a ghost investigation. I was the first official ghosthunter to go into Boone Tavern with such a task. I wanted our investigation to be as thorough as possible, so I decided to bring in a psychic/medium, Ginny Drake. She has worked in the field of education for over thirty years and holds a master's degree in education from Georgetown College, a teaching certificate from Eastern Kentucky University, and a B.S. in social work from Murray State University. Ginny had become my mentor while teaching me to work with energies, so I felt she would be an asset to the investigation. I must say that when we arrived and parked in front of the Boone Tavern, I was impressed with the grandeur and magnificence of the Southern Colonial hotel and restaurant. As I stood looking at all the scrolled details and other features, I was fascinated to learn that the bricks used in the construction of the building in 1909 were made by the students attending Berea College.

Built on a prominent location, the hotel sits where the old Dixie Highway intersected with the campus of Berea College. This highway was planned as one of the first automobile highways in 1914 and was constructed to connect the Midwest to the Southern states. This was also another factor in the growth of Berea and the popularity of the Boone Tavern. Laden with bags of ghosthunting equipment, we made our way into the lobby of the hotel. We approached the front desk to let the staff know that we were ready to start our investigation. The front desk clerk looked at the registry to find where the empty rooms were. She gave us several keys to rooms on the second and third floors for us to enter during our investigation.

While we were standing in front of the registry desk, Ginny asked me to come and stand by her. I walked over to her, and, wham, it hit me. We were standing in what I would refer to as an energy vortex. It felt like there was an oscillating energy field spinning in a spiral motion, making me a little giddy. I enjoy finding these spots that tend to make me rock back and forth when I stand in the middle of one. There is more than one theory about how these vortices evolve, but I feel it may have to do with the energy of the land coming up through the building. Ginny asked the desk clerk what area was immediately below where she was standing. She told us it was the basement. Ginny looked at me and said, "We must go down there before we leave. I think we might get some good evidence there."

I bent down to retrieve my bags, and Ginny said, "I'm picking up on a young child." She hesitated and then continued, "It is a young boy. I think he is about nine years old. He likes playing tricks on the staff." I turned to look at the clerk, and she was smiling. "Yes," the clerk said. "We have heard of sightings of a little boy from our guests and staff over the years." At that point Ginny predicted that we might get some more information about the little boy if we went to the basement right away.

We headed to the basement to see what might happen, and we captured a special spirit orb and a child's voice. We found the energy vortex and stood in that area as we took snapshots with our cameras and performed a couple of EVP sessions. Ginny began to communicate with the playful and happy child. I asked Ginny to hold up her hands as I instructed the little boy to show himself around her hands. As I continued to talk to him, I snapped a shot with my camera and captured a spirit orb close to Ginny. What makes this capture so unique is that the orb is behind an object, which contradicts the theory that all orbs are dust reflecting back as globe-shaped anomalies in the flash of the camera. If that were the case, this orb would be in front of the barrier instead of behind it, revealing only half of its shape. This was a rare and super capture of a spirit orb. We continued to talk to the little boy, and behind us a box scooted across the floor and startled us. We swung around, and no one was there. We laughed and thanked the little boy for causing the commotion. I asked him if he would speak to us, and I captured an EVP of a child's voice that said, "I can see you." This spry spirit was having fun with us, and Ginny said she felt he must have lived in the early part of the 1900s. I thought that he might have been a child of one of the earlier staff members when the hotel first opened. It felt to me that he was allowed to play throughout the building while his parents worked. Ginny and I agreed that he was of African American descent. Since this was a place where one could be who they were without the fear of judgment about race or gender, I'm sure the atmosphere here was one of comfort and joy.

We didn't want to spend our entire two hours in the basement, so we ventured to the second and third floors to check out the other rooms. We stepped into the elevator and started our journey to the top. As the elevator was moving, I said, " Did you know that I was in a falling elevator once?" Just as I said that the elevator stopped abruptly between two floors and started to jerk as if it were going to fall. Everyone gasped and looked at me. The elevator made another attempt to readjust itself to the next floor and jerked again. I said, "When I get off this elevator, I'm taking the stairs down." It finally leveled with the third floor as the doors opened to let us out. When we returned to the front desk, I asked the clerk if there had been reports that the elevator dropped or jerked before getting to the top floor. She looked puzzled and said, "Not since I've been here, and I've been here for over four years."

The rest of our investigation continued on the second floor, as we entered the different rooms to see what we could find. After about four rooms, we went into one where I picked up on a male ghost through my dowsing rods. He didn't know he had died and seemed to be confused as I continued to ask yes and no questions. Ginny was standing by the bed and noticed an indention, as if someone had been lying on the bed. She told us that the ghost just sat up in bed and asked her, "What are you doing here?" She continued to communicate with him until he was calmer, and then he left the room. We concluded our investigation and took the stairs to go back to the lobby. The staff was interested in knowing if we had gotten any results from our equipment. I shared with them the EVP I had gotten of the little boy who said, "I can see you." They were thrilled to hear it.

In 2010, I thought it would be nice to do a follow-up on the hauntings at Boone Tavern. I learned that a few months earlier, a

The spirit orb of the little boy hiding behind a barrier was photographed near Ginny as she called him forward.

renovation of Boone Hall was completed to preserve and enhance the historic character of the hotel. The Boone Tavern has earned the Leadership in Energy and Environmental Design (LEED) certification from the U.S. Green Building Council. I couldn't help but wonder if the paranormal activity increased during this time and thought an investigation would be in order.

I called the manager, Gary McCormick, and he was open to having me do another ghost investigation. I arrived at 9:30 on a blistering cold and snowy morning. As I opened the entryway door to the tavern, I could see the wonderful new decor and colors that complimented the expansive lobby. The deep gem colors of blue and gold were rich, warm, and inviting. I loved all the changes and could hardly wait for lunch to check out the menu.

We were greeted by a wonderful staff, and I was impressed to see the bellman dressed in a sharp, top-notch, white uniform that made him look distinctive and proud. His name was Fred

Baker. He informed us that Gary was running late because he was held up by the snow. Two other employees, Anita Ridgeway and Tucker Collins, were standing next to Fred. Anita was gracious and offered us coffee while we waited for Gary. While we were drinking our coffee, I explained to them that I had completed a ghost investigation in 2005 and wanted to check to see if the same type of activity was still present. I asked Anita, "Do you have any knowledge of strange activity that might be the result of a haunting?" She answered, "I have witnessed a few things that I can't explain how or why they happened. There is a common occurrence in the dining room that has us baffled. Several servers will be setting up the tables with napkins and silverware when the silverware will start to drop onto the floor in a domino effect as it goes from one server to another. It's as if a small child is having fun by running from one server to the other and knocking off the silverware.""Have you ever heard of a guest having an experience?" I asked. "Yes, I have," she answered. "I was standing by the front desk one morning when a woman came down dressed and ready to check out. It was early, around 5:00, and we thought it was strange to have someone checking out so early. The lady explained to us that while she was asleep, she was awakened by a touch on the hand. When she sat up in her bed, there was a man in her room. As she focused on him, he disappeared. That's when she got up, got dressed, and got out of the room. She was a bit shaken. I believe the woman was in Room 206."

When I heard about this account, I thought that Ginny was going to be thrilled to hear this story since we were in Room 206 when we found the male ghost that didn't know he had passed away. I thanked everyone for their stories and walked over to the front desk. I asked a pretty young lady, with a big smile, if she would be willing to do an interview about the hauntings of the hotel. She told me that she was the desk clerk and her name was

Jordan Perry. "Jordan, can you tell me what you have observed while working at the Boone Tavern?" I asked. "Well," she started with hesitation, "on my third night of training, I was sitting here at the desk by myself. It was around 2:00 in the early morning when I heard a crash coming from the Skylight Room. Since the hotel was so quiet, it really startled me. I wanted to find out what made the sound, so I went into the room to see what had happened. As I looked around, there was no one in the room, but I did see the big black ice scooper lying on the floor. The scooper is kept on top of the ice-maker machine. I know it causes a vibration when it is running, but the scooper had landed all the way across the room from where the ice machine was. When I asked the other kitchen staff if this had happened before, they laughed and said that it happens a lot. That's when I started to suspect this place of being haunted." I asked Jordan, "Have you ever seen or heard what you thought might be a ghost?" "Yes," she quickly answered. "One morning while standing at the desk and check-ing on room availability, I heard a little boy laugh. I looked up to see if a child had come into the lobby, but there was no little boy. I looked back down at my computer to start my search and heard the sound of a little boy laughing again. This time I noticed that the sound came from the Skylight Room, where the ice machine is. I guess that room gets a lot of activity. There have been other times during the day and night that I've heard him laughing in the lobby. Several times I've heard the sound of someone run-ning back and forth in front of the desk and on those stairs, " she said, pointing to the stairs behind me. Jordan added, "Everyone who works here seems to know of the little boy. They think he's around nine or ten years old. He seems to be happy and very mischievous."

While Jordan was telling her accounts of the activity, Fred walked up behind us. He informed us that he would be join-ing us when we went upstairs into the guest rooms. We were

Fred Baker standing in the middle of the vortex near the front desk

delighted to have his assistance. He also asked us if we would mind doing him a favor. "What do you want us to do?" I asked. Fred said, "Please stand right here and tell me what you feel." Fred had Chuck stand in an area in front of the desk. As Chuck stepped into the spot, Fred noticed that he started to rock back and forth. "Do you see Chuck rocking?" he asked. This brought back memories of my first visit to Boone Tavern when Ginny had discovered the energy as a vortex. I asked Fred how long he had been employed at the Boone Tavern, and he said about two years. That told me that he did not learn about the vortex from us, since he wasn't there the first time we came. I asked Fred, "How did you find out about the vortex?" He said, "I discovered the energy by walking through the area and noticing the pull it had on my body."

By now Gary had arrived, and after our introductions, I was able to continue my interview with him in the comfort of a big, padded chair in the lobby. I said to Gary, "Tell me what you have experienced since you became the general manager of the Boone Tavern." Gary began, "When I came here in 2007, many of the employees told me about hearing the little boy laugh and seeing him standing behind them in the freight elevator. At first I was a skeptic and didn't pay much attention to their stories. My office was on the second floor before the renovation, and sometimes at night I did hear footsteps outside my office door. When I would go to see who was walking around, there would be no one there. Sometimes, while sitting in my office, I would hear paper shuffling or rustling, and when I would turn to see what was making that sound, there would be nothing there, and the paper was not moving either."

Gary asked us if we wanted to go up to the second floor where he could show us where he had his experiences. We picked up our equipment bags and headed for the second floor. When we got there Gary pointed down the hall and said, "Before the renovation started, we had the furniture removed from the rooms. I went down this hall to the room at the end to check on things after the movers left, and I could hear the boards in the floor squeak. I didn't hear footsteps, but instead I heard the sound that the boards would make if someone were walking on them. I turned and said out loud, 'I guess it's you and me. I know this place is going through some changes, but we promise to keep its charm.' I thought that if anyone could hear me talking to these unseen figures, they would think I was crazy."

As we walked toward the stairs, Gary asked if we would mind taking the stairs back down. Later, at home, when I played back my recorder to listen to my interviews, I picked up an EVP of the little boy. After I say that we have no problem taking the stairs, the little boy's voice can be heard saying, "No problem." I was extremely pleased to have captured the unexpected EVP of him.

Gary took us down into the basement so he could show me where he had a bold encounter with the little ghost boy. He said, "I was standing here in front of the caged area when I heard the loud laughter of a small boy behind me. The hair on the back of my neck stood straight up, and I swung around quickly, expecting to see a little boy, and, of course, there was nothing there. Feeling a little unnerved, I went upstairs to the kitchen, and as I entered the room, the ice scooper that was sitting on top of the ice maker came flying across at me and barely missed my head. I walked up to one of the kitchen staff and told them about the little boy laughing, and she said, 'Wait until the ice scooper hits you in the head.' Then I immediately told them that I had just witnessed the ice scoop flying over my head a moment ago."

By now it was getting close to lunch time, so we decided to finish our investigation and have lunch at the restaurant. The food was a delicious Southern style, and I had the fried green tomato salad. It was truly yummy. Of course, the biggest treat was the spoon bread that they brought out in a basket and served by dipping a big spoon into a soft cornbread pie and placing it on your plate. It has a great history and has been served as part of the meal since Boone Tavern opened in 1909.

Before we finished our lunch, I looked up and there stood the chef beside our table. He had seen us come in and recognized us from long ago. I was shocked to see that it was Jeff Newman, who was now the executive chef. For years he had been the chef at another haunted establishment known as the Mansion at Griffin Gate in Lexington, Kentucky. We began to compare notes about the different hauntings, and I thought it was weird that he would end up in both places as the chef. You might call our meeting a coincidence, but since this type of thing happens to me so often, I no longer believe in coincidence. It was also a wonderful conclusion to a successful day of ghosthunting at the Boone Tavern.

CHAPTER 3

Buffalo Trace Distillery
FRANKFORT, FRANKLIN COUNTY

A GOOD FRIEND OF MINE, Fiona Young-Brown, an author from the Bluegrass State, called me one evening for an interview. I had met Fiona a couple of years ago through her husband, another friend of mine. She explained that she was writing an article for the September issue of *Kentucky Monthly* about haunted distilleries. "Patti," she said in her English accent, "when I got this assignment, the first person that came to mind was you." I told Fiona that I had completed two ghost investigations of a distillery named Buffalo Trace with great success and would love to share my story with her. At one time there were many bourbon distilleries located in the limestone-enriched soil of Kentucky, but now only eight distilleries are left: Buffalo Trace, Four Roses, Heaven Hill, Jim Beam, Maker's Mark, Tom Moore, Wild Turkey, and Woodford Reserve. They can be found on the world-famous Kentucky Bourbon Trail, a fun excursion and a way to learn about the heritage of Kentucky bourbon. According to the Kentucky Distillers Association, about 95 percent of the world's bourbon is made in Kentucky from traditional recipes from master distillers that have been handed down through the generations. Buffalo Trace took its name from the huge herds of buffalo that formerly roamed Kentucky, carving paths, called "traces," through the wilderness. In the late 1700s pioneers came to a wide area that had been cleared out by the buffalo on the banks of the Kentucky River. A distillery was started there in 1787, and it is known today as Buffalo Trace Distillery.

When I first got the call from Theresa, a former employee at Buffalo Trace, inviting us to investigate the distillery, I remembered that I had a student, Bobbie Vereeke, whose husband also worked there. Bobbie told me that her husband knew about the ghosts that haunt several of the buildings on the property. While she was a student in my ghosthunter course, Bobbie shared with me her unusual talent for automatic writing, in which a spirit takes control of her hand and writes out messages. I knew she would be a great asset to the investigation since she used that method to communicate with the spirits.

I organized a group of forty ghosthunters from my organization to investigate the distillery. When we arrived on the property we drove through the entrance into a beautiful, natural, and rustic setting. It wasn't hard to imagine herds of buffalos grazing along the traces that lay before us as we circled around to the back of the original main house to the company parking lot below.

When we met our tour guide, she asked us if we wanted to know the history first or did we want to wait until after the investigation. I like to go into an investigation without being briefed about the place beforehand so that if a name or event is revealed to us, we will not be influenced by it until it is later validated through reliable sources. We opted not to get the history until after our investigation and went forth with our ghosthunt.

The guide led us up to the main house, called Stony Point Mansion, since that was where so many of the employees had experienced unexplainable and illogical activity. With our cameras, camcorders, audio recorders, and EMF meters in hand we started our investigation, moving down the hall towards the back of the house. My EMF meter started to register a disturbance by beeping and flashing a red light. I wanted to electric dowse with the EMF meter so I asked the invisible entity to stop making the meter go off by backing away. The meter came to an abrupt stop. I thanked the spirit and asked it if it would answer my questions by making the meter beep for "yes" and remain quiet for "no." It beeped once to agree. This is a method I call electric dowsing. The tour guide was delighted to see this result. I asked if the spirit was a female, and the meter remained silent. I asked if it was a male, and the meter immediately beeped twice for "yes." Several gasps came from the group. I continued to ask yes and no questions in order to find out as much as I could about this personality that was coming through for us. When the session was over I asked our guide if she had any idea who we might be communicating with. She replied, "All of the information that was validated through the meter matches that of a former president by the name of Colonel Blanton. When Blanton was sixteen years old, he started to work at the distillery, and by the time he was twenty-four he became president of the whiskey plant. His leadership allowed the company to survive the Great Depression, the Great Flood of 1937, and World War II. His love for people and the company inspired him to build a clubhouse so that employees could have a place for social and community functions. All the employees wanted to work hard and please Colonel Blanton."

We left the first floor of the mansion and descended into the basement to see what else our instruments would reveal. This time, Bobbie Vereeke felt a strange urge to go into one of the back offices. She sat down at the desk with pen and pad and went into a mild trance so she could give in to the movement of her hand. Soon the writing began. It was amazing to see the words start to appear across her pad. After the session was over she revealed that she had been in communications with a lady named Anna, a former employee of Colonel Blanton. She wanted to make sure all was well at the distillery. Her job had been to keep the place clean, "spic-and-span" were the words Bobbie wrote, and to keep the Colonel happy. Anna's words read, "I worked here. I don't have anywhere else to go. He was a great man and I just want to please him."

We left the basement and headed for another building, known as the Riverside house, opposite the boiler room. This house was built in 1792 and is the oldest recorded building still standing in Franklin County. The house is being renovated, but at the time of our investigation it was in a deteriorated condition. We were not allowed to go inside for fear of injury, so we stood at the doorway and took pictures of the shabby structure's interior. As we backed away from the house, I looked up and saw a face looking down at us from the second floor. I pointed my camera and took a shot but was not able to capture the face in the photo. Another member of my group took a shot and got a faint outline that appeared to be someone looking back at us. It was a good piece of evidence in the camera, but it just didn't show up once we printed it out on paper.

It has been over eight years since I did that investigation at Buffalo Trace, so I thought I would call to see if any of the employees were still experiencing any ghostly activity. After

The Riverside Home is a place where apparitions and EVPs have been captured.

introducing myself and explaining the reason for my call, I was routed to Angela Traver, the public relations manager. Angela was attentive and once I asked her if she had experienced any type of paranormal activity, she was gracious enough to share her story with me.

Angela's office is located in the sunroom of Stony Point Mansion. It was a wintery morning, still dark, when she arrived at her office. Soon after entering the room, she sat her computer case on the floor beside her desk so that she could remove her coat and scarf. As she bent down she saw a tall, dark figure pass by on her right side. She jerked round and quickly reached for the light switch to see who else was in the room. Once the light was turned on, she could see that the room lay quiet before her with no sign of a dark figure. She told me, "Knowing that Colonel Blanton was a tall thin man, and the fact that he died in this same room, made me think that maybe he was still making

A spirit orb is captured when Patti asked the spirit to come to her hand.

his rounds in the manor. I was okay with that thought and proceeded to get ready for the day's business."

On the last leg of our investigation, we entered the Buffalo
Trace Gift Shop. The sales staff gathered around us to tell us about
the weird experiences they had had while working in the shop.
Most of them agreed that the most common occurrence was the
sound of footsteps above the gift shop. It sounded as if three or
four men were walking around wearing heavy boots. The area
above the shop was a storage space. No one was assigned to that
area unless they were adding more items to storage. Sometimes,
the employees would hear the sounds of objects being dragged
across the floor. They said that sometimes it sounded as if the
items in storage were being rearranged, even though there was
no one on the second floor at that time.

Our group was anxious to get started upstairs. As we ascended
the stairs we were met with a blanket of hot still air that took my

breath away. It was roasting up there. I didn't know how long we could last in such heat, so we started immediately gathering evidence. Bobbie held her notebook in her hand, and I took pictures as I recorded my requests of the spirits to speak. My husband, Chuck, took a picture of me just as I asked the spirits to come to me, and he captured the image of a spirit orb hovering over me. I glanced over at Bobbie and saw that she was starting to write. I went over to where she was standing and looked over her shoulder to see what information she was getting. It was hard to make out some of the words, but she later translated them for us. This is what she wrote: "Must be careful here. We know that it is hot, but you need to spend time . . . ." and the message stopped. Then it started back up again: "Four of us are here for work. The big man came to see us daily. He wants to make sure things are done right." There was another break in the writing and then she continued again: "John, Amos, Fred, and Ralph." Another pause: "There are secrets in this building. You can find them, but you must look carefully. I found them long ago and protected them. The stone walls are built to hide . . . ." There, the communication stopped.

By this time most of us were about to pass out from the heat. I knew it would not be good for any of us to remain there any longer, so we concluded our investigation and returned to the gift shop below. It was a super experience for all of us. The best part was hearing all the stories and experiences of the employees that helped validate the data that we collected while investigating the distillery.

Colonel Blanton passed away in 1959, after spending over fifty-five years doing what he loved best, in the home he loved the most. During his time at the distillery, he went from being office boy to company president, and he was credited with preserving and enhancing one of Kentucky's historic landmarks. It seems as though the Colonel has made Buffalo Trace Distillery a paranormal landmark as well.

CHAPTER 4

Colville Covered Bridge
RUDDELLS MILLS, BOURBON COUNTY

ONE AFTERNOON I DROVE to Collectors Gallery, where Chuck was waiting for me to pick him up for lunch. I went inside the building to get him, and while I was walking down the hall I noticed a new art photo hanging on the wall ahead of me. It caught my interest right away because it was a collection of old covered bridges photographed by one of my favorite Lexington photographers, Jeff Rogers. I have always found covered bridges fascinating whether they were haunted or not. Folklore is full of eerie tales about such bridges. It's fitting to hear scary stories of unearthly specters appearing on these bridges because the bridges are a passage for crossing over to the other side.

While I was studying the photo of the bridges, I came across the name of the Colville Covered Bridge. I remembered one of my students, Eddie Rassenfoss, from Paris, Kentucky, telling me about this covered bridge. He claimed it was haunted. As Chuck walked up to me to let me know that he was ready to go, I said, "Road trip, it's time to go and check out Colville Bridge to see how haunted it really is."

In the late 1700s covered bridges were being built in small towns all over Kentucky. At one point there were over four hundred of these magnificent wooden, covered passages that provided protection for travelers, wagons, cargo, and cattle as they crossed a river or creek. Of all these bridges, there are only thirteen left, and of the thirteen, only four are still open to vehicular traffic. Most of these covered bridges were lost to fire, burned by troops on both sides during the Civil War. Today, all the remaining covered bridges are listed with the National Registry of Historic Places.

Stories are told about the bridges as stages for hanging a slave, or hacking off someone's head, or losing control of a car and crashing into the water below. There are bridge stories about Civil War ambushes and unwanted babies tossed into the water. Such incidents are the source for many ghost stories. I called the Kentucky Heritage Council and State Historic Preservation Office and spoke to Patrick Kennedy. He was extremely helpful in providing me with the facts about the Colville Covered Bridge. It was built in 1877 by Jacob Bower, and it traverses over Hinkston Creek in Bourbon County. The bridge featured truss construction and a multiple king post style with a single 124-foot span. During this era the Kentucky wilderness was covered with an abundance of poplar trees, so the truss structure was built with poplar timbers. After many years, the bridge was in dire need of repairs and was restored by Louis Bower in 1913. His son, Stock, restored and raised the bridge to its present height in 1937. Sadly, the rough-hewn structure that served its community so well was dismantled in 1997 and had to be totally rebuilt. It didn't open to traffic again until 2001.

I contacted Eddie since he knew about the ghost stories connected to the bridge, and he had conducted several ghost investigations there. I asked him to tell me some of the ghost stories he'd heard about the bridge.

Eddie said, "Back in the 1930s or so, a young woman and her boyfriend were driving home from their high school prom. It's not clear if they had been drinking or if they just weren't paying attention, but for some reason, the young man lost control of the car just before entering the covered bridge. He swerved and the car plunged into the waters below. The next morning it was reported that the two of them had drowned. Some time after their deaths, stories about travelers seeing mysterious and unexplained lights coming from underneath the bridge started to surface. These stories started rumors about the bridge being haunted. Curious youths began to come to the bridge to see if they could witness these bizarre lights appearing around the bridge. They would wait until dark and then drive their cars to the center of the bridge to see what would happen. After a while they would notice what looked like car headlights coming up from behind their car. When they turned around to see the lights, the lights would disappear. Moments later lights would shine through the bottom of the bridge as if a car had gone into the creek, and the car lights were shining up through the water."

I asked Eddie what kind of evidence he recorded during investigations at the bridge. "I love to come here and get EVPs," he said. He told me about one of his investigations where he parked his truck in the center of the bridge to see if he could witness the lights. His mini audio cassette player was recording in the seat beside him. As he patiently waited for something to happen, he thought he heard a rustling sound that seemed to come from behind his seat. He glanced in his rearview mirror and thought he saw something behind him and, for a split second, thought about getting the heck out of there. Then he asked, "Is there a sweet spirit in this truck with me?" He waited a few seconds, to give the ghost time to answer, and then he rewound the tape in his audio recorder to see if the ghost had answered. He played back the question, and within a few seconds he got a very breathy "Yeessss." It sounded like a female's voice, so he thought he might have captured the voice of the girl who had drowned on her prom night.

This experience ignited Eddie's desire to find out all he could about the bridge. He began to ask people in his community if they knew of any death associated with the bridge. He was told by one of his friends that in the 1970s, a teenager had hanged himself in the middle of the bridge from one of the high rafters. The father of Eddie's friend was ten years old when he heard police sirens heading out to the bridge one evening. Then he found out the next day that the police had discovered a teenage boy hanging from the rafters. Another story that Eddie uncovered was about an elderly lady who was walking across the bridge and fell ill and died before she could get across. Her name was Ms. Mitchell and the date of the incident was 1933.

Feeling confident that he had enough information to try another EVP session, Eddie and a friend went back to the bridge. To his amazement, he captured sixteen EVPs during his question session. Each time he would ask a question, he would stop the recorder to see if there was an answer. He continued this procedure for a couple of hours, and even though he did not get a response to every question, he got a lot more than he had anticipated. One of Eddie's first questions was, "What was the name of the boy who hung himself in 1977?" After a few seconds he played the recorder back and heard a whisper that sounded like "Jonathan." He stopped the tape and pressed record again and asked, "Is your name Jonathan, yes or no?" Again, he listened to his recorder to see if there was an answer and got another whisper, "Yes." He continued with five more questions but didn't get any more answers. Patience is one of the biggest assets a ghosthunter can have, and Eddie was quick to learn this lesson.

Eddie was pleased with the results he had gotten with this investigation and decided to return another night. On his return, he didn't get any responses during his EVP session until he started home and decided to ask questions while his friend drove the truck. He asked, "Are you inside the car or outside?" He got a response, "Outside." He continued and asked, "What side of the car are you on?" The response was, "Your side." Eddie was a little creeped out about this and wanted to find out who this ghost was. He asked the entity to identify itself but after about three more attempts, there was no response. With his patience growing thin he commanded, "If there is someone here, say something or forever hold your peace." He was shocked at the reply: "Get out of the car." He explained to the ghost that he was not getting out of the car and continued with more questions, but didn't get an answer until he started to ask some questions about Ms. Mitchell. He found out through the answers that were coming through the recorder that Ms. Mitchell had been riding with them in their truck when they would leave the bridge for home. She admitted that she liked talking to Eddie but also wanted him to take her back to the bridge.

Once I had collected my information about this haunted location, Chuck and I drove to the Colville Bridge by the way of Paris Pike, one of the most scenic roadways in the Kentucky Bluegrass Region. This quiet route affords spectacular views of horse farms amidst the historic rock fences that line the road for twelve miles. These classic natural beauties reminded me of the stone fences I passed as I traveled the roadways while I lived in Scotland, and there is good reason for that. The rock fences of Kentucky were first constructed by Scotch-Irish who brought this tradition of dry stone masonry from their country and used slave labor and Irish immigrants to build these barriers. What I find so amazing about these fences is that they are constructed without using any mortar. The secret lies in the skill of how they are stacked, so that the force of gravity and frictional resistance holds them in place. If they are built correctly, these fences will be resistant to fire, water, insects, and earthquake and can last up to 150 years.

A blanket of shadows formed around us as we entered the blackness of night along the country road. We turned off onto a more primitive road, and shortly the headlights revealed a bright white-and-green covered bridge directly before us. Why was it painted white and green? I learned from Patrick that when these bridges were built, it was decided to give each state its own bridge color. Kentucky chose white and green.

We pulled off the road and stopped before entering the bridge. I grabbed my flash light and left the car to go stand in the middle of the bridge. It was a cool October evening with a slight breeze that carried the scent of the water below. There was no moon that night so the only light that brightened my path was the torch in my hand. Chuck called out from the car, "Hey, Patti, don't go too far, I don't want to lose sight of you." I yelled back, "I'm okay, don't worry about me!" and at that moment I felt a slight touch on my shoulder. I jerked around and flashed the light towards where I was standing. Nothing was there. Just about that time, a set of headlights came up behind me, and as I turned I could see that it was the rest of my investigation team. I had decided to invite Pete Eclov and Mary Beth to join us at the bridge. They were two of my newer ghosthunters and needed to get more experience in the field. I knew their expectations

Patti captured this spirit orb hovering near Chuck Starr and Pete Eclov as Pete recorded an EVP that says, "Yes," when Patti asked if Ms. Mitchell was present.

would run high, which, to me, seems to render better results on a ghost investigation. It sure did pay off because we started to get results as soon as we began gathering our data.

After we had discussed some of the bridge legends, which included the teenage couple who drowned under the bridge and Ms. Mitchell, we decided to turn on our EMF meters, recorders, and the Ovilus. While walking down the center of the bridge, our EMF meters started beeping, alerting us to a disturbance in the electromagnetic field. Even though the disruption only lasted for a couple of minutes, we were able to get responses to a few of our yes and no questions. The Ovilus, which indicates energy through reciting words, started to talk shortly after the meters registered. As I lifted the Ovilus up, it spouted out, "Car lights," and we looked at each other in amazement, since one of the stories involved car lights coming up behind a parked car on the bridge.

Then I asked if Ms. Mitchell could come through, and shortly after that question the Ovilus said, "Sarah Mitchell." This name is not programmed into the vocabulary of the Ovilus, so you can understand our astonishment. Mary Beth said, "Are you here with us, Ms. Mitchell?" Pete decided to rewind his audio recorder to see if we got a response to the question. Sure enough, we heard a woman's voice clearly answer "yes" to Mary Beth's question.

I always tell people that I do not have proof that ghosts exist, but I've been known to get some pretty convincing evidence. I feel the evidence we collected that night at the bridge was a good indication that the Covered Colville Bridge is definitely haunted and worth the trip to investigate.

CHAPTER 5

Hall Place Bed-and-Breakfast
GLASGOW, BARREN COUNTY

ON OUR WAY TO SCOTTSVILLE, to speak at the Allen
County Public Library and complete a ghost investigation of
The Haunted Hospital, Chuck and I arrived in Glasgow and
checked into our place of lodging. David Dinwiddie, owner of
The Haunted Hospital, had graciously booked us at Hall Place,
which is about twenty miles from Scottsville. I told him I was
looking for places to write about in my next book, and he felt
that we would love this old historic and possibly haunted bed-
and-breakfast.

Glasgow is located in and is the county seat of Barren County,
Kentucky. It was established in 1799 and was named Glasgow by
John Matthews, who was from Glasgow, Scotland. That is why

the city is well known for its annual Scottish Highland Games. The Highland Games are a way of celebrating Scottish and Celtic culture and heritage. They hold competitions in piping, drumming, dancing, and Scottish heavy athletics. The games also include entertainment and exhibits related to other aspects of Scottish culture. The Kentucky Tourism Council named the Glasgow Highland Games as one of the "Top Ten Festival Events" for the summer.

Our trusty GPS brought us to our exact destination of Hall Place, located in the historic downtown district on Green Street. As we drove up to the front yard, we saw a tall wooden sign that read Hall Place at the top. Below that it said Theodosia's Tea Room. I learned from Gary and Karin Carroll, the owners of Hall Place, that the house was built in 1852 as a dowry for Theodosia Tompkins, who married Dr. James Hall. The Carrolls named their bed-and-breakfast and tea room in honor of the Halls. We parked the car in back of the building, amidst a beautiful garden and seating area. Even though it was dreary and raining, I could imagine how romantic it would be to sit in the garden and enjoy a glass of wine and watch the fireflies on a warm summer eve.

We grabbed our bags out of the trunk of our car and headed for the entrance. As the door opened, a delicate ringing sound came from a small bell that was placed at the top of the door to alert the innkeepers of our arrival. A tall and slender lady wearing a blue floral blouse and a long, dark midi-skirt joined us at the front desk. She introduced herself as Karin Carroll and welcomed us to Hall Place. Seeing our ghosthunter vests, she realized that we were the ghosthunters she was expecting, and she seemed genuinely excited to finally meet us. She was quick to share some of her stories about weird and strange events that she and her husband had experienced in their inn.

After hearing a few of her stories, I looked at Chuck and said, "Honey, I think we need to book another night so we can investigate this place while we are here." Chuck agreed and we signed in for two nights instead of one. We went up to our room, which is called the Theodosia Room. It was a large suite with a queen-sized, antique half-tester canopy bed, covered in a finely stitched quilt. The room was furnished with an antique armoire, fireplace, and an oversized private bath that used to serve as a treatment room for the doctor when he owned the home.

The next morning we woke up to the wonderful aroma of a home-cooked Southern breakfast, complete with fruit, yogurt, eggs, bacon, and waffles, served with a hot cup of coffee. When we got to the dining room, Gary asked us how we'd slept. I decided this would be a good time to share with him something that happened to me during the night. I was suffering with a sore back from a fall in a cemetery during another ghost investigation a few days before. While sound asleep, lying on my side and turned towards Chuck, the pressure of what felt like two hands pressing on the lower part of my back woke me. At first I thought it might be Chuck checking on me, but when I reached out, I could feel Chuck still beside me in bed. I lay still and noticed that my back started to warm up as if someone had held their hands against my back for a while, creating this heat. When I rolled over to take a look, I noticed that my back muscles didn't seize up and cause me pain as they had been doing over the last few days. It was a relief. I rolled back over and within minutes I fell back to sleep.

Gary smiled and said, "Well, that doesn't surprise me. You see, you are staying in the same bedroom where Dr. James Hall used to sleep. The other room beside your room is where he kept overnight patients. He was in the habit of getting up in the middle of the night to check on his patients. You may have experienced the good doctor's concern for you and his checking to make sure your injury was being addressed." I loved that explanation.

The rest of the day Chuck and I visited with Gary and Karin

The haunted Victrola that starts up on its own

at different times because of their busy schedule and the fact
that the inn was booked for the weekend. While Chuck was with
Gary I would be with Karin and during that time, with recorder
in hand, we would ask questions about the activity they had
experienced. Karin's first story was about the Victrola she had
displayed in the parlor. It was a beautiful antique phonograph
with a large, polished external horn in a deep rust color that
amplified the playback sound.

Karin explained, "I was sitting in the parlor beside the fireplace one evening while working on some needlepoint when I
heard the sound of the Victrola's wheel spinning. I walked over
to it, and it was spinning very fast without any logical reason.
Usually when you start a Victrola it will start to spin slowly and
then speed up, but this was not the case—it started up in a fast
spin. I called out for Gary and when he came into the room
he was shocked to see the wheel spinning. The Victrola has a

broken spring and the wheel had seized so that it could not be moved, even if you tried to force it. Gary placed his hand on the moving wheel and it stopped. He tried to move it again to see if he could recreate the movement, but it wouldn't budge. It has never moved again." Gary laughed and added to her story, "After that happened I looked at my wife and said, 'If the pump organ starts to play, I am out of here!'"

Karin and Gary also discovered a trap door in the floor of the porch that is now the front room where guests check in. Beneath the trap door they found a cave that went under the house. They discovered that the house had been used as a stop on the Underground Railroad. The cave under the house extends twelve miles out and opens onto a spring on the other side of town; it was a perfect passage for conducting escaped slaves to freedom. Karin said that she had met African-American travelers who had heard about her inn being used as part of the Underground Railroad from stories that had been passed down to them from family members. Karin told me that she had found records revealing that Dr. Hall also had slaves and that he gave each one of them his surname. He treated them with kindness, and when he gave them away to his relatives, he made them promise to always take care of the slaves.

"Did you know that Vicki Lawrence, the comedian who played Mama on *The Carol Burnett Show,* and her husband, Al Schultz, stayed here a few months ago?" Karin asked. "Vicki was in Glasgow doing a performance, and she and Al stayed here while they were in town. When they came down for breakfast we asked them how they'd slept, and Al said that in the middle of the night he was awakened by a woman standing at the foot of his bed. She had on a blue dress, and he thought she was a black woman. He said that she looked at him and begged him to hide her, that they were coming to get her. Then she started to crawl in bed with them, and Al told her she couldn't do that and asked

The trap door
that leads to the
old Underground
Railroad tunnels

her to leave. She disappeared and then two men, dressed in uni-
forms, appeared standing at the foot of the bed. He thought that
maybe the woman was a slave and was being chased by these
two soldiers. Al looked at the men and noticed that they were
tall, and he told them that even though they were bigger than he
was, they couldn't hurt him because they were ghosts. Within
a few seconds the two men disappeared and things were quiet
again, so Al went back to sleep."

I asked Karin if there were any unexplained sounds that
they have heard in the inn. She told me that they constantly
hear someone walking upstairs. She added that even the previous owners warned them about the footsteps. The former owners said that once they called the police, thinking there was an
intruder in the house. The policemen also heard the footsteps on
the second floor, but there was no one there. Karen told me that
she thought the footsteps are the most common ghostly sound
they hear. Karin remembered: "A female guest was watching TV
one evening, and she heard someone walking outside her door,
talking loudly. She turned the volume on the TV to mute so she
could hear what they were saying, but then the voices stopped.

Later the next morning, the guest commented to me that the people who came in late last night were really noisy. I had to tell her that no one else had come into the inn at that time, and there were no other rooms rented."

In between our interviews I decided to take a break and go up to my room to relax. I love to work Sudoku puzzles so I grabbed an apple, propped myself up on my bed, and started my game. A wooden chair with a burgundy seat cushion stood across the room from me. While my eyes were focused on my Sudoku book, I could see a man sitting in the chair. I would raise my head to look at the chair, and, for a split second, I saw a man in a dark suit sitting with his legs crossed before he would disappear. I lowered my head and started my game, and, again, I could see a man sitting in the chair. As before, when I would raise my head, he would disappear. I had already learned that this used to be Dr. Hall's bedroom. I thought it might be Dr. Hall, but I expected to see him in a white doctor's jacket instead of a black suit.

When Chuck came back into the room I told him that I had seen a man sitting in the chair but was puzzled why he would be in a black suit. Chuck told me that Gary had just given him a tour of the inn, and while in one of the rooms, he saw a group picture of the doctors, and they were all dressed in black suits. "Okay, that works for me," I said. When we came down for breakfast on the second day of our stay, we joined a mother and daughter who were traveling from Alabama. They had come to Glasgow to join a scrapbooking seminar. When the daughter, Shannon Gibson, saw my T-shirt, she commented on the ghosthunter. com that she observed on the back. I told her that I was a professional ghosthunter, and we were here in Glasgow to investigate haunted locations. Shannon looked at her mom, Lisa Sweet, and said, "Oh my gosh, I so totally believe in ghosts. Do you think this place is haunted?" I glanced over at Gary, and he gave me a wink and a nod, so I answered, "Well it might be, but I don't think you have anything to fear."

Shannon said, "Last night while in my room, I felt as if I were being watched, and once I fell asleep I kept waking up from bad dreams. Since we are in adjoining rooms, I would go and look around the corner to see if Mom was okay. When I told her about my restless night, she said she had experienced the same thing and would come around to check on me. How weird is that?"

I asked them to tell me about their dreams. "I dreamt I was in a car," Shannon said, "driving with someone in the back seat who was complaining and making me angry, so I said to them, 'Stop your complaining and do something about it.' At that moment the person took a gun and held it under his chin and shot himself, which woke me up immediately." Lisa said, "In my dream I kept seeing injured animals, and I remember there was lots of blood all around me."

I mentioned to them that it was interesting to note how their dreams related to physical injuries. I told them that the house once belonged to a doctor, and the house served as a place where the injured would come for treatment. At times they would have to remain overnight. Once we finished visiting with our new friends, we left the second floor and met with Gary and Karin one more time in the parlor. They told us that they had purchased another historic home not too far from Hall Place. It has been labeled by the community as an old haunted house, and Chuck and I are already making plans to go back and investigate the Carrolls' newly acquired property that they will convert into another bed-and-breakfast, which they hope to have finished by 2012. They have named the future bed-and-breakfast "1854 Bryan House." They plan to have ghosthunter tours and overnight ghosthunts while the home is being renovated. Maybe we'll find even more Glasgow ghosts.

CHAPTER 6

The Haunted Hospital
SCOTTSVILLE, ALLEN COUNTY

"HELLO."

"May I please speak with Patti Starr?"

"You are speaking to Patti Starr."

"I know you probably will not remember me, but my wife and I took your Bardstown Ghost Trek last year. After spending the evening with you and learning about ghosts and the many ways to communicate with them, I became hooked."

This phone call was the start of a new friendship. While sitting at my computer, I was attempting to answer my e-mails when I got a phone call from a man who introduced himself as David Dinwiddie. He explained to me that he had leased an old, abandoned hospital in Scottsville, Kentucky. He and his son, Chris, were going to turn it into a haunted attraction for Halloween, but it seemed that the haunted part was becoming more real than fantasy. I was totally thrilled that I had influenced someone to start a new business and to think it was going to be opened in my favorite month of the year, October.

David had a few concerns he wanted to share with me. "Patti, when we first started to clean up the debris that had accumulated over the past several years, our volunteers noticed strange noises. They would stop their work and turn towards the sounds and listen. Then, if they heard it again, they would move towards the sound to see if someone had come into the building without permission. They told me that as they started to walk towards the sound, it would stop only to start back up again after they went back to work. Sometimes the sounds would be so loud and clear that the volunteers would become so upset they would pick up their tools and leave for the day."

"What kind of noises did the workers hear?" I asked. David explained, "There were several different sounds reported over a four-week period. It started with the sound of babies crying. The volunteers would go over to where it sounded like a child was crying out in pain, but when they searched the area, there were no children in the hospital. They would even go outside and check the perimeter of the building to see if children were playing close by and found nothing to explain the sounds of children crying. When we started to research the building, we found where the different stations were located. It was very unnerving when we found out that the area where we heard the sounds of babies crying had been the nursery."

"Your hospital sounds like a great place to investigate for ghosts," I replied, and he continued, "That is exactly why I'm calling you. I would love for you to come to the hospital with your various equipment and instruments and do a ghost investigation." I told David that I would be honored to do this, but I'd have to wait until after ScareFest, our horror and paranormal convention in Lexington, and that I would come after September.

It seemed like a matter of a few days instead of months before it was time for Chuck and me to leave for Scottsville to investigate the haunted hospital. David was very kind in arranging for me to stay the night in a very haunted bed-and-breakfast about twenty miles outside of Scottsville in Glasgow, another haunted location in this book. We were driving deep into the beautiful Kentucky countryside, our first trip in that area. When I asked David about the location and history of Scottsville, he told me that it was near the border of Tennessee about sixty miles from Nashville. He bragged about the closeness and fellowship of his small town with pride. I remember the first time I saw David; he reminded me of a character from my childhood. Mr. Brown was a deacon at our Baptist church, and he played the part of Santa each Christmas. I'm not saying that David was as big as Santa, but he had this perfect, jolly round face that made me think of what the real Santa would have looked like.

When we entered the city of Scottsville, which is the county seat for Allen County, we passed a welcome sign with Scottsville's motto, "The Friendly City." Soon after that we found ourselves driving through the public square, admiring the concentration of delightful and colorful retail shops. The courthouse sits in the center of the turnpike leading from Louisville to Nashville. It was one of the most pristine small towns, reflecting a loving history, that I had ever visited.

I called David so we could meet before my seminar at the local library that David's wife, Julie, had arranged for me. He gave us directions to check out the hospital grounds before the investigation that was scheduled for the evening. As we pulled into the driveway, I was rather surprised at the sight of the hospital. It looked more like a one-level office building, with tall weeds and lots of winding vines growing all around. It looked very small for a county hospital until we drove around back and could see that there were two stories to the building, as the basement was exposed at ground level and made another floor. The windows were broken out, and you could see the old, white, iron-framed beds that were forgotten in time and left behind. To the right of the drive, in the back of the hospital, was a strange metal structure. David walked over to this rusted-out structure and explained that it was a specially built incinerator that burned all the body parts from surgery and possibly the embryos from miscarriages. It did give me an eerie feeling just standing beside it. On the other side of the incinerator was a wooded area, and as we stood beside this devise, the wind picked up and blew cold through us. That didn't help my feelings at all.

I asked David about the history of the hospital, and he told me that it was opened to the public in 1952. He said that during the hospital's construction, there was only one fatality. One afternoon, a laborer was sent into the back part of the basement to work. As he reached down to move some wood panels, he was shocked to find a copperhead snake coiled to strike under the wood. He jumped back but it was too late—the copperhead bit the worker. He died shortly afterwards.

David also pointed out that because EMS was not allowed to pronounce anyone dead, all bodies had to be brought to the emergency room for a doctor to make that call. Because the hospital had two emergency rooms, one for spillover, they would put the bodies in emergency unit two until the funeral home employees could pick them up, since there was no official morgue in the hospital. If the bodies belonged to families in another county, the bodies would remain in this room until they were retrieved by family.

As the hospital aged and become more and more outdated, it merged with a new hospital in 1993, and in 1994 the Scottsville maternity and nursery wards were closed. Soon after that, nurses who worked in that area would comment on hearing the sounds of babies crying, although the nurses knew that there were no

The hospital's body-part incinerator

babies there. A man whose mother had been a nurse at the hospital told David that sometimes his mother would take him to work when she couldn't get a sitter, and he would stay in one of the rooms where the nursery used to be. He would be awakened by the sound of a baby crying. He would leave the room to find his mom. When he would find her, she would explain that it was a common sound that everyone heard when they stayed in that room and that he should not be afraid. He would go back to the room and go back to sleep without being awakened again.

For thirty years David was an EMT stationed at the hospital. Sometimes when he was scheduled for a twenty-four-hour shift, he would go back into the basement area where there was a room for the EMTs to sleep between calls. He remembers that once, after he woke up in the morning, one of the nurses asked him how he'd slept. He told her that he was kept awake most of the night by doors slamming and objects being moved and dropped on the floor. He asked her who was so busy down there, and she replied that there was no one there but him.

Before we left the hospital and headed for the library, I asked David if I could interview his son, Chris, and some of the volunteers. He called them over to the car, and they were all anxious to tell me about their own ghostly experiences.

Chris started, "One afternoon, while I was working at one of the nurse's stations where all four halls meet, I heard a clear voice of a young child say, 'Hello.' I turned to see who was behind me, and I noticed a broom closet. I thought that maybe a child had gone inside there and was playing a trick on me. I walked over and opened the closet but found nothing there that would have made that sound. This freaked me out so I picked up my tools and left for the day. From then on, when I worked in this room I propped the door open so that if anything like that happened again, I could easily run out of the room."

David interrupted and added, "I was in what used to be the waiting room for the CCU patients, and while I was working, the door to the room slammed. I went over to open it, but it was stuck. I figured that it must be due to the dampness that the door was swollen and that was why I couldn't get it opened. I tried for over fifteen minutes to get the door to open. I began to feel a little panicked and realized that the only way out was through a window. I had to hold on to the gutter that gave way as I jumped to the ground. The gutter is still hanging outside the window. I walked around the building and went in through the front to get back to the room, and, to my amazement, the door was standing wide open. And, Patti, I just remembered this," David continued. "I was working in another one of the rooms to get ready for the Halloween tours. I was standing in the corner of the room with my arms up while attaching a string of lights to the ceiling. All of a sudden, a big splash of water hit my side where I was standing next to the wall. I lowered my arms and

looked at my side, and it was soaking wet while the water continued to flow down my legs into my socks. I looked up to see if the
ceiling was leaking, but it wasn't. Anyway, if the water had come
from the ceiling, it would have landed on my shoulder, not come
from a side angle and hit me in the side just below my armpit.
The wall that I was standing close to did not have any signs of
water on it. Now that was a totally unexplained experience, and
it scared the heck out of me."

Chris prompted one of the volunteers, Travis Ford, to share
one of his experiences. Travis, a bit reserved, began, "I was walking down one of the hallways getting ready to enter one of the
rooms where we were working to get it ready for the Halloween
tours. To tell you the truth, I have never liked that room. While
I'm working in the room, I feel like there are eyes staring at me,
so I'll turn around, and there is no one there but it still creeps
me out. Anyway, as I turned to go into the doorway of the room,
I stopped immediately. It felt like someone was standing in front
of me, but there was no one there. All of a sudden, with a mighty
force, I was pushed out the door and landed against the wall in
the hallway. Once I realized what had happened, I turned and ran
down the hall until I reached the lobby. I was out of breath and
scared out of my mind at what had just happened. I remained in
the lobby for a while with all sorts of thoughts going through my
head, trying to make sense of what had just happened to me." I
asked Travis if he has gone back into the room since then, and
he said he had. He told me that he still feels creeped out when he
has to work in the room, but nothing has pushed him again.

Once I had finished with the interviews, we left for the
library where we had a full house in attendance. While I was
there I was able to meet Julie Dinwiddie and she told me about
her interests in the haunted hospital. She is a first grade school
teacher with a love for ghost lore and ghost stories. She told me
how she and David loved to travel, and at each destination they

try to find a ghost tour they can go to. Julie and Tallauh, Chris's wife, complete this family venture by selling tickets for the ghost tours and booking the various ghost groups for overnight investigations.

Now comes the fun part. We left the library and headed out for The Haunted Hospital, as it has now been officially named. We had about forty people waiting to go into the unknown dark site to see what we might experience together. After our prayer of protection we headed down the road that leads to the back of the hospital. As we were walking, I stopped the crowd and told them I had heard voices coming from the wooded area. This caused a few gasps within the crowd. I took my recorder to see if we could capture an EVP. Sure enough, on playback we heard children talking. We couldn't make out what they were saying, but it was definitely children's voices. The crowd was thrilled and frightened that we were already getting evidence.

We continued through the back doors of the basement and entered a dark, damp, and moldy area that seemed more like a dreaded dungeon than a former hospital ward. As we continued down the hall, a woman in the group screamed and said that something like a cold hand ran down the back of her leg. This made the atmosphere even more fearful as we continued with our investigation. All in all, it was a good night for us ghosthunters. We were able to pick up unknown energies that made our EMF meters sound out and register a disturbance. We picked up a couple of names, revealed through the use of the Ovilus. Chris is going to research to see if he can find a connection to persons associated with the hospital. I can't wait to return and continue my investigation of this newfound treasure that appears to be full of ghostly activity.

Jailer's Inn Bed-and-Breakfast
BARDSTOWN, NELSON COUNTY

AS I WALKED THROUGH THE PUB, making sure all the guests had their needs met, I noticed a fair-haired, slim gentleman sitting at the bar. As I approached him I recognized him as the owner of the Jailer's Inn. Since I had became the general manager of The Old Talbott Tavern in 1996, I had not taken the opportunity to go next door to introduce myself to the owner of the Jailer's Inn. This was a perfect time for us to meet. Just as he reached for his drink, I introduced myself and we started to chat.

I learned that Paul McCoy had purchased the Jailer's Inn Bed-and-Breakfast from his parents, Challen and Fran McCoy. They had purchased the county jailhouse when it went to auction after it closed in 1987. I asked him about his business because I was trying to improve the Tavern's business and thought we could partner on some ideas. I suggested to Paul that we might promote something special together to bring in more guests. We talked about several promos that would include a wine tasting, or mystery dinner, or romantic get-a-ways. He invited me over to his place to see his facilities and that's when I discovered something really unique about the Jailer's Inn. It is haunted! As I entered the front door, I was hit with an impression of a woman who was in charge and guarding this space. From the corner of my eye, I saw figures dart back and forth in the hallway. "Paul," I said, "I don't mean to alarm you, but do you know that this building has spirits?" He smiled and almost reluctantly admitted that he did think it might be haunted. I took the opportunity at that time to tell him about my other profession as a ghosthunter and asked him for permission to do a ghost investigation of the Jailer's Inn. Quietly, he agreed.

Before the building was a bed-and-breakfast it served as a jailhouse for Nelson County from 1819 until 1987. The jailer's office was on the first floor, and the prisoners stayed on the second floor until 1874 when the county built the extension on the back. They also added a tall stone fence and gallows for hanging the convicted. Once they moved the prisoners to the back of the building, the jailer and his family lived in the front part of the jail.

We set a date and I returned to the Jailer's Inn with my small Bardstown group of ghosthunters, which included two close friends, Melody and Gary. We started our investigation on the first floor in the Library Room that housed many older books and included a king-size poster bed and sofa. We continued our search for the spirits into the next room called the Colonial Room. It offered a rustic feel with the natural limestone wall and the hand-hewn timbers that ran across the ceiling. While working in these rooms, I felt as if I had time-traveled back to the late 1800s. Since the first floor didn't seem to be very active. we decided to move on to the second floor in hopes of finding some paranormal activity.

At the top of the stairs and to the right, we entered the 1819 Room. This room was once referred to as the dungeon. It seemed funny to call an upstairs room a dungeon, but at one time it was dark, with thick hand-hewn timbers all along the walls and ceiling with no windows to let in the light. This is the room where the jailer would shackle the criminals who had committed the most heinous crimes. At one time, the only way to get to this room was to put a ladder up on the side of the building and corral the men up through a window. Then they were chained to the walls in this dark room. The window was closed off by another door to create a secure hold with no escape. Now, it is a beautiful room with white sheer curtains flowing across the walls for a beautiful, calmer ambiance. We had great hopes that this room would be the one where we would find the most evidence of ghosts.

We set our audio recorders out, positioned our camcorders in the corner of the room, and continued to ask for the spirits to communicate with us through sight or sound. As I turned to walk into the bathroom, I felt a strong cold spot and asked one of the team to take a picture of me where I was standing. When the photo was developed, there was a thick, dark mist to the right of where I was standing, which indicated to me that we had possibly captured spirit energy.

I felt that it was the presence of a woman but couldn't make out who she was or why she was there. I grabbed my dowsing rods and started to dowse in the room. I asked if the spirit was a female and got a "yes" response. I asked if she lived there and got a "no" response. This answer eliminated the ghost as a member of the jailer's family. I asked her if she died there and she responded "no." I asked if she was a visiting spirit and got a "yes."

The last hanging at the old county jail that is now the Jailer's Inn

Then her energy seemed to leave the room. Later on I asked Paul if a woman had ever been hanged at the jail, and he said he did not have a record of such an incident. I asked him if a woman had ever been incarcerated there, and he said that a couple of women had been arrested but not for any major crimes. My curiosity was about to get the best of me, so after the investigation I went to the local library to see if I could find out who this woman might be. After hours of searching the microfilm, I found an article in the newspaper that dated to 1909. The title read, "Is the Bastille Haunted?" Wow, I thought. They were writing about the jail being haunted all the way back then. The story was written by a reporter who had heard reports that the inmates were complaining about ghosts waking them up at night from loud banging, screams, and the sounds of chains dragging across the floors. He decided to research some of the prisoners who had died at the jail to see if one of them was haunting this place.

One story that caught my interest was about Martin Hill, a man who drank too much bourbon, who had been arrested in 1885. His wife was greatly afraid of him when he drank because he became so mean and violent. As I was reading this story, I closed my eyes and could feel her fear, and I started to envision what she had gone through while married to this man. He would beat her so badly at times that he would break her arm or a few ribs. He would hit her in the head until she would lie unconscious. One night Martin came home drunk and grabbed his wife to start another brutal beating, but she jerked away from his grip and ran out of the house. She ran into the woods to the other side of the hill to a neighboring farmhouse. She knocked on the door and begged the farmer to let her stay with his family until morning because her husband was drinking and she feared for her life. Martin was furious that his wife had run from him. He grabbed his rifle and stormed out of the house in hot pursuit of her. It wasn't long before he came to the farmhouse. He stood outside in the front yard waving his rifle around while swearing to kill everyone if his wife didn't come out. The farmer came out and pleaded with Martin to go home and sleep it off. He promised him that his wife would return to him the next morning. Martin refused and before he could cause any more ruckus, his wife stepped out on the porch to plead with him. The moment Martin saw her, he lifted his rifle and shot her dead before she could speak. Martin was arrested and taken to the jail. While awaiting trail he became ill, so the jailer sent for the doctor. Martin told the doctor that he was in great pain. He said his head was throbbing, his arms ached, and it hurt for him to take a deep breath. After the doctor examined Martin, he couldn't find anything wrong with him. All he could do was give him some pain medication.

A few days later Martin's condition worsened, and the jailer sent for the doctor again. Martin had to be strapped to his bunk because he was growling, cursing, and writhing in pain. The doctor examined Martin and again could not find a reason for his pain. Later that night Martin died, and the doctor commented that he had never seen anyone die in such horrific pain before.

I now think I understood what had happened. As a ghost-hunter, through my experiences and communication with the spirits, I learned that sometimes people who die a quick or violent death may not realize at first that they have passed and are now in spirit. I believe that when Martin shot his wife, and her body fell to the floor, her spirit continued to follow Martin as they took him away to jail. It didn't take her long to realize that something was different about herself and that she could have an effect on him. She might have felt that she could show Martin how much pain and fear he had put her through during all those years of abuse. I think he probably knew it was the ghost of his wife causing his pain, and this traumatized him to death.

This helped me to understand why the female ghost that I was communicating with in the 1819 Room indicated that she did not live in that structure or die there. She just followed Martin there and then remained. I feel she protects the Inn as she has gained the confidence to know that she can no longer be hurt or abused, and that is why she is there.

A few years later, Paul told me that a couple had come to the Jailer's Inn and stayed in the 1819 Room. They told Paul what a wonderful time they had while there, and before leaving they took some pictures of their room. When they got home and had the photos developed, there was an apparition of a woman standing in the same corner where we had captured the dark mist while experiencing the cold spot on our investigation. She sent the picture to Paul and he placed it in his desk drawer.

He was excited to get such evidence, since the Travel Channel was scheduled to come in a couple of weeks to film the Jailer's Inn for a ghost special. They had named the Jailer's Inn as one of the ten most-haunted places in America. When they got there, Paul pulled open the drawer to show them the photo of the female apparition, but the picture was gone. He couldn't believe it, and to this day he has never found the picture.

I did my first ghost tour in Bardstown in 1997, and I included the Jailer's Inn as one of the stops. Since then, Paul keeps updating me with many ghost stories from his guests and employees. One of my favorites is about a salesman who came to Bardstown to serve his clients, often staying overnight at the Jailer's Inn. On one of his many trips to the Inn, he was sitting in a chair in his room reading a newspaper. Out of the corner of his eye, he saw someone walking by. He lowered his newspaper and saw a man walking past him, headed for the other side of the room. The guest turned his head to see if he had left his room door open, but it was still closed. He turned back and watched the man continue to walk forward until he passed through the wall and disappeared. The salesman was completely dumbfounded by what he has just witnessed. He got up from his chair and left his room. He found the manager and asked if he could go out behind the building. The manager took him to the back door and told him to go out and enjoy the private courtyard in back. As he walked alongside of the building and turned the corner, he saw the same man sitting on a wrought iron bench positioned across the courtyard. The salesman wanted to meet the man who could walk through walls, so he slowly walked over to him. The closer he got to the man, the more faded in appearance he became until finally the guest couldn't see the man any more. He was so impressed by this experience that for three years he would return on the same date at the same time, hoping to experience this man's visit one more time.

Paul later told me that when his parents bought the building and starting renovating it for a bed-and-breakfast, there used to be a door in the wall where the man had passed through.

They decided to close off the door to make it part of the wall. Maybe what the guest witnessed was a previous jailer making his rounds to secure the jail. In some of my investigations where I get reports of ghosts walking through walls, I have found through research that at one time there was a door there. The spirits seem to continue to use the old portal.

Once when an employee was cleaning an upstairs bathroom at the Inn, she leaned over to scrub the sink and happened to look up into the mirror. She gasped at the sight she witnessed: a big man with a decayed face standing behind her. She screamed and ran out of the room and back downstairs. The next day she did not show up for work. She had quit her job.

In the early years of justice, lawmen didn't always imprison the right man. It wasn't common, but every once in a while they would accidentally hang the wrong man. The cell would be full of criminals. When the officials would come to get their man for execution, sometimes all of the men in the cell would point to the nervous one in the corner. They would grab him and hang him only to find out later that they'd hanged the wrong man. It is believed that this mistake may have happened at one time or another at this county jail. Maybe the employee had seen one of those men that had been hanged by mistake.

Since my first investigation of the Jailer's Inn, Paul has continued to let other ghosthunter groups come to his inn to investigate for ghosts. All of us continue to find more spirits. During our annual Bardstown Ghost Hunting Get-A-Way Weekend in November my group buys all the rooms at the Jailer's Inn and The Old Talbott Tavern, and it is amazing how much evidence of spirit activity we get over this three-day weekend. We have found children who speak to us through EVPs. We capture children's faces in photos and see apparitions of children. Why would we get children's spirits coming through in a jail, you might ask. When the jailers and their families lived there from 1874 until

1987, many children were born and died there. It would stand to reason that we would find children's ghosts there.

A good friend of mine, Frances Etienne, heads a group of ghosthunters called Afterdark Paranormal Investigations. She told me about an amazing investigation her group conducted at the Jailer's Inn. At about 1:00 A.M., Frances and her team were sitting in the courtyard with their audio cassette recorder on. Since this was the area where the hangings had occurred, they were hoping to get an EVP that would be significant to the history of the executions. When they went inside the Jailer's Inn and rewound their recorder, they were shocked at the EVP that came through. It was a man in a deep voice that said, "May the Lord be with us." Imagine a criminal standing on the gallows with the black bag over his head and the rope pulled tight around his neck just seconds away from a horrible death. The priest walks over to the subject and says, "May the Lord be with us and have mercy on your soul." This EVP was a great piece of evidence of such a scene.

Even though I can see why the Jailer's Inn was named one of the ten most-haunted places in America, it now offers another unique and more luxurious way to do time. The courtyard offers a private, sunny garden where you can sit and relax while listening to the birds and breezes that blow through the trees. Each guest room is decorated with antiques and heirlooms. The breakfast is bountiful in flavor and Southern pizzazz. It is the perfect place to be incarcerated after being found guilty of having so much fun and relaxation.

CHAPTER 8

Kentucky Theatre
LEXINGTON, FAYETTE COUNTY

FOR TWO YEARS JEFF WALDRIDGE, one of my GCI members, Chuck Starr, my husband, and I planned the future of ScareFest, a horror and paranormal convention to be held in Lexington, Kentucky. Since the historic Kentucky Theatre was going to show the movies that featured the ScareFest horror stars, we thought the theater would be a good place for the fans to have a ghost investigation.

I met with Fred Mills, the manager of the Kentucky Theatre, to talk to him about the history and hauntings of the theater. The theater was in pristine form the day I entered the ornate Italian Renaissance lobby. Its rich, golden colors and magnificent marble floor were stunning. I had never before seen such a luxurious movie theater. While talking with Fred, I learned that he had been with the theater since 1963. He told me that the theater opened in October 1922, with a special feature that made the Kentucky Theatre stand out from all the other theaters in Lexington: a house orchestra and a Wurlitzer symphonic organ that played before every movie. Could you imagine being seated in such a luxurious and elegant theater as the curtains opened to a musical overture played on the Wurlitzer organ? As you looked forward you saw lyrics flashed upon the huge white screen as everyone joined in to sing "My Old Kentucky Home" before the movie started. As they say, "Those were the good ol' days."

"Over the years the theater became one of the most popular places to go in the evening for entertainment," Fred said, "since there were no cable TVs, VCRs, Internet, Netflix, and so on. Back in the 1970s we started to offer the midnight movies hosted by WKQQ radio. We called it the "Double Q Midnight Movies," and it became a popular social event. Later we brought in the *Rocky Horror Picture Show,* which became a cult movie with a huge following. Even today it still brings a good crowd."

"In all the years that you have worked here have you had any experiences with ghosts?" I asked. Fred thought a moment and then said, "I have heard stories from some of the employees, and they seemed to think the theater is haunted. The most-often-talked-about experience among the staff is the apparition of a man sitting by himself in the lower seating area of the old theater. The ones who saw him said that he always sat in the number-two chair. One day, when one of the guys was telling this story, RT Baxter, the projectionist at the time, laughed and told us that he knew who the ghost was. He was a former projectionist who worked at the theater for many years. One evening he died of a heart attack while running a movie up in the projection room. RT told us that after this guy started the movie he would go down into the seating area and sit in seat number two to make sure the sound was good. He didn't want anyone to complain about the sound being too loud or too low. After a few minutes he would get up and go back to the projection room. RT told everyone not to be afraid of him and to go on about their jobs."

Fred agreed to allow our group to do an investigation after the midnight movie on Friday and Saturday night during our ScareFest event. I was planning on being the lead investigator, but as things became far to hectic for me at ScareFest, I asked Serena Gordon, a member of GCI, if she would take my position of lead investigator for this event. She agreed and reported back to me some amazing results from the investigation. Serena told me that they went upstairs into the projection room. She knew that back in the 1940s, the projectionist had died in this room. Previous employees had reported cold spots in the room and the feeling of being watched. Serena, a psychic/medium, felt a heaviness in her chest while walking around in the room. Even though she knew that someone had died in this room, she didn't know he had died of a heart attack until later.

When the investigators started to leave the room, a man in the group stepped in front of Serena to open the door. As soon as the door swung open, both Serena and the man saw a full apparition, male, dressed in a tan jacket white shirt and black pants. The man holding the door slammed the door shut and jumped back, bumping into Serena. She asked him what he had seen. He didn't respond to her question and she thought that maybe he was in shock. She asked him again and this time he said, "I think I saw a ghost." She asked him to describe what he saw, and it was the same description that Serena gave me when she reported the sighting.

They opened the door again and there was no one there, so they proceeded down the stairs to go back into the old theater, a second, smaller auditorium that used to be the State Theater but is now incorporated into the Kentucky Theatre as one theater with two seating areas. Serena led the group down the aisle to the stage. Some of the theater employees had seen a male apparition walking across the stage while they were standing at the top of the aisle during clean up. The apparition was reported to be wearing a jacket and baseball cap. Of course, when the group went down to the stage to see who was there, they couldn't find anyone else.

The group joined Serena on stage for an EVP session to see if she could get the ghost to respond to a question and capture it on her digital audio recorder. She started out with, "Who are you?" No response. She asked, "Did you die here?" Again, no response, but on the next question she asked, "Can you tell me the street where you lived?" A male voice coming through the recorder answered, "Tenth Street."

Continuing the investigation, Serena led the group behind the stage where the lights were off. There was enough light coming from the door of the stage to walk around without bumping into each other. Serena asked, "Can you make a sound to let us know you are with us?" Just at that moment a piece of ceiling tile that was stacked on the floor lifted up and flew across to the other side of the room, startling everyone. When they examined the ceiling tile they could find no evidence to explain why it went flying across the room.

By 4:00 A.M. everyone was ready to call it quits, so Serena concluded the investigation. She contacted me later and gave me a full report on the evidence they had captured. I was thrilled to know that the investigation was successful in getting such good evidence of a haunting at the theater.

Over the years my name and business have become so synonymous with ghosts that I get a lot of requests to be featured for Halloween specials. When I got a call from Greg Stotelmyer, a reporter for ABC's local affiliate channel 36 TV, I wasn't surprised when he asked me if he could follow me on a ghost investigation for his show called, *Kentucky's Back Roads*. The first place that came to mind was the historic Kentucky Theatre. It had good history, good ghost stories, and good ghost investigation results. I called Fred again and he agreed to allow the TV crew to film me doing a ghost investigation at the theater.

When Chuck and I arrived at the theater, we were joined by Fred and Greg with the film crew. Raymond Mitchell, the projectionist, and Bill McCray, the security guard, along with his wife, Sylvia, were also there to join us. Bill and Raymond had stayed late one night and had captured some strange anomalies and a couple of EVPs that Bill had burned to a CD to share with me. Since Raymond had been with the theater since 1962, I felt he could share even more ghostly experiences from the theater.

Once I had my microphone in place we were ready to start our investigation. We went down into the basement where Raymond led me into a small room that used to house the boiler. He said that many years before he joined the theater it was rumored that a man was murdered here. I was hoping to get some strong evidence that might reveal a ghost haunting this dark, secluded room. My meters were not accurate indicators of activity because the ceiling of this small room was lined with electrical wiring. The energy from the wires interfered with the meters and they beeped constantly, so I had to turn them off. When I used my infrared thermometer, I noticed a quick drop of twelve degrees. I turned on my audio recorder to see if I could pick up an EVP. During the session Bill turned to me and said, "The last time I was down here with my recorder I got a clear EVP." I asked him what it said. Bill told me that it said, "Help me. He's got me."

We left the basement and went back upstairs to the auditorium. As we walked down the aisle to the stage, Raymond said, "The old projectionist used to come down and sit in chair number two at the beginning of the movie to make sure that the sound was perfect. Sometimes at night I have come into the auditorium and seen a human form sitting in the number-two chair. Then it will disappear. I believe it is the old projectionist still checking to make sure the sound is good."

After hearing that story, I stood on stage myself and looked down at the seating area by the number-two chair. I said, "If the spirit of the projectionist is here and you would like to show yourself, could you create enough energy to appear in my photo?" Then I took a shot with my camera while pointing it in the direction of the chair. I was excited to see a perfect spirit orb stationed beside the number-two chair. This was a great shot for the TV camera man, and they used it in the show.

I wanted to go up into the projectionist's room to see what we could get there. I pulled out the Ovilus to see what words might come through. I was surprised when it said "death" since this was the room where the projectionist had died. At that moment Raymond told Greg of an incident that had happened to him one night before closing. "I was getting ready to leave the projection room," Raymond said "and when I went to open the door, a dark shadow was looking back at me. It reached for me and gave me a push. My first reaction was to slam the door shut." "What did you do next?" Greg asked. Raymond said, "I threw the door open and slid down the banister without my feet touching a step. When I got to the bottom, I ran out of the theater." Raymond's story validated what Serena had told me about her experience with the same door. The ghost did not touch her, but she and the other ghosthunter had seen a full apparition when they opened the same door during their investigation.

Our last place to investigate was the balcony. We walked around and at one point my EMF meter started to beep. It was a slow and irregular beep, which is a good indication of spirit energy trying to come through. I asked if it was male and got a positive beep. I asked if it died there and got another positive beep. I continued with another question but noticed that the meter was not responding and the short session was over. I asked Chuck to stand in the area where I was picking up the EMF disturbance and took out my camera. I asked the spirit, if he was still with us, to please appear near Chuck's left hand. When I get this specific, and then I actually get something in the area I asked for, I think this is good evidence that the spirit is communicating with me. Just as I snapped my camera, a spirit orb appeared over Chuck's left hand as I had instructed it to do.

Our time was running out, and I figured this would be a perfect time to end our investigation. I was pleased with all the readings and data that I had collected during our investigation. Greg was also pleased and was sure that the investigation would make a super story for his TV show. The clip of us at the

In the balcony, a spirit orb appeared next to Chuck's hand.

Kentucky Theatre can be viewed on www.youtube.com. In the search box enter "Ghastly Ghosts" and scroll down to find the video with Greg Stotelmyer.

The historic Kentucky Theatre is a grand old building that has survived a flood, fire, and changing times. In all these years it has continued to serve the community with popular movies, indie films, concerts, galas, and midnight shows. The historic Kentucky Theatre has become a beloved landmark to generations of people living in Lexington and is sure to carry on in its glorious tradition.

CHAPTER 9

Lock and Key Café
GEORGETOWN, SCOTT COUNTY

CHUCK AND I HAD BEEN TRAVELING out of town and on our way home we decided to make a stop in Georgetown, Kentucky. We were in the middle of a home remodeling project, and I needed to look at some antique furnishings. I had heard that Georgetown was known for antique shops and malls downtown so I wanted to check them out. I had heard about a particular unique antique shop called The Vault and wanted to visit it first while we were in the vicinity.

As we drove into the downtown area I couldn't help but notice the rows of colorful shops that represented the height of the Greek Revival period of architecture in Kentucky. Georgetown is also where Kentucky bourbon was born. Located on West Main Street are the Royal Springs where Reverend Elijah Craig used the water to enrich his brew of bourbon back in 1789.

When we arrived at The Vault, we were lucky to get a parking place in front of the shop. I couldn't wait to start browsing for treasures and valuables that I seemed to find in these mystical, old antique havens. The bell over the door rang out our entrance. A senior lady, the shop manager, welcomed us as we started our journey through the store. When we got to the middle of the building I noticed a vault. I looked at Chuck and said, "So that's why they named it The Vault. This must have been a bank at one time."

As I continued to go deeper into the back of the building, I began to feel a bit dizzy. This is always a good indication for me to start paying attention to my surroundings. When I'm in an older establishment with old and odd items, I can pick up on the energy of those who previously owned them. I decided to go back to the front of the shop and find the lady who was in charge. I asked her, "What did this building used to be?" She said, "It has been many businesses. It has been a furniture store, and at one time it housed a funeral home. I think the building is most remembered when it was the Georgetown National Bank." I said to her, "I thought as much since I saw the huge vault in the back." It would be hard to miss, with the huge metal doors opened and rows of books stacked on the shelves instead of money. I asked the manager, "Can you tell me anything interesting about the building?" She said, "Years ago a bank manager committed suicide here." After hearing this, I thought that may be why I became so dizzy when I walked through the shop: maybe I was picking up on the suicide. My head started to feel weird again

The framed area of where the bullet and blood went into the wall during the former bank president's suicide

so I asked, "How did he die?" She said, "He took a gun to his head and pulled the trigger. Would you like to see where he did this?" "Oh, yes," I said, "If you have the time." She led us over to a small restroom and opened the door. As she stepped inside she pointed and said, "Look at the wall there, and you can still see the stain of blood surrounding the hole in the wall where the bullet passed through his brain."

I walked past her to go inside the room. I immediately felt every hair on my body stand straight up. I believe I was picking up on the residual haunting. When an event happens that causes a high emotional-energy level, it is sometimes imprinted on the surrounding area. It's as if the event left behind a memory to be experienced by others. If you could just imagine what someone might have felt just before taking his own life, you might be able to understand the uneasy feeling I was experiencing. I turned and looked at where she was pointing. There was a glass and wooden frame that had been secured over the hole in the wall to protect it from damage but still allow the view of the blood and hole caused by the bullet.

This was a great time to ask, "Do you think this building is haunted?" The lady looked at me and sternly said, "Yes, I do." "What makes you say that?" I asked. "We hear things all through the shop," she said. "Sometimes it sounds like a shelf of dishes fell and crashed to the floor. When we go to the area where the sound came from there will be nothing on the floor, no broken anything. Other times we have seen kitchen utensils like spoons and forks fly across the room. When we see customers wander into that back room, we join them while they are there because sometimes items will fly across the room, and we don't want them to get hurt. Also, in the evening before we close, we can hear noises upstairs over the top of the shop. It sounds like they are very busy, and we can hear them dragging heavy objects across the floor. When we go upstairs to see if a customer went up without us seeing them, there is no one there. We think that now and then, George, the bank president, likes it to be known that he is still here, and I think that is why we experience these noises."

I thought this would be a good time to introduce myself and ask permission to come back and do a ghost investigation. I was pleased by how quickly the manager agreed to let us come back that weekend. On our return to The Vault we began our investigation about 2:30 in the afternoon. I prefer to perform my ghost investigations during the day, since I'm an early-to-bed-and-early-to-rise person. I get great results, especially around 3:00 P.M. I was curious to see if I would feel the same dizziness that I felt the first time I was in the shop, so I ventured over to the same area. Sure enough, when I got to the area I started to get dizzy again and noticed that I was standing in front of a large, wooden armoire. I decided to test the area with my EMF meter, and as soon as I turned it on I got a quick spike and a couple of irregular beeps. I took the EMF probe and placed it up towards the ceiling and then down to the floor and did not pick up any disturbances. I took the probe and again pointed it towards the armoire which made it beep twice, stop, and then beep once, stop, and then beep again. When this happens I believe that what I'm picking up might be more paranormal. A steady fast beep usually indicates an energy field emitted by electrical objects or other man-made mechanisms. Since I was getting such an irregular beep, I believed that it might be a ghost.

After several minutes of examining the armoire, I asked the store manager if she had ever felt anything strange around the armoire. "Why?" she asked. I explained to her that it made me feel dizzy and confused when I was standing near it. I also described the reaction I was getting with my EMF meter. I told her it was enough of a reading for me to think the place is haunted.

She said, "The armoire belonged to the lady who the TV movie *Sybil* was named for. Remember her? She was the one with sixteen personalities. Sally Field played the part of Sybil." "Oh, my goodness. Yes, I remember that movie. I had heard that a doctor from Lexington had treated her for the disorder," I said.

Because I had such a connection with the energy around that armoire, I wanted to find out as much as I could about the real person who owned it. The true identity of Sybil was a well-kept secret, and I could not find any information at the time about her. All I knew about her was what I had seen in the movie. I had heard a rumor that she lived in Lexington, but without knowing her real name, I couldn't confirm this either.

It was not until July 27, 2009, eight years after my first investigation at The Vault, that I discovered the identity of Sybil. Early that July morning I was reading the *Lexington Herald-Leader* and found an article of interest. I read that a Woman's Exhibit at the Dodge County Fair was presenting drawings from a famous unknown artist who was a resident of Lexington. Her name was Shirley Mason. This still didn't ring a bell for me. As I continued to read the article, I was shocked to find out that this artist, Shirley Mason, was the woman known as Sybil. She suffered from a multiple personality disorder and was treated by Dr. Cornelia Wilbur, a University of Kentucky psychiatrist. The artwork was found in her Lexington home after her death in 1998, at the age of seventy-five.

Once her identity was exposed, more articles were published on the Internet, and I learned that she was born in Dodge Center, Minnesota, as an only child. Her mother suffered from a mental disorder that caused her to abuse her little girl physically and sexually. After Shirley grew up and became a teacher, she would black out and not remember what happened to her during the lost time. In the 1960s she moved to Lexington, where she was treated by Dr. Wilbur.

I went back to the armoire for one last attempt to see if I could pick up anything that might help me understand the feelings I was getting from the area that emitted the energy I was picking up. It was as if I could feel despair or deep sadness as if it were ingrained into the wood of this beautiful piece of furniture. I feel that I might have been picking up on the owner's energy at the time it was in her possession. I came very close to buying that piece because I felt drawn to it, but for some reason decided to let it go and continue my investigation.

Once we were finished with our two-hour search, I thanked the manager for letting us conduct our investigation. As we left The Vault I had no clue that we would be back five years later when it would be yet another business, The Lock and Key Café. I was putting together a list of places for GCI to check out and decided to call The Vault to see if I could bring my group there. The phone number had been disconnected so I went online and found that the Vault was now a café called the Lock and Key Café. I called the owner and, after introducing myself, got permission to come back to conduct another ghost investigation. I took a small group consisting of me, Chuck, Jeff Waldridge, and Cindy McFarland. When we arrived I noticed that new front windows had been installed but the overall appearance of the building was pretty much the same. The inside was a different story. It was bright, upbeat, and sported a colorful decor. There was a chic leather sofa to the right as you entered the café, which invited you to sit and listen to live music. The atmosphere was stylish, modern, and hip, with New Age coffees and teas and a few unique crafts and gifts. The first thing everyone in the group wanted to do before starting our investigation was to check out the bullet hole in the lady's restroom. Again, I got the same feeling that I got the first time with the hair raising up on the back of my neck as we entered the room. Jeff and Cindy were surprised at how much blood was visible after seventy years.

When I talked to Colleen, the owner of the Lock and Key, I told her that I had not been able to find any information about the bank president committing suicide and asked her if she knew the story. She shared with me an article that was written in the *Georgetown Times* on January 16, 1930. The headlines read "G. T. Hambrick Took His Life January 10th." The article stated that Mr. Hambrick asked one of the clerks to assist a customer just before he left the banking room. A moment later they heard a loud shot coming from a back room. The janitor rushed to the room and found Mr. Hambrick collapsed on the floor, dead. They found a note in his vest pocket that indicated his suicide was due to ill health, and there was no financial shortage. It was reported by those who knew him that he had been suffering with severe head pains over the last few weeks. I walked the group over to where the vault was, now a quaint dining area. As I stood inside I thought about the door closing shut and locking us away forever. That would be scarier than seeing a ghost! I was relieved to know that the door couldn't accidentally be shut because the lock had been dismantled. While standing in the vault, one of the servers told us that there was another vault in the basement that we could check out. Since we were not getting any EMF readings in the vault or in the area where the armoire once stood, we decided to go in the basement to see if we would have better luck there.

It was a typical dark and dusty basement, and we decided to start our investigation by trying to get some EVPs. We had three recorders going, so we walked around, in, and out of the other vault. I would ask a variety of questions to see if we could get an EVP on all three recorders. Usually when we do a group EVP session, the EVP will only be heard on one recorder. After several attempts and no results, I asked the spirits if they could tell me who they were, and my recorder picked up a male voice that said, "I am here." Could this have been George speaking out to us? When Cindy and Jeff listened to their audio recorders, they did not pick up the same EVP. We finished gathering our data and returned to the café above.

During my interview with the owner, Colleen London, I asked, "Have you had any experiences in the café that you would consider paranormal?" "I've had a couple of things happen," she said. "Once, in the early morning, I was in the back of the café and heard a sound coming from the front of the building. It made me think of a jar falling to the floor and then rolling forward for a few moments. I walked to the front and searched the area and never did find the jar or anything that might have made that sound. A few days later I was talking to one of my staff and asked if she had experienced any strange sounds. She said that she had heard a sound like a glass container rolling on the floor. I had not told her about what I had heard, so I was a little surprised that she described the same sound that I had heard.

Another time, while working up front, I heard the sound of dishes crashing to the floor. I went back to where the sound came from and didn't find any evidence that anything had fallen or broken. This is a sound that I have heard more than once, and every time I go to check it out, there will be no evidence of dishes falling on the floor."

"It's interesting to me that you heard the dishes crashing. I investigated this place years ago when it was an antique shop, and the manager said that she and her staff had heard the sound of dishes crashing," I said. Colleen responded, "Well, it's good to know that we were not the only ones to experience this."

I asked Colleen if any of her staff had experienced any other strange activity, and she said, "You might want to speak to Crystal Burge. She has told me about a few things that have happened to her." When I spoke with Crystal, the café manager, I asked, "Have you had any personal experiences that you would consider strange or eerie while working here?" "Yes I have," Crystal answered. "A few times, after arriving in the morning, I have heard my office chair rolling around on the floor. When I reached my office the sound stopped, and I found my chair under my desk as I had left it. It was obvious that it had not moved, but I would have sworn I heard it rolling around. There have been instances when I have heard a glass object fall to the floor and roll around, but when I go and look where the sound was coming from, there was nothing rolling around on the floor."

"This is the same sound Colleen told me that she had heard, and she said it sounded like a jar hitting the floor and rolling around," I said. "Yes, exactly," Crystal agreed. "I have also heard the dishes crash to the floor and so has Colleen. On our front doorknob hangs a bell so that if anyone enters the café, we will hear the bell ring. On occasions, the front doorbell will ring, and when I look up from the counter to see who has walked in, there is no one there. In a joking way I'll say, 'Hello,' and go back to my chores. I want to make everyone feel welcome here, even if it might be a ghost."

I asked Crystal if she knew when she first started working at the café about the suicide that had been committed at the location years earlier. She said that she did not find out about the suicide until later. A fellow came into the café and asked if he could look inside the ladies' restroom to see the bullet hole. She then told me that she preferred to go into the men's restroom and avoids the ladies' restroom all together. She doesn't like the way it makes her feel.

I asked Crystal, "Have you noticed items being moved, changed, or disappear without an explanation?" Crystal thought for a moment and replied, "Yes, I had bought a package of paper muffin cup liners, and when I got ready to make the muffins I could not find the liners anywhere. I went to the storage where I was sure I had put them, and they were not there. I called Janet, one of the staff, and asked her if she had by chance moved the liners, and she said that she had not touched them. She said they were on the shelf the last time she looked. I told her that they were not on the shelf, and she insisted that they were there. So I figured that they, the ghosts, had moved them. I continued to search with no success in finding the liners and had to go out and buy more before I could make my muffins."

It's always a real treat for me to return to a haunted location years later to see if the paranormal activity still exists. I found it rewarding to hear that the current employees of the Lock and Key had some of the same experiences as the former employees of The Vault. Even though this old building has been many different businesses within its 111 years of existence, it continues to produce enough evidence to support a possible haunting.

CHAPTER 10

Mammoth Cave National Park
MAMMOTH CAVE,
EDMONSON COUNTY

MY SON, SHANE, and his family came for a visit from Texas. He told me that on his way back home he was going to stop at Mammoth Cave to take his wife, Sarah, and their sons, Connor and Liam, on a tour. This got me thinking that maybe the cave would be a great place to look for ghosts. Surely such a place, hidden in the dark belly of the earth, would hold some sort of paranormal activity, so I decided to take a road trip to Mammoth Cave.

It was a cold and rainy day in October when Chuck and I arrived at Mammoth Cave. I was surprised to see how many people were standing in line waiting for the next tour to begin. I thought to myself, "They are going to freeze down there," not knowing until later that the temperature in the cave system remains constant, usually in the mid-fifties. We approached the visitors' center, which was buzzing with many people signing up for the tours while others were shopping at the gift shop. Although we were unable to book a tour of the cave at that time, we were able to spend some time at the visitor center. There, I learned that Mammoth Cave was the largest cave system in the world, with a total of 367 miles of caves. It is also the oldest tourist attraction in North America, first opening in 1816. I was delighted to learn that Jules Verne wrote about the cave in his book, *Journey to the Center of the Earth,* in a chapter titled "The Central Sea." There were fifteen different tours ranging from thirty minutes to four hour tours and traveling from three-quarters of a mile to four miles.

The history of Mammoth Cave is intriguing. It is estimated that the cave was first discovered by humans about four thousand years ago. In the 1800s the cave became a tourist attraction, using black slaves as tour guides. Some of these guides chose to explore the cave and found new routes for the tourists to experience. The most famous of these explorers was Stephen Bishop. He was the first black slave brought to the cave as a tour guide and started to explore it right away. Bishop was credited for finding several popular areas, including Fat Man's Misery, Cleaveland Avenue, and Mammoth Dome, which are among the most outstanding features in the cave. Even after the Civil War, when he and the other slaves were set free, many of them chose to remain as guides because of their love for the cave and the joy it brought them.

Another famous explorer was William Floyd Collins. He was a renowned cave explorer in Kentucky during the early 1900s. He was on a quest to find a better tourist entrance for his newly discovered Crystal Cave, which was a part of the Mammoth Cave system. After he found what he was looking for, he set out to return to the surface but became stuck while crawling through a narrow tunnel. As he struggled to free himself, he dislodged a rock that fell on his leg and trapped him. When he was noticed as missing, a search was started. The search party heard him yelling through a small opening. For a few days the rescuers passed food and water to him while they tried to figure out a way to free him. Suddenly, the cave collapsed around Collins, closing off any contact with him other than his voice. After seventeen days trapped in the cave, he died of starvation and dehydration. His body was not recovered until two months later. For many years Collins's body was displayed in a class coffin for the tourists to see. It was later removed and is no long available for public view.

With two thousand years of guides, explorers, and visitors passing through the trails of dark, silent, and spooky passages, some lost their way, were trapped, died of fright, or fell into deep pits. This type of history might be the cause of a haunting or two. The people at the visitors' center had given me the names of some people to contact about ghosts at Mammoth Cave. One of the first people I talked to was Charles Hanion, a career park ranger and the co-author of *Scary Stories of Mammoth Cave,* along with author Colleen O'Connor Olson. He has worked at the site for a total of twenty years and has a BA in anthropology from the University of Tennessee.

I asked Charles, "What is it you like best about working at the cave?" His response was, "I am proud to be a part of the human and natural history filled with tradition and success that surrounds Mammoth Cave." I told Charles that I had read the book he co-authored and found it captivating. I didn't know that tuberculosis patients had been kept in the cave as part of their treatment for the disease. The doctors had hoped that the condi-

Mammoth Cave encompasses 367 miles and may be haunted by ghosts, such as a former explorer known as Floyd.

tions in the cave would aid in the healing of the patients with consumption, TB, and other respiratory ailments. He told me that patients were brought in a few at a time, but most of them did not recover and died there. Tourists are reminded today of this era by the remains of a consumption cabin and the doctor's cabin. There is also a stone that rests beside them, called Corpse Rock. When a patient died, his body was laid out upon the rock; it was the patient's final resting place before his corpse was removed for burial.

I asked Charles if he would tell me some of his own personal experiences involving ghost sightings. He chuckled and said, "Well, I can't prove that what I've seen are ghosts, but I can tell you some things that have happened to me. During the late 1980s, I had taken a lantern tour down to an area called Chief City. It is a huge area, two acres in size." "Wow," I said, "I can't imagine a cave being that big." He continued, "We stopped the group to rest in front of Sacrifice Rock." I interrupted and asked, "Why was it called Sacrifice Rock?" expecting to hear a morbid story to serve as part of my ghostly report about the cave. He answered, "As I and the other tour guides lead our group into the cave, we carry a bucket filled with clothes soaked in a fuel to use as a torch. Once we light them, we throw them ahead of us to create more lighting on our path. When we get to the rock, we try to throw our torches to the very top of the rock so it will better illuminate the area. So many times we throw the torch, and it exceeds our aim and falls over to the other side, or it never makes it to the top of the rock and bounces off. This act causes us to sacrifice our torches—hence the name, Sacrifice Rock." That wasn't the story I was hoping for. "Okay, that makes sense. So, what happened once you stopped the group at the rock?" "On this tour we were lucky. The other guide threw the torch that landed perfectly on top of the rock. I turned at that moment to check out the rock, and to the side of the rock I could see a man standing there looking back at me. I could see that he was wearing a hat and a jacket and held an old lantern in his hand. At first I thought it was the other guide but when I glanced over to where I last saw him, he was still standing there. I turned my head back to take a closer look at the figure, but this time he was gone." "Did anyone else see this man?" I asked. "Yes, there was a woman in the group who pulled me aside after the tour and said that she saw a man standing by the rock and then he disappeared. She wanted me to tell her if she had witnessed a ghost," he said. "When we got back to the center, I asked my partner if he had seen what I had seen by the rock, and he said yes, but he didn't want to say anything in front of the tourists." I asked Charles, "Do you have any idea who it was that you saw?" Charles replied, "I'm not sure, but one of my first thoughts was that it might be one of the black slave guides who worked there for many years. These men loved their jobs, leading folks into the cave and telling them the history and stories. It would make sense that they loved it so much they chose to stay, even in spirit."

"Have you ever seen anything move or disappear to reappear someplace else?" I asked. "One day, when another guide and I were walking down one of the passageways, I glanced over and noticed a bench with an old whisky bottle sitting on it. Since I was in the midst of a conversation, I didn't pay it much attention. On the way back, as I was nearing the bench, the whisky bottle flew off the bench and landed in front of me. I looked down, and for a second I thought that maybe someone was playing a trick and had rigged the bottle to fly off the bench. I examined the area and could not find any evidence of tomfoolery. I figured that it might be one of the ghosts having a little fun with us," Charles said.

Still wanting to hear more stories, I asked him if any of the staff had shared any experiences they'd with ghostly activity. Charles said, "When we get new rangers we tell them that when they go into the caves, they should ask Floyd to go with them for good luck. You know who Floyd is?" he asked. "Yes, I read about him," I answered. "We warn new rangers that if they don't ask Floyd to go with them, he might get back at them by playing a trick or two while they are down in the cave. One day a group of new rangers had started to do a little exploring on their own. When they got to the same area where the whisky bottle had fallen in front of me, they turned the corner and went down a smaller avenue. As they went deeper their cameras stopped working, their flashlights started to flicker, and their cloth torches started to sputter as if they were running out of fuel. Believe me, you don't won't to lose your light source in the cave. They became spooked and came back to the surface looking confused. Their flashlights were working fine, and the cameras were taking pictures with no problems. I asked them if they forgot to ask Floyd to go with them, and they just stared at me as if to say, 'Are you serious?' Then they turned and looked at each other and vowed they would ask Floyd to go with them from now on."

"What is the most common experience that you hear among the guides?" "The most common unexplained happening is when the guides get pushed on the right shoulder," Charles said. "They looked around, thinking it is a buddy, but there is no one there. It is a pretty hard push and not mistaken for imagination. Another spooky experience is hearing heavy boot steps walking up behind them only to turn and see no one standing there. Sometimes these steps will become so loud that guides would leave the area and not turn out the lights on their way out for fear that whatever is there would follow them if it were dark."

After talking with Charles it made me want to learn more about Mammoth Cave's history and myths. Rich in history, the cave holds many stories about the lives of the people who traveled the passageways, leaving their mark behind. There also seems to be strong evidence that some of them chose not to leave their mark and just stay there forever instead.

CHAPTER 11

Mansion at Griffin Gate Resort
LEXINGTON, FAYETTE COUNTY

WHENEVER I WANT TO ENJOY the atmosphere of gracious dining, I go to the Mansion at Griffin Gate, where my dining experience is always an unforgettable one. The drive up the hill landscaped with ancient trees of blue ash, burr oak, Kentucky coffee and hackberry standing guard over the magnificent four-column, antebellum mansion, lures me into a bountiful time of long ago. Once I'm inside this four-star, four-diamond restaurant, the state of pleasure continues as my eyes scan the lavish rooms filled with antiques, paintings, carved fireplaces, and glorious crystal chandeliers that reflect the era of the 1800s.

Most of the paintings hanging in the rooms and in the foyer are replica lithographs that include John James Audubon's birds and wildlife, old English country scenes, and, of course, lots of images depicting horses and Thoroughbred racing. After all, Lexington is known as the "Horse Capital of the World." There is no wonder why Middle Eastern sheiks and other wealthy buyers of Thoroughbred race horses prefer to dine at the mansion after a successful day of buying at the famous Keeneland Sales.

I feel that whenever there is such a combination of beauty and history as we find at the mansion, there will usually be mysteries and sometimes hauntings to follow. Since ghostly activity has been experienced by many of the staff and guests at the mansion, the stories have become numerous over the last few years. Of course, with most hauntings, you experience the sound of footsteps, cold spots, doors mysteriously opening, dishes clinking, silverware falling onto the floor. But from the stories I hear, there seems to be much more ghostly phenomena at the mansion.

Sometimes, late at night when the staff is cleaning up, they hear the faint sounds of an old Victorian harpsichord. When they stop what they are doing so they can get a better sense of where the music is coming from, they are usually drawn to the air shafts from the heating and air conditioning units. The sound is eerie. When it starts to play, the staff says the hair on their arms and on the backs of their necks will rise, and they feel goose bumps. They have never been able to find the source of this music.

While a group of ladies were sitting at one of the dining tables, a cup and saucer that had been sitting on the fireplace mantle suddenly flew off and landed on the other side of the room. They were jolted in their seats but also amused by what had just happened. They had heard that the mansion was haunted, and they had been coming to the mansion for many years, and so they were delighted to have finally witnessed such evidence of the haunting.

Another time, a lone gentleman came to dine at the mansion, and while he was sitting at his table, checking out the menu, he noticed someone approaching him from across the room. He looked up and saw a beautiful lady dressed in a long, flowing, ballroom-type gown, which appeared to predate the early 1900s. She made eye contact with the gentleman, and as he smiled at her, she returned the smile as she passed his table and went into the adjoining dining room. He thought to himself how delightful it was to have reenactors walking through the dining rooms for ambiance during your meal in a place rich in local history.

When it came time for the gentleman to pay for his meal, he told the server how much he enjoyed the added entertainment of the lovely lady reenactor walking through the dining room in full period clothing. He said it was the first time he had ever been to a restaurant where they created such a complete atmosphere of a time long passed. As he was expressing his gratitude and describing the young woman he'd seen, the server stared at him as if to say, "What in the world are you talking about?" The gentleman noticed the young man's facial expression and asked, "Is there something wrong?" The server explained to him that there were no reenactors or models or anyone of that description walking through the dining area that evening. The guest was thoroughly amused by the possibility that he had most likely witnessed the presence of a ghost.

One afternoon, I was at the mansion with my husband to help him hang some framed artwork that the restaurant had ordered from his art business, Collectors Gallery. I met the security guard walking through the foyer. We introduced ourselves and I asked Eric, the guard, if he had ever experienced any ghostly activity in the mansion. He was eager to share several stories, but my favorite one was about the security system going off several times in one week while he was on duty.

After the restaurant was closed, Eric would make his rounds to ensure that the building was empty of guests and staff, and he secured the building by checking all the doors that were to be locked. On this particular evening, a series of false alarms had gone off with no apparent reason. Just a little after 2:00 A.M., the alarm went off and Eric once again followed procedure by checking the doors, which were all locked. He entered the dark building with his flashlight glaring ahead and started to check out all the dining rooms on the first level. Finding no evidence of a disturbance, he turned to start up the stairs to the second level.

As he entered the common area that was connected to four dining rooms, he shined his flashlight into the center of the space. There was nothing out of place so he proceeded in and out of the four dining rooms. All was as it should be. He returned to the common area, and there in the middle of the floor was a lone dining room chair. He was taken aback, and as he regained his composure, started to walk towards the chair for a closer look, realizing that it couldn't have gotten there on its own. As he approached the chair, it began to shake and rock back and forth, which was enough to convince him to get out fast, and away he ran.

One day as I was running an errand at Walgreens, a fellow stopped me on my way into the store. He asked me if I was the ghosthunter who was investigating the Mansion at Griffin Gate, and I told him I was. He wanted to tell me about an experience he had at the mansion the day before. I was grateful that he wanted to share his experience with me, but I was on a tight schedule and didn't have time to listen to his story, so I gave him my business card and asked him to please e-mail me his story. He insisted that he couldn't wait to tell me the story and begged me to give him just a moment. He was so insistent that I agreed and turned my complete attention to him.

He began by explaining that he was the maintenance man at the mansion and that his boss had called him into the office to give him a list of projects that needed to be completed by the weekend before a huge wedding was to be held. His boss emphasized to him that he must take care of the burned-out light bulbs in the upstairs chandeliers first. He gathered the new light bulbs and ladder, then headed upstairs to attend to his chore. He turned on the chandeliers so he could see which ones needed to be replaced. He counted how many he needed to take to the top of the ladder in order to save time from going up and down the ladder each time. He changed out the old bulbs for the new ones. Once he descended from the ladder, he looked up one last time to make sure he had not overlooked any of the burned-out bulbs. Once he saw that they were all working, he moved on to the other five chandeliers to complete his project.

The next day, just hours before the big wedding, the wedding director complained to the manager that the chandeliers were still in need of new light bulbs. The manager called his maintenance man into his office, irritated at the fact that his request to change the light bulbs had not been completed. The maintenance man assured him that he had changed all the burned-out light bulbs and that he had also checked each chandelier before he left to make sure they were all working,. The manager told him about the wedding director coming into his office to complain about the chandeliers, so he sent him back to get the job done before the wedding party arrived.

The maintenance man grabbed his ladder and more new bulbs and headed for the chandeliers once again. He turned on the lights, and, to his amazement, the same bulbs that he had replaced the day before were burned out again. When he got to the top of the ladder and reached to remove the fist bulb, he noticed that it was not screwed into the socket very securely. When he turned it to tighten it, the light immediately shown brightly. He didn't know what to think as he proceeded to touch each light bulb to discover that they were all loose and needed to be tightened in order to work.

He pondered over what had happened, and it came to him that the experience might be linked to the ghostly activity that so many of the other staff members had witnessed. His thoughts of ghostly interference increased as he proceeded to the other chandeliers to find that the bulbs he had replaced and were working the day before, were now loose, but once tightened, worked just fine. He couldn't imagine anyone getting the ladder and climbing up to six chandeliers, picking out the new light bulbs and unscrewing them so they would appear burned out. It would have taken too much time to undo the bulbs, and someone would have noticed what he was doing and would have stopped him. After all, everyone was aware that things needed to be in perfect order for the big wedding the next day. That's when it came to him that he had to share this ghostly experience with Patti Starr, the ghosthunter of the mansion.

Sometimes the radio, which is set up in the bar of the mansion, would come on abruptly without anyone near the radio to turn it on. One evening it turned on and started to change channels and settled on a theme that was not programmed into their DMX. The song was from the popular TV series Mash and was titled "Suicide is Painless."

One evening as Ron Bradley, senior captain server, was setting out the wine glasses on the table before the restaurant opened, he was startled by a sound behind him. He knew he was the only one in the dining room at that time, so when he heard the flash of the fire being ignited in the fireplace behind him, he was shocked. He went over to the fireplace to look at the gas log unit, but just before he got to it, the fire went out. He looked down and saw that the fireplace was not yet connected to the gas pipes. The contractor was still installing the new log units in the other fireplaces and had not started the connection to the gas lines. So how did this fireplace manage to light itself without being connected or having a source to burn a fire?

Ron told me that even after the gas log units had been connected to the gas lines that sometimes the log units would come on in the fireplaces without any of the staff turning them on. The management even had the company that installed the units come back to check them out. They could find no logical reason for the gas logs igniting a fire without being turned on.

One of the most popular ghost stories about the mansion concerns a female ghost (lovingly named Greta by the staff) who committed suicide. The story goes that this young woman was deeply in love with a soldier. He had promised her that someday he would return so they could marry. Instead, the soldier betrayed her love by running away with her sister. The shock was too much for her to handle, so she hung herself in her upstairs bedroom, which is now referred to as the Blue Ash Room.

A survey record from the Historical Preservation Society reveals that Nora and John were listed in the History of Fayette County in 1882 as the children of David Sutton Coleman and Judith Ann Coleman who lived in the mansion from 1850s through 1880s. The record referred to her as "Miss Nora." Since records of children were sometimes omitted back then, it is not known what happen to Nora or when she died. There is no other mention of her in any of the family history or memoir. According to the Griffin Gate Survey, there is one room listed as "daughter's bedroom" in the mansion, which is now the Blue Ash Room. That could have been Nora's room. This room is also considered the most haunted of all the rooms at the mansion. The staff did not have this information when they dubbed the ghost Greta.

A former manager came into the mansion one afternoon to work on a wedding. Once she got to the top of the stairs she noticed that the shutters in the Blue Ash Room were closed. This was highly unusual since the employees were told to always leave these shutters open to allow lots of sunlight into the upstairs rooms. She thought that maybe they had been closed the day before for a meeting that needed the room to be darkened for a PowerPoint presentation. She walked over to each window, unlatched the hook holding them shut and opened each of the four shutters. She turned to walk away and decided to go to the restroom, which was located just outside the Blue Ash Room. As she was leaving the restroom something prompted her to turn and look back into the Blue Ash Room. She stepped back into the room and was shocked to find all the shutters closed and locked again. She decided to leave the shutters closed since she felt that maybe Greta was at it again, and it was obvious that she did not want the shutters opened. It was her room and she didn't want the sunshine to brighten up her mood.

Another spirit that seems to play havoc with the staff and guests is that of a little girl. She has been seen briefly running in and out of the dining rooms upstairs and sometimes as a shadowy mist running up the stairs to the third floor where the children's nursery used to be. Once, during a ghost investigation that I conducted at the mansion, I was able to capture the voice of the little girl on my recorder. At the time, the lighting above the staircase and the chandelier were turned off so that electrical energy would not interfere with our other sensitive equipment. At one point I turned around to take a picture of the staircase, and just before snapping my camera, I noticed that the sconce lights above the staircase were blinking on and off. I was startled to see them come on and off three times. I became very excited and called the other participants to come and see these lights blinking off and on. Since the power was off, I knew it was not because of a power surge or faulty bulbs. As I was explaining to the others what was happening, unbeknownst to me I was at that moment picking up the little ghost's voice on my sound recorder as she explained, "Daddy was causing the lights."

On another ghost investigation of the mansion, I brought along two psychic mediums, Jason Lewis and Jim White, who both came to me at different times without comparing their findings with each other. Each of them identified the ghost as Alice, a vixen of a child around the age of nine or ten years. Research reveals no mention of an Alice in the history of the mansion, but a neighboring farm family had a little girl named Alice, who was ten when the census was taken in 1850. Maybe this child came for a visit to play with the other children, Nora and John, and her spirit remains there today. This information was provided to me by Eric Duckworth, one of the ghost investigators with me that day. He took a special interest in finding history about Alice and went in a different direction on the research when he decided to look up the data on the neighboring farm.

The mansion's beauty is magnified during the Christmas season by all the stunning Christmas décor and the huge Christmas tree laden with awesome ornaments and big, brightly colored ribbons displayed in the foyer. Back in the early 1900s, due to travel distance and money, people chose to go back home to visit their family members during Christmas. This was the time to catch up on all that had been happening to each other during that year. This was also before radio and later television were the center of entertainment, so during these Christmas visits the children would gather around the fireplace and the elders would entertain them by telling scary ghost stories to pass the time before going to bed and waiting for Santa's arrival. It sounds strange to tell ghost stories at Christmas, but for some it was the only time of the year they could share them with each other.

For two years in a row, Ron Bradley and David Singleton have had firsthand experience with the spirits of Christmas at the Mansion at Griffin Gate. One of their favorite tasks was to decorate the huge Christmas tree in the front lobby. Their talents were truly reflected in the outcome—a marvelous and stunning Christmas icon glistening in bright colors and sparkling lights. One morning when they came into work they were surprised to see that most of the ornaments were missing. They thought that someone had stolen them. Since the tree looked so sparse, they bought new ornaments and added them to the tree for the remainder of the season.

Within a week, it was time to take the Christmas décor down. The remainder of the original ornaments along with the new ones and the bright red ribbons were put in a big cardboard box marked "Christmas décor for tree" and stored away in the attic for the next year. When the Christmas season rolled around again, Ron and David prepared to decorate the mansion. They went to the attic to retrieve all the Christmas decorations and noticed a box that they didn't recognize. The strange thing about this particular box was that it was not marked as to what was inside, and it had the ribbon from the Christmas tree the prior year wrapped around it. When they opened the box, they found all the ornaments that had disappeared the year before. Since Ron and David have been with the mansion for many years, this was validation for them that the ghosts were having their way again.

CHAPTER 12

Maple Hill Manor
Bed-and-Breakfast

SPRINGFIELD, WASHINGTON COUNTY

SOME OF THE MOST BEAUTIFUL scenic country roads in Kentucky are found in the Bluegrass region, which offers rolling hills, an array of trees and flowers, and horses running in fields corralled by white wooden fences. One sight that most likely will not be seen while driving in this region is a herd of alpacas. That is unless you are traveling on the dirt road that leads to the stateliest Greek Revival plantation you could ever hope to visit: the nationally recognized, award-winning bed-and-breakfast known as Maple Hill Manor.

The Manor was built in 1851 on nearly six hundred acres and is listed on the National Register of Historic Homes. Over the years this historic grand manor, accented with Italianate details, has been featured in many travel and home publications, including the popular *Southern Living*. The manor was also voted Kentucky's Best B&B in 2004, rated number one in the U.S. as the B&B with the Most Historic Charm in 2003, and the Best Breakfast in the Southeast in 2005 and 2006. My husband and I got up one October Sunday morning and discussed over breakfast what we wanted to do on our sunny day off. We decided to take a drive into the country to see where these beautiful roads of Kentucky would lead us. As we started our road trip, I couldn't help but notice that the leaves on the trees were already transforming into rich colors of red, purple, crimson, burgundy, radiant yellow, deep gold, warm brown, and ruddy orange as they glimmered in the sun's rays. Orange is one of my favorite colors, and according to some color experts, stimulates creativity, energy, and is the symbolic color for autumn. I remembered one fall afternoon when, my grandson, Liam, age four going on twenty, was looking out the window of the car and discovered that the leaves were turning orange on the trees. He turned and said to me, "Look Granny! The leaves are rusting on the trees." And proud Granny said, "Liam, I couldn't have said it better." Now that's creativity. It wasn't long before we found ourselves in the quaint town of Springfield where most of the stores on the main street were closed. Unlike the big cities, these smaller Southern towns were closed in the observance of the Sabbath. This enhanced our ride, since we could drive around without the hassle of a lot of traffic getting in the way of our country sightseeing trip. While we were patiently waiting at a red light, Chuck suddenly remembered our conversation with an interesting lady at the Campbell House Restaurant in Lexington a few weeks before. She had noticed that Chuck and

I were wearing T-shirts that displayed "Ghost Hunter" on the back, so she decided to walk over to our table to ask us if we were really ghosthunters. Once we validated that question she sat down at our table and proceeded to tell us about her son Todd Allen and the manor.

Todd had just bought a beautiful B&B outside Springfield. Over the last few days he had been telling her how he thought his new property might be haunted. We both remembered that she said the manor was located on Highway 150 between Springfield and Perryville, the site of one of the largest Civil War battles in Kentucky, so we took our cue to turn there in hopes we would be lucky enough to find this location. We soon saw the Maple Hill Manor sign on the right side of the road as we headed east. Turning onto the private road and driving up the hill, we were pleasantly greeted on the right side of the road by a herd of alpacas that were enjoying a romp in the fenced area. We learned later that the alpacas were brought to Maple Hill Manor by the owners, Todd Allen and Tyler Horton, when they discovered the many uses of this exotic animal's fur. It is spun into a fiber that is comparable to cashmere and made into sweaters, capes, caps, throws, and teddy bears just to mention a few items.

As we reached the top of the hill, covered in tall autumn-colored trees, we were greeted by a very happy, tail-wagging, golden retriever, Sampson, who seemed so pleased to have visitors. I noticed three cats behind him, lying on the outdoor furniture while grooming themselves. We got out of the car and started walking towards the front entrance of Maple Hill Manor as Sampson joyfully accompanied us to the door.

We knocked on the huge, tall door that showed signs of age through its many cracked layers of white paint. The door opened and there stood a very distinguished and handsome young man that we correctly presumed to be Todd Allen. After a brief introduction, Todd graciously invited us into the manor. We shared our story with him about how we met his mother and what she told us about his recent purchase of the manor. Todd was excited about his new venture as innkeeper of Maple Hill Manor, and with great pride began to tell us the history of his home.

In 1848 Thomas McElroy started the construction of this beautiful home for his seventeen-year-old fiancé, Sarah Maxwell, and once it was completed in 1851 he presented it to Sarah, who was now his wife. They moved into their magnificent home and started their life and family together. They were blessed with seven children but unfortunately, four of them died there between the ages of one and four years, and later they lost one teenaged child. When Sarah was forty-eight, she died in the home as did her husband, Thomas, when he was sixty-nine. On October 8, 1862, the Civil War battle at nearby Perryville took place, involving about 75,000 soldiers. Many of the wounded were taken to a makeshift hospital at the courthouse in Springfield, six miles from Maple Hill Manor. Courthouse records state that many of the plantations along the road to Springfield were pressed into service as temporary hospitals for the wounded and dying soldiers. It is believed that one of these plantations was Maple Hill Manor. In the years that followed, the manor has gone through a few incarnations. It was home to former New York Giants quarterback Phil Simms when he was a child. It was at one time a fine dinner hall and then later a home for children.

We couldn't wait to have Todd explain to us what he was experiencing in the way of haunting because we hoped that he would invite us back to do an investigation to see if we could document any evidence to support his findings. He explained that shortly after he and Tyler moved into the manor, they realized that the old house held many mysteries and secrets. After the innkeepers had heard the laughter of invisible children; seen dark figures moving from the dining room to the kitchen; glimpsed a woman walking up the stairs then disappearing; noticed doors

opening by themselves; their beloved golden retrievers, Sampson and Sophie, scurrying away as if something had just frightened them; they thought they had reason to believe that ghosts
haunted the place.

The hardwood floor in one of the upstairs rooms does not
gleam like the floors in the rest of the manor. When the owners
moved into the manor, they noticed that this floor was blood-
stained from the soldiers' wounds. They stripped the floor and
refinished it only to find that, in a while, the blood stains would
come back. They realized that if they painted the floor a dark
hunter green, it would not only compliment the colors in the
room, but it would also solve the problem of the bloodstains.

The sounds of footsteps walking back and forth in this room
can be heard by persons on the first floor, even though no one
is present on the second floor. Sometimes the footsteps would
be so loud that the former owners thought they had a break-in.
They would grab their guns and dog and head upstairs to investigate who was in this room. After a thorough search, they found
no evidence that anyone had gotten into the house. They were
convinced that it must be the ghosts of the soldiers who had
been brought to this room during the battle of Perryville.

Todd made the comment that each year when the Perryville
State Park has its reenactment of the Civil War battle on October 8, the activity in the upstairs room seems to become more
intense. The sounds of the footsteps are heard more often than
any other time of the year, and the other spirits seem to be more
excited, causing unexplained disturbances in other areas in the
house, including the basement.

Over the years, some guests have claimed to experience
the presence of a black Civil War soldier's presence. They have
actually seen him or sensed his presence in one of the upstairs
rooms and sometimes in the kitchen. One guest was in the
kitchen, and as she turned she thought she saw one of the black

Union soldiers looking into the window. She could make out his uniform and cap as he glared back at her through the closed window. Others have picked up on the personalities of plantation slaves. In the cellar is evidence of slavery, including shackles hanging from the hewn log beams.

In Allen's research of the historic home, he learned that Sarah McElroy had a little boy who died in the house from a tragic accident. One afternoon, while Sarah was tending to a few of the household affairs, she noticed that her four-year-old son was playing a game of peek-a-boo from the upstairs landing. As she came out of a room the little boy would hang over the railing with a "peek-a-boo, mommy." Sarah would look up and laugh and say "peek-a-boo" right back at him, then she would enter the next bedroom just under the stairwell. When she turned to walk into the other bedroom, a tragic thing happened in a matter of seconds. The upstairs banister above where her son had been leaning over to play his game suddenly gave way, and the little body tumbled and landed with a heavy thud a few feet behind his mother. Sarah turned and found her precious baby on the floor. She screamed for help and tried to revive her son as she lifted his frail little body.

It's not clear if the child died on impact, but one of the mansion's psychic guests felt that his death came after two days. Sarah never got over the death of her son, and walked the floor and stairs in grief for many months. During a couple of ghost investigations, a little boy's voice has been captured on sound recorders calling out to his mommy. Other convincing data has also been collected as evidence that the little boy is still haunting Maple Hill Manor. On one of my favorite ghost investigations of the manor, Chuck was filming me just after I had communicated with the little boy through electrical dowsing. He captured a wonderful anomaly in the shape of a vortex (thought to be the energy of a spirit) on our Sony infrared camcorder that appeared

The stairs where the little boy fell to his death. Patti captured these orbs as she asked the spirit to show himself after getting an EVP from a child that said, "Mommy."

to come from behind me and then through my chest as it continued its path on past the camcorder towards the front door. This was a very emotional time for me, and I was so fortunate that Chuck was able to capture this evidence on film.

While doing my own research, I found a story about another previous owner who had experienced a variety of ghostly activity while living in the manor. He claimed that sometimes at night he would hear a bang like something heavy falling and hitting the floor with great force. It would be so loud that it would wake up everyone in the house. The family noticed that the sound seemed to be coming from the foyer just below the stairs. They would look up to the top of the stair and realize that, if someone were to fall from there, it would cause a similar sound. They also made note that the banister that followed up the stairs and turned to continue to the landing was not the same height as it was on the stairs up. It drops in height from thirty-six inches to about twenty-eight inches, which would not prevent someone from falling over the railing.

This family did not know about the history of Sarah's son falling from the banister at the time they heard the sound. This piece of information was not found until they had moved away and the new owners, Todd and Tyler, found the history of the little boy's tragic death. When you visit Maple Hill Manor, be sure to look at the banister at the top of the stairs, and you will see a section of the banister is a slightly lighter color wood, indicating that it had to be replaced for some reason.

After visiting with Todd I asked him for permission to have a Ghost Hunting Get-Away-Weekend at the manor. I explained that I would present a seminar to describe the history of the manor and how to conduct a ghost investigation in a safe and appropriate way. Todd suggested that he would prepare a dinner for everyone on Saturday night. After dinner we would proceed to investigate the manor for ghostly activity. He happily agreed to all of our plans for the ghosthunting weekend and scheduled us to return in six months for the event. When we returned to Maple Hill Manor, we were thrilled to learn that Todd had completely sold out all of the rooms in the manor. We unpacked and started on schedule.

We started our ghosthunt on the second floor beside the banister where the little boy had fallen. I asked Todd to hold his hands above his head while I coached the tiny spirit to come to Todd's hands. I do this type of experiment at most of my investigations to demonstrate how the ghosts are communicating with us by appearing in the photo as anomalies near the person's hands. Within a few shots I was successful in capturing several big yellow orbs around Todd's hands. I was also recording the photo session with a cassette recorder when I captured a very soft voice of a small boy calling out, "Mommy."

We decided to continue the investigation by going to the first-floor foyer. While I was standing close to the spot where the little boy had fallen, my EMF meter sounded a couple of beeps. I started my question session again with the little boy and asked him if he was the one making my meter go off. I got a "yes" response. During my questions I learned that he had not died instantly as was thought. The little boy lived two more days after his fall while in great pain. Once the session stopped, I turned and faced my husband, who had started filming with our infrared camcorder. Feeling a bit saddened by my conversation with the little boy, I looked up at my husband just as he gasped. He had captured a strange white anomaly coming from my heart area that moved towards the left of the camera and then disappeared. I asked him, "What did you see?" as we all ran over to look into the small viewer on the camcorder. Everyone was thrilled to see such evidence on their first ghost investigation. The anomaly was shaped like a small white boomerang with small orbs within the shaft of the energy. We watched it over and over to make sure it wasn't atmospheric contamination or a bug. We checked it for other possible explanations and could not find anything that would clarify the anomaly. I must confess that I enjoyed that ghost investigation at the manor more than any other investigation I had ever done. The people were fun, the ambience was perfect, and the ghosts were actively taking part. I don't think I could have asked for a better evening than that.

CHAPTER 13

Mud Meeting House and Cemetery

HARRODSBURG, MERCER COUNTY

I REMEMBER WHEN I WAS ABOUT ten years old I joined a group from my church, Jackson Mill Baptist, called the GAs, (Girls Auxiliary). It was designed for girls between the ages of ten and sixteen, and we'd meet at church on Wednesday nights to study Bible scriptures. Our group leader, Mrs. Wilson, thought it would be nice to have a pajama party for us to relax and get to know each other outside the church. We all met at her place at 7:00 on a Saturday evening for a barbeque, which included hamburgers, potato salad, baked beans, and corn on the cob.

During the first few hours we giggled and played together until all the adults went to bed. Then we got bored, so we had to think of things to do to stay awake all night. Mr. Wilson's property backed up to an old cemetery so one of the girls, Nancy, came up with the idea that we should go to the cemetery. She thought up a game where the unlucky chosen one would be led to the center of the graveyard blindfolded. Then she would take off her blindfold as everyone else ran away. It was up to the girl to find her way back to Mrs. Wilson's house. Nancy had a bit of a mean streak, but the other girls still followed her lead.

Nancy decided that she would be the one to pick who would go into the cemetery. I knew she would pick me, since I was not one of her groupies. All the girls squealed with delight, since they weren't the target. They grabbed my arm and pulled me to the front porch. I stood there as they put the blindfold around my eyes and waited for them to lead me down the steps. I could hear the crunching of the leaves as we walked for a distance until Nancy said, "Okay, this looks like a good place." She placed the flashlight into my hands and said, "Count to ten and then take the blindfold off to find your way back to the house."

Off they scampered as I listened for their footsteps to fade away. I slowly lifted the blindfold from my eyes and with the flashlight pointing ahead of me looked to see where I was. It was a clear night with a bright, almost full moon. The headstones were scattered ahead of me in different shapes and sizes, some were leaning with age. Even though I felt nervous as I saw eerie shadows that seemed to dart back and forth between the headstones, I was also intrigued. I flashed my light on the headstones and read off the names and dates of the deaths. As I walked deeper into the cemetery I was drawn to certain headstones, and sometimes I heard my name being whispered behind me, "Patti." After about twenty minutes the other girls got really worried and thought something terrible had happened to me. I could hear them in the distance calling my name. Then I heard Mrs. Wilson firmly yell, "Patti, where are you?" The girls had gotten in big trouble for taking me out into the cemetery and leaving me. I realized I had better start back to the house and had to chuckle a little about the trouble that Nancy had gotten the girls into. This was a night I would never forget and that I would revisit over and over again as I grew older.

One of my favorite things to do as a ghosthunter is to visit cemeteries. I feel that you can walk around the dead and still feel them there. You can say their names and talk to them. I think they hear us, and they appreciate that they have not been forgotten. I get wonderful EVPs and great photos in cemeteries that help me with my collection of evidence of life continuing on after death.

Now that I'm always looking for cemeteries to investigate, another one of my students and good friend, Lee Kirkland, told me about a graveyard he visited as a child. He said he would go there with some of his school buddies, and they would walk around after dark with a flashlight. They were looking for spooks. They wanted to see or hear these ghosts for themselves. As they huddled together, they would walk over to the old Mud Meeting House and flash their lights into the windows, hoping to see signs of a "hant."

I asked Lee, "Did you ever see anything while you were there?" He said, "Yes. We would see shadows at the top of the hill walking between the trees and headstones. We had heard that if you walk up to the Old Mud Meeting House, you could hear the voices of a sermon going on." I asked Lee, "Did you hear anything?" "You bet," Lee said, "I would hold my ear to the door or sometimes the back wall, and we would hear muddled voices that would sound like a church sermon. It was moments like that, which happened to me as a kid, that made me want to become a ghosthunter."

I wanted to find out about this historic place, so Lee, Chuck, and I met at the Dairy Queen in Harrodsburg, and then we followed Lee to the Old Mud Meeting House Cemetery. We pulled out of the parking lot and drove through a busy part of Harrodsburg to make our final turn. Then we drove into the countryside. We passed a few cattle farms until the winding road took us to a short turnoff to the right, where we pulled into a driveway guarded by a huge white iron gate.

Lee's wife, Jennifer, was on her way from work to meet us, so while we waited, we walked behind the car to the side of the road and read the historical marker that detailed the history of the church. The Old Mud Meeting House was the first Dutch Reformed Church west of the Allegheny Mountains. It was established by fifty members who came to Mercer County from Pennsylvania in 1781. The church was built in 1800 on land that also provided space for a cemetery located in the city of Harrodsburg, which was founded in 1774 and was the first town in Kentucky. The members built the church with their own hands, and mud was used inside the walls, giving the church its odd name. As the men laid the first planks they stopped to pray for God's blessing. Before the church was finished, a member of the congregation died and was buried in the cemetery on the hill. Later, as the aging members were passing away, many were buried in the cemetery. Among these people who were laid to rest in the cemetery were Revolutionary War veterans who had nearly starved with Washington during that terrible winter at Valley Forge, some who faced the British at the battle of Monmouth and Brandywine, some who crossed the Delaware River to storm the Hessians at Trenton, and others who fought in the trenches of Yorktown. Some of them no longer have headstones, but I did find a listing of all those who are buried in the cemetery at the Harrodsburg Historical Society.

Jennifer arrived just before dark. As we were walking up the hill I could see that the Old Mud Meeting House was under

The haunted cemetery behind the Old Mud Meeting House

renovation. Once this project is finished, it will reopen to the public, but the cemetery is open at all times. We had planned to get there before dark to take pictures of the building. It was getting darker sooner than usual because the day was heavy with clouds and the threat of snow.

I suggested that we go inside the cemetery before it got too dark to see. We walked behind the building, where there was a somber, ascending knoll with many headstones peering out beneath sprawling trees advanced in years. They seemed to be shielding the graves. The hill was surrounded by a stone fence with a closed, wooden gate at the entry. We unlocked the gate, walked forward a few steps and stopped. We said a prayer of protection and asked permission to enter this scared ground. With great respect, we walked forward into the graveyard.

We used our flashlights to avoid tripping over the smaller headstones. I looked up and saw a ball of light fly across my path. It startled me. And a few seconds later, Lee saw the same anomaly fly past him and said, "This reminds me of the first time we brought my son, Mason, out here. He was about two years old and it was just before dusk. We were walking around looking at the headstones when I heard Mason laughing behind me. When I turned to see why he was laughing, I saw him running with a stick. I asked him what he was doing, and he said he was chasing the ball. At that moment I thought that maybe he was seeing a spirit orb."

I aimed my flashlight over the west side of the stone fence because I thought I saw a dark, shadowy figure pass from one tree to the other. There was nothing there. Lee called me over to look at a photo he had just taken. Coming off two headstones was a fine, misty form located close to the edge of the stone fence. Lee said, "I have a friend who is a deputy sheriff, and he was out riding his horse one afternoon. The property that he was riding on backs up to this cemetery. As the horse approached the stone fence, where these two headstones are close to, the animal stopped suddenly. The deputy tried to make the horse go forward, but he wouldn't budge. When he gave him a firm command to go forward, the horse reared and threw him off his back. The sheriff lay on the ground and the horse galloped away. Since we both grew up here, he knew the stories of this place being haunted but never really gave it much credence. That was until that day. I guess it was a good experience because he has now joined our group, SHOCK [Spirit Hunters of Central Kentucky], and often goes ghosthunting with us."

Jennifer said, "Hey, guys, are you ready for us to do an EVP session?" We crowded around her in the area where we were getting the strange activity. She pulled out her digital sound recorder and began by saying, "My name is Jennifer and I would like to communicate with you. We are not here to hurt you, scare you, or exploit you; we just want to talk to you. Can you send your energy through this little box in my hand and tell me your name?"

Within about seven seconds, my EMF meter started to beep and Lee's K2 EMF meter registered a hit. The K2 EMF meter became a popular instrument to use on a ghosthunt once it was seen on the A&E Network show, *Ghost Hunters*. We were far out into the country and there were no electrical wires close enough to cause these meters to go off. We looked at each other but did not make a sound so as not to interfere with the spirits that might speak into the recorder. Jennifer waited for another twenty seconds and stopped the recorder. She hit the play button and we all listened, hoping to hear a voice telling us a name. When the recording came to the part where our meters went off, both our meters went off again in unison with the recorded beeps. We were shocked to get this type of results. After the meter stopped, a voice answered Jennifer's questions for a name by saying, "Tom." Jennifer said, "Good job and thank you, Tom, for letting us know your name."

We were happy to get these extraordinary results considering we had only been there a few minutes. Jennifer started her recorder again for more questions. Lee asked, "Are you a soldier?" After waiting about ten seconds, he asked another one, "Are you connected to the church or the land?" We waited another ten seconds, and I asked a question: "Will you give us permission to be here?" Jennifer hit the "play" button. When Lee asked if he was a soldier, we didn't get a voice but heavy static came through the recorder for about four seconds. The next question Lee asked was about being connected to the church or land. We heard a strong answer, "I am." When I asked for permission, we heard a response that said, "Yes, you do." We were thrilled with this excellent EVP session.

The only interference we had while doing our EVP session was the mooing of cows from a neighboring farm. The mooing was really creepy; they sounded possessed. I asked what was wrong with those cows, and Lee said they were in heat. Knowing this, we discounted any weird sounds that were picked up while recording. Jennifer said, "Cows freak me out. I don't like them and to hear them moo like that is wigging me out. I wish they would hush." We all laughed at Jennifer's comment, a welcome bit of comic relief in a night that was becoming eerie.

Unlike my first time in a cemetery with a bright moon, this night the moon was in a new moon phase, which is good for ghosthunting results, but we had no light coming from anywhere. It was, as they say, "pitch dark" by now. I pulled out the Ovilus and began to walk around asking questions to see what words we would get from this instrument. In a few moments we heard the words, *stone, people,* and *light.* I felt this was appropriate considering we were in a cemetery with headstones with people's information written about them on the stones. I asked if we could have the names of the ones with us tonight, and the names that came through were "William," "Richard," and "Lee." I'm always amazed that when I ask for names, they will start to come through the Ovilus. I discovered these same names listed on the cemetery roster that I found on the Harrodsburg Historical Society's Web site.

I put away the Ovilus and reached for my camera. I continued my conversation with the spirits and asked them to show themselves in energy form. After a few snaps of my camera, I started to get a few orbs. They were very light, so I told them that I could barely see them and asked them to show themselves a bit stronger. When I snapped my camera again, I got a very bright, white, spirit orb over a headstone and close to where Lee and Jennifer were standing. I handed the camera to Chuck and asked him to take a few shots of me, Lee, and Jennifer to see if he could continue getting spirit orbs around us. Chuck spoke to the spirits and asked, "Can you show yourself in a color that might tell

us about your personality or mood that you are in?" Just as he
shot the picture, he got a blue orb. When he told us what he had
captured, Lee took his camera and asked for the same spirit to
appear to him for his shot. When he snapped his camera he also
got a blue orb. I considered this another good piece of evidence
that we captured during this investigation.

I asked Jennifer if we could do an EVP session with her digital
recorder since we were getting these spirit orbs. She agreed and
turned on her recorder and asked, "Do you want us to know that
you are here?" Again my EMF meter sounded a couple of beeps,
and on playback you heard a voice answer after the two beeps and
say, "Hello." Jennifer asked two more questions, "What is your
reason for being here? Are you the one that formed the energy of
a blue orb?" On playback we heard a voice of a male answer her
question. The words were muffled, and we could not make out
what he was saying, but at least he was trying to communicate
with us. The same voice answered, "Yes," to the questions about
being the spirit of the blue orb.

Since it was so cold we decided to call it an evening. We
were happy to get such great results in our short time there.
We headed for the gate and once we got there, I stopped and
suggested that we do one more session with the Ovilus before
leaving the cemetery. We stepped outside the gate and closed
it. I turned the Ovilus on, and the first thing it said was, "Harrodsburg." Chuck asked, "Did it just say Harrodsburg?" Lee and
Jennifer both agreed that it said Harrodsburg, which is not one
of the words programmed into the vocabulary of the Ovilus. I
asked Jennifer to please turn on her recorder to see if we got any
spirits responding to the words of the Ovilus, and on playback
we got a couple of hits. During the playback we confirmed that
the Ovilus did say, "Harrodsburg." It also chattered out the name
"William" again and the number "eight." I said that we were
leaving and asked if it had a parting message for us. The Ovilus

answered, "Bill, get up." After that, Jennifer's recorder picked up a male voice that said, "Damn, Jennifer." Then the Ovilus said, "Alone somewhere is Sam." This was the best playback so far. The Ovilus is not programmed to speak in complete sentences, so how we got them was a mystery.

We turned away from the gate and headed towards the back of the church. Lee suggested that we place our ears to the wall to see if we could hear any voices or a sermon. He told me that it was common knowledge throughout the community that voices can be heard in the Old Mud Meeting House. I placed my ear to the wall and turned my recorder on. I thought I heard a single voice, and while Lee had his ear to the wall facing me said, "What was that?" I knew at that moment he heard what I heard. I couldn't make it out, but it had a rhythm to it as if a poem or maybe scripture was being quoted. When we played the recorder back, it was on the recorder but so faint we couldn't make out the words.

I couldn't have been more happy with a ghost investigation than with this one. I can't wait to go back for another investigation since we got so much evidence our first time. If anyone were to ask me about this sacred place, I would have to agree that we got strong evidence of a possible haunting.

CHAPTER 14

Mullins Log Cabin
BERRY, HARRISON COUNTY

SOMETIMES WHEN I'M SEARCHING for a place where Chuck and I can go to escape from our busy schedules, I like to find out-of-the way places. I love staying at places like Natural Bridge, going hiking, taking pictures of the beautiful countryside, and just getting away from the hustle and bustle of life. The smell of fresh air, letting the sun warm my skin, and listening to the gentle breeze as the birds chirp out their melodies is the best way for me to recharge my energy. Sitting out in nature, reading a good book while snacking on cheese and grapes is heaven to me.

While searching for a getaway destination, I found an unusual place called Mullins Log Cabin Country Getaway. The destination was an 1850s cabin located in the small town of Berry with a population of only 307 people. The cabin has no electricity and comes with coal oil lamps and candles for light and a stone fireplace for warmth. I loved imagining staying in an original dovetail log cabin like the one my great grandparents had. The cabin would allow me to spend a day as they would have. The cabin sits on six acres of land with a creek flowing behind it. You can enjoy a comfortable hammock that is set up in an area across the creek called Walnut Grove. There is no running water or a bathroom in the cabin. If you look under the bed, you'll find a chamber pot for nighttime use. If you need to relieve yourself during the day, there is a contained outhouse to the left of the cabin, about fifty yards away. Boy, did that bring back memories! Believe it or not,

I lived in a house without indoor plumbing or a bathroom the first six years of my life. We had an outhouse to accommodate us during the day and a chamber pot to use at night. The cabin has a loft with a double bed, and downstairs there is a sofa that turns out into a bed. Plus there is enough room to place sleeping bags around. This was a perfect place for the next time Chuck and I decided to get away.

A former student of mine, Joe Clark, sent me an e-mail to check out some of his investigations he had listed on his Web site. As I checked the list, I saw that he had gone to the Mullins Log Cabin Getaway. I called Joe and he told me that his investigation yielded great paranormal results, and he felt the cabin was haunted. He told me that Judy Mullins, owner of the cabin, was ghosthunter friendly, and she rents out the cabin to people hoping to experience ghostly activity. He suggested that when I call, I should let Judy know that Joe Clark recommended me to her.

Since it was way too cold for us to rent the place during December, I decided that this cabin would be a perfect chapter to include in the book I was writing. I called Judy to see if I could come and do an investigation at her cabin. Judy was receptive and welcomed my visit. We made an appointment to meet the first week in January for an interview and ghosthunt at the cabin.

We never expected an arctic cold front to be gripping our area, with temperatures in the teens and single digits at night. When we got to the cabin, we saw that Judy had started a big fire in the stone fireplace, but even after being there for almost two hours, the heat from the fire had only raised the temperature to thirty-two degrees. It was around eighteen degrees with a wind chill factor of nine degrees outside, so it was a little warmer in the cabin.

When we first walked into the cabin, my eyes were not adjusted to the low light, since I had just walked in from the bright, white, snow-covered yard. I thought, "How will I be able to see my way around?" It didn't take long for my eyes to adjust to the coal oil lamp and candle lights. After we said our hellos and intros I started my interview with Judy as we sat huddled close to the fire. I sat in a rocker with a hand-woven reed seat in a herringbone design that Judy had made. As Judy sat across from me, she looked as if she were planning a skiing trip, with her bright red down jacket, thick woven gloves, woolen cap, and fur lined boots. She was dressed to stay warm and was a real trouper to allow us to come to the cabin in such cold.

I wanted to know about the history of the cabin, so I asked Judy, "When did you become the owner of this cabin?" Judy answered, "In 1991 I overheard a conversation about an old log cabin. A neighbor was telling the local country storekeeper that he was thinking about burning it down to get it off his property. That's when I spoke up and said that I would love to have it. He was happy to know that it would be preserved, and I was happy to get a nice piece of history and heritage. We dismantled the cabin log by log and stone by stone as we numbered each piece. Within a year I had it completely restored and we had guests staying overnight by 1992."

As I looked up at the tall ceilings, I noticed the wood was different from the rest of the cabin. I asked her if the roof was new and she said that it was. "We added the loft with the stairs and roof, but the logs and limestone fireplace are all original." "Do you know the history of this place?" I asked. "I don't have a lot of direct history, but I did find out that I had a third cousin who grew up in this cabin. Her name was Lily, and she died long before I was born. When I was researching the cabin, I did find out that the property where the cabin sat along the Cynthiana Turnpike was close to three Civil War battles fought in the Cynthiana area. Soldiers traveling through this area would stop at these local residences to get food and fresh horses as they continued their journey. Since the cabin was located in that area and was dated to the 1850s, I felt sure that the soldiers probably stopped at this cabin as well." Judy replied.

"My real interest here today is to learn about the haunting experiences you, your guests, and some of the other ghosthunters have had. What can you tell me about that?" I asked. Judy chuckled, "Well, I do have one ghost that I feel is quite a character. He likes to pinch and not only me. He has also pinched guests and ghosthunters. The first time it happened to me, I had crossed the creek that runs behind the cabin to the land on the other side that I call Walnut Grove. I have some hammocks set up for the guests to enjoy. While I was walking around I looked down and saw what looked like very old headstones. They were small and I couldn't make out if there was any writing on them because of the age. I thought that I might be walking around in a family cemetery. As I stood still at the foot of one of the headstones, I was pinched really hard on the back upper part of my arm. I yelped out and turned to see if my nephew, Toby, had come up behind me. He can be a real practical joker, and I thought that he might have pinched me, but he was not there."

I asked Judy, "Who else has been pinched by these unseen hands?" She replied, "One night a few of us, including my daughter, Janessa, and Toby, were visiting at the cabin. All of a sudden Janessa screamed out, 'Toby, quit pinching me!' He said, 'How can I be pinching you when both my hands are on top of the table in plain sight?' He made a good point." I said to Judy, "And that happened here in the cabin unlike when you were outside?" She said, "Yes. Another time when someone got pinched, it happened to one of my guests. This lady was standing behind the cabin looking around at the peaceful scenery, and she was pinched on the arm as well. She is a very spiritual lady, and she told me she turned to see who was pinching her, and there was no one around to blame it on."

Judy also told me, "I remember when Joe Clark brought Chris Dedman with him to do an investigation. Joe was the first ghost-hunter to do an investigation of this place, and now he brings others to witness the activity here. While Chris was sitting in a chair over by the door, he said, 'Ouch,' and Joe asked him what had happened. Chris said, 'I just got pinched on the arm.' I'm not sure why this ghost always pinches on the arm. There is another family that comes down from Frankfort a couple of times a year. They were raised in an old log cabin and told me that when they stay here they feel like they have come back home. During one of their summer visits, they were sitting out on the front porch with the door open so they could see back into the cabin. Inside the cabin there was a paper bag filled with a few snacks sitting on the hearth of the fireplace. They heard a noise and looked inside the door and saw the paper bag dancing across the surface of the hearth. They started to laugh thinking that maybe a mouse had gotten inside and was causing the commotion, but when they entered the cabin and looked inside the bag, there was nothing there. They looked at each other and didn't think that it was funny any more."

I thought this was a good story, and it would be difficult to explain what was causing the paper bag to dance across the hearth when there was nothing in the bag. "Do you have any other personal stories that have happened to you while you were in the cabin?" Judy replied, "Yes, I just remembered what happened to me and my nephew. We were sitting in the cabin and talking, when we heard a strange sound that we had never heard before. It seemed to be coming from the rafters above and sounded angelic, like a falsetto. We glanced at each other, realizing we both were hearing the same sound. It wasn't so much like a song but more like a running of scales and lasted for about thirty seconds. It was really beautiful music."

"Judy, before we start our investigation, can you think of any other activity that has been witnessed here by you or your guests," I asked. "Yes," she said, "I rented the cabin to a Kentucky author who writes books on hauntings and ghost stories, and he and his girlfriend stayed here one evening. While they were sitting around the cabin's fireplace, they heard someone walking across the front porch. When they got up to see who might have stopped by, there was no one there. They stepped out on the porch and looked all around at the open yard, and did not see anyone. If someone had walked up on the porch, they would have seen them leaving the area, but there was no one there.

At this point I advised Chuck to get our equipment out of the car, so we could start our own investigation of the cabin. I started out with my EMF meter sweep, knowing there would not be any false positives, meaning that I would not be picking up any manmade energy from wiring or appliances to make the meter go off. I knew if the meter went off, it would have to be paranormal since there was no electricity.

While I was setting up my other instruments I decided to place my digital recorder on a small table to record any unusual sounds and hopefully capture some EVPs. Even though my fingers were freezing in the cold cabin, I took many shots with my camera, hoping to capture a mist, form, apparition, orb, or any other shape that I might be fortunate to get. I took a couple of snap shots of Judy, who had moved to sit on the hearth to get closer to the warm fire. I walked to the other side of her and said that if there was a spirit in the room, would it please form next to Judy—and I got a spirit orb to the left of her. It was the only orb that I got during the entire investigation, and I took close to eighty pictures. Later when I went through my pictures, I was excited to see a face that seemed to glow in the background of the fire next to where Judy was sitting. It looked like a male face with his mouth open getting ready to speak.

I continued to walk around the dimly lit cabin that was now hazy with smoke that had crept out of the fireplace. I went over to

Judy Mullins sitting on the hearth at the Mullins Log Cabin. Patti captured a face in the blaze of the fire.

one of the front windows were the couch was and turned on the Ovilus to see what words would come through. I was surprised to hear how chatty the Ovilus was. I thought with no electricity in the cabin it might not say much. I started the session by asking if there was someone there who would like to communicate with us, and the names that came through were Kevin, Roger, Jimmy, and Mike. The names did not come through in a consecutive order, because some of the words in between were not clear. I always find it amazing that when I ask for names, the next words that will come from the Ovilus are usually names. While still standing by the couch I thought it was strange that I got the word mattress, because earlier Judy told me that the couch turned into a comfortable bed. We had a good laugh over that word. I continued to walk around and ask questions about the lives of the spirits, who they were and why were they there. Judy spoke up and told me about the Civil War soldiers coming through Cynthiana and staying in the cabin. While she was telling her story the Ovilus remained quiet, but as soon as she was finished, it started reciting "war," "state," "soldier," and "stabbed." I was pleased to hear these words since they resonated with the story of the War Between the States and the soldiers. I decided to change my instruments and use the Ghost Radar from my iPhone. It is an application that employs a proprietary algorithm to analyze the quantum flux in a close area. The readings are displayed graphically as blips on the radar screen, along with numeric and textual readouts. When I turned it on, within a few seconds, there were three bright yellow dots on the radar screen indicating a strange energy. I walked over to the fireplace, and the Ghost Radar spouted out, "fire," "hearth," and "basket." When Judy heard the word "basket," she looked at me and nodded her head to say yes, because we had been talking about her basket weaving workshops.

As I continued to walk over to the stairs, I got the word "music" from the Ghost Radar, and I thought that was a good clue since I was standing under the rafter where Judy and Toby had heard the musical notes sung in the beautiful angelic voice. When I decided to put the instrument away I said, "I must go now." And it said, "Away." I said, "Yes, I'm going away now. Goodbye." The Ghost Radar said, "Bye." I just about fell over, and Judy was also amazed at the response. When I get this type of response from these instruments, and the words coming through are related to what we were talking about or doing, I feel we have a spirit that is trying to communicate and let us know they are of an intelligent energy.

We concluded our ghost investigation, and I thanked Judy for her gracious hospitality. I told her that I would be calling Joe Clark to compare my data with his results to see if we had any similarities. Judy told me that she was thrilled that we had gotten some good evidence in such a short time. We gave each other big hugs, and I promised to come back in the spring when it wasn't so unbelievably cold.

I called Joe Clark when I returned home so I could share with him some of the names we picked up while in the cabin. While on the phone I asked Joe, "We got the names Kevin, Roger, Jimmy, and Mike. Did you get any of these?" Joe answered, "No, we got Derrick several times and Isaac Angel." I asked Joe, "How did you come by your names?" Joe answered, "I was with Tommy Jones of Para-X and some members of his group, KAPS. They were using the Hack Shack Ghost Box and an audio recorder to capture EVPS."

When I told Joe about the words that fit with the belief that soldiers of the Civil War stayed at the cabin, Joe told me that the best EVP they got that night was a female voice that said, "Hurry up, boys." I told Joe that maybe the lady of the house was hurrying the soldiers on.

Joe told me that they had several spikes with their EMF meter, and since there was no electricity or any other type of manmade energy in the house, he felt the spikes to be of a paranormal nature. He also said that they noticed temperature fluctuations and battery drainage as well.

Once I documented all my calculations and data and comparing my notes with Joe, I would have to agree with him that the Mullins Cabin has a great potential for being haunted. It does seem to be a peaceful and gentle haunting, so I don't think anyone would be frightened while staying there. They may be startled or even amazed at some of the ghost's shenanigans, and that would be thrilling—at least it would be for me.

The Old Talbott Tavern
BARDSTOWN, NELSON COUNTY

BARDSTOWN, SETTLED IN 1780, is the second-oldest city in Kentucky and boasts of being the Bourbon Capital of the World, with distilleries such as Maker's Mark, Heaven Hill, Jim Beam, and Four Roses. It's a town appreciated for its spirits in drink and its spirits of the ghostly kind. Many of the town's Federal and Georgian architectural buildings dating from the 1780s to 1850 are still standing strong and tall today, full of history and hauntings.

The Old Talbott Tavern, circa 1779, has placed journals in each of its rooms for guests to write about their experiences there. This may include a brief explanation of their visit or why they came to the Talbott, but most of the time they write about their ghostly encounters and what happened to them during their stay. Once you check into your room at the Tavern, not only can you read about these experiences, you can also bid the staff to tell you some of their own experiences.

I hold The Old Talbott Tavern dear to my heart. I will never forget the first time I stepped through its ancient portal in June of 1995. My sister, Wanda Belcher, who lived in Bardstown at the time, had convinced me to move to Bardstown after our mother's passing. Shortly after I had moved in and became settled, Wanda picked me up and took me out for lunch. She understood my absolute joy in discovering haunted places, so with all the town's ghost stories and folklore of the Tavern, she knew this would be a perfect place for us to dine. The minute I entered the lobby, I felt totally overwhelmed with the presence of many ghosts. Even before we were seated at our table, I had to ask the host, "Is this place haunted?" and I got an unusual response. She looked at me and said, almost with a chuckle, "Are you kidding me? This place has many ghosts, and they play havoc on the staff and guests who stay here." I couldn't wait to hear all their stories.

A few weeks later I saw an advertisement in the local newspaper for a bookkeeper position at The Old Talbott Tavern. I jumped at the chance to get this job, and off I went to place my application. The interview went so well, and with my many years in retail management, I knew I would be chosen for the position—and I was. Once I started to work, it didn't take but a few weeks until I had reached my goal to become the General Manager of The Old Talbott Tavern. I was employed by the Kelleys, who owned The Old Talbott Tavern for three years. I was also the manager when the great fire of 1998 burned through the Tavern, destroying many priceless antiques, old clocks dating to the 1840s, wall art of John James Audubon dating to the

1800s, and old records, registration logs, and photo albums that dated to the 1800s.

One of my favorite duties as manager was choosing the weekend entertainment for our pub. When you step into the pub, the present day seems to melt away to make you feel as if you had just stepped through a time warp to another time and place. The whole atmosphere seems to represent a piece of Old World history right in the heart of Bardstown. The dark, hewn-log beams overhead are original, and occasionally you can see a handmade nail from the 1800s, sticking out of the wood where they used to hang hams to cure in the 1930s. To the right of the entry there were two stone fireplaces that acted as early hearths, providing heat for weary travelers who came into the pub from their stagecoach ride. I was thrilled to see the food warmers that were built into the stone wall on the side of the fireplaces. They displayed their original shelving and cabinet doors, which have warped and split due to age and the heat coming from the fireplaces. The floor is laid with thick, wide timbers, and in 230 years there have only been two floors. The present floor is nearly one hundred years old. The bar was built by a local carpenter, and over the many years the wood has seasoned with the many people who have sat at the bar while sharing good fellowship, jokes, and occasional gossip—well, maybe a lot of gossip.

One of my favorite entertainers was Mike McGrath with his guitar and list of songs you could pick for him to play. His music was varied, and he could replicate just about any song from the oldies to the most recent pop with his talent as a singer and musician. Mike had always been a little curious about the ghost stories he had heard, so on Halloween night, 1997, he decided to stay after closing so we could do an investigation. With his 35mm camera, he took pictures of the areas I'd told him stories about and where sightings of ghostly apparitions had occurred. Later, after he developed his film, he was amazed to discover

A misty form of the little girl ghost is captured in the chandelier.

that he had captured the form of a little girl sitting in one of the dining room chandeliers. When he shared the picture with me, it validated my suspicion of a little girl haunting The Old Talbott Tavern. Many times I would walk into this empty dining room at closing to see this same chandelier swinging by no apparent means. The chandelier on the opposite side did not move—only the one closer to the fireplace. There had also been other times when I heard children laughing in that same area of the building, even though no children were present. I felt that Mike's picture was a great piece of evidence that the little girl ghost had revealed herself to us that night.

Over the years, this little girl has continued to show herself to guests and employees, who light up as they tell of their encounters with her. One guest tells how she woke up to the sensation of a small child spooning her back and twiddling her hair through its fingers. She said for a moment she thought she was home in her bed, and her four-year-old daughter had crawled into the bed with her. When she turned over to find no one there, she remembered that she was not at home. Was this the little girl ghost that she had been warned about? The room where she stayed, the General's Quarters, is where the little girl is seen the most because she loves the canopy over the twin beds in this room.

Now that I have my own ghost walk business, Bardstown Ghost Trek, I take the walkers with me into The Old Talbott Tavern, and we stand in the most haunted room there. The crowds are amused when they witness the spirit of the little girl answering my questions by making the light on my EMF meter go off and on for the answer "yes." She will even open the door on request and turn off the lights to the chandelier, but only if it suits her fancy. Some staff members appreciate her little antics but others become weary of them and quit their jobs because of her frequent interaction with them. She has been referred to as Annie, Becka, and other names, but none of these have been validated. The only connection is that she may have been one of the twelve children born there in the 1800s to the Talbott Family.

The Talbott Family bought the place in 1885, and George and Annie Talbott lived there and ran a restaurant and hotel in this building until 1916 when it was sold to T.D. Beam, the distiller, Jim Beam's brother. Only five of the Talbott children survived to adulthood. Could the girl ghost be one of their little ones who decided to stay and play? Another time when ghostly activity revealed itself through unexplained phenomena was when a guest in the dining room asked to speak to the manager about his meal. When I responded to his request, I asked him how could I help him. The guest asked me to do something I found very strange. He said to me, "Can you make my fork stop moving?" I looked down at the table and saw his fork was balanced on the rim of his salad bowl, rocking back and forth. Reaching down with my hand, I pushed the fork off the rim so that it rested in the bottom of the bowl. I turned my attention back to the guest and asked, "Is this what you wanted me to do?" He responded, "Wait and watch the bowl." I again turned my attention to the bowl as he requested, and within a few seconds, without any assistance from anyone, the fork slid up the side of the bowl and was once again balanced on the rim of the bowl, rocking back and forth as it was when I first arrived at the table. I was thrilled to see this blatant attempt from the spirits to get our attention, and with a bit of a laugh, I said to the guest, "Oh, it must be one of our ghosts having some fun." The guest was taken aback by this remark and insisted that he and his family would be leaving right away. I guess not everyone is as happy as I am when the ghosts decide to come out and play.

Over the last few years, the ghostly activity around this same area still persists. Many times I have had guests and employees approach me with new stories of objects moving on their table. Sometimes it is about a plate that slides from one end of the table to the other with no visible means for it to move. Other times it is a story about a glass of water levitating off the table and landing in the middle of the floor without a single drop of water spilled. I have even heard repeated accounts of the silverware moving on its own.

History notes that many famous people from all walks of life and various eras have passed through the door of The Old Talbott Tavern. Washington Irving wrote a story titled "Stolen Kiss," which he was inspired to write while having lunch at the tavern. He witnessed a young man coming in off the streets and stealing a kiss from a very pretty miss who was having lunch there. The artist John James Audubon loved having his lunch at the Talbott. Folklore says Abraham Lincoln stayed at the Tavern when he was a boy of nine, traveling through Kentucky with his parents. The local newspaper of 1945 reveals that

Roy Rogers came through Bardstown on his way to Springfield to buy horses, and he stayed at the Talbott and enjoyed a breakfast there. Revered food critic Duncan Hines enjoyed a meal at the Tavern and gave the experience a rave review. During the 1930's one of America's most famous generals, George S. Patton, frequented the Tavern, and as a result of his many visits, the management gave him his own table with a brass plate that reflected the name of General George S. Patton. Last but not least, outlaw Jesse James used to come to Bardstown to visit relatives and friends and to enjoy an evening of drink and card playing at The Old Talbott Tavern.

James's connection to the Talbott came from the fact that his mother was born in Midway, Kentucky, which is only a few miles from Bardstown, and it was believed that she went to grammar school in Bardstown. His cousin, Donnie Pence, was the local sheriff of Bardstown at the height of Jesse's notoriety. As a matter of fact, the sheriff used to run with the James boys but soon realized that this was not the life for him, so he decided to become a lawman instead of remaining an outlaw. When he died, he had been Nelson County's trusted and beloved sheriff for thirty years. Jesse also spent some time with Donnie at the jail, located on the other side of The Old Talbott Tavern, but only as a visitor and not as a prisoner.

When Jesse James stayed at the Tavern, his favorite room was the one with murals painted on the wall by a mysterious and unknown artist. It was thought that the murals dated to the middle 1800s, but there is no written history revealing who painted them. They were discovered in 1926 when the wallpaper was being replaced. One night Jesse woke up in the middle of the night, after a little too much bourbon before retiring. He thought he saw the birds fly out of the murals, so he grabbed his gun and shot a round of bullets at the birds. Three of the bullets went into the murals on the other side of the room, and the holes remain there today as a reminder of Jesse's night at The Old Talbott Tavern.

In the late 1980s, a manager named Gloria and one of the cooks were getting ready to close for the night. As they walked up the stairs to take the money to the safe, they both saw a man in a long coat walk across the top of the landing. They were both surprised because no one else was supposed to be in the building. As they continued up the stairs they saw the side door to the left close shut, as if the stranger had gone to that room and closed the door. They opened the door to see if he had gone into the room, and just as they did, the door on the other side of the room closed, as if the stranger had gone out the door. By this time, curiosity had taken hold of them, so they hurried over to the back door to see if they could figure out who he was. When they opened the door, they saw him walking down the hall. He continued out the fire escape door to the fire escape landing outside. With the door still opened, he turned and looked at the two of them looking back at him, flipped his head back, and laughed raucously. When he brought his head forward he completely disappeared. Gloria and the cook were stunned. Without a word, they turned and walked down the hall, put away the money, locked up and left the building.

A couple of weeks later, Gloria and her husband were watching a TV special about outlaws of the Wild West, and as they were showing pictures of Wyatt Earp, Billy the Kid, and Jesse James, she jumped to her feet and said, "Oh my god! That picture of Jesse James looks exactly like the face I saw the other night when the cook and I followed that man out on the fire escape where he disappeared. Now I know that the stories must be true, and I finally got to meet Jesse James's ghost."

In 1998, a fire broke out at the tavern. At 5:00 A.M., I received a phone call from the fire department that The Old Talbott Tavern was on fire, and they needed the names of all the guests staying there. Luckily for me, I had planned a murder mystery dinner for that evening, and I knew exactly how many guests and in what rooms they were staying. After I hung up the phone I hurried down to the tavern to see how bad it was and nearly collapsed in horror at what I saw. The building was blazing; fire was shooting out the windows, and a gaping hole had opened up in the roof. The first thing I asked about was the safety of the guests; all had gotten out safely with no injuries. This ancient building had not been closed for business since the late 1700s, and in the 1950s made it into the *Guinness Book of World Records* for being open as a business for over 150 years. There was so much damage that I wasn't sure if The Old Talbott Tavern would reopen its doors, but after almost two years of planning, it reopened in November of 1999, even more beautiful than before. The ghostly activity continues to reveal itself through unexplained phenomena as usual. It appears that the ghosts are still just as active as they were before the fire and eager to show themselves to anyone wanting to find them.

CHAPTER 16

Perryville Battlefield State Historic Site

PERRYVILLE, BOYLE COUNTY

ONE DAY I RECEIVED A PHONE CALL from a lady who introduced herself as Joan House, Program Coordinator and Preservation Specialist of the Perryville Battlefield State Historic Site. She had heard about my profession as a ghosthunter and was interested in setting up a seminar about ghosts for the site's next October events and reenactments program. We agreed to an hour-long seminar about ghosts and hauntings followed by taking the audience on a ghost investigation through the battlefield. I was interested in learning about the history of the battle of Perryville, so I set up a time to meet with Joan and talk to her.

When I met Joan standing tall in her tan uniform, her sandy blonde hair pulled back, I could see that she was passionate about her work. She told me, "I fell in love with the park when I was young, and my dream was to work here one day. Every morning while I'm getting ready, I feel very blessed to have such a beautiful place to come to work."

The first thing that I wanted to know was the history of the battle and the impact it had on Kentucky. Joan told me that Kentucky had desperately tried to maintain its neutrality during the Civil War. Since both Abraham Lincoln and Jefferson Davis were native-born Kentuckians, neither one wanted to provoke Kentucky into taking a stand on one particular side. As a result, both Confederate and Union troops set up camps in Kentucky by 1861.

On October 8, 1862, one of Kentucky's biggest Civil War battles was fought just west of Perryville when Confederate forces
under General Braxton Bragg and Union forces led by Major
General Don Carlos Buell clashed. It was unusually hot for that
time of year, and there was a drought. The soldiers were racked
with heat, thirst, and exhaustion while fighting the enemy. The
battle lasted over five hours, and when it was over, more than
7,600 soldiers lay dead, wounded, or were missing.

After the battle the Union soldiers were buried in a cemetery
along the Springfield Pike. The Confederate soldiers weren't so
lucky. For three days, both the dead and wounded lay in the
roasting sun. During those three days, the local farmers' hogs,
which had escaped from broken fences as a result of the battle,
came out of the forest and fed on the decomposing bodies. The
local men and slaves would run them off so they could bury
the bodies at the Bottom Family's farm, which later became the
state park.

The Union dead did not remain at the cemetery long and
were moved to Union cemeteries at Camp Nelson and Lebanon,
Kentucky. It was not until 1902 that the Perryville Commission
placed a monument dedicated to the Confederate soldiers who
fought and died at the Battle of Perryville. On February 26, 1936,
this battle site became a part of the Kentucky State Parks system
known as the Perryville Battlefield State Historic Site. The Perryville Battlefield site has become a favorite for reenactors, who
come to the park for the annual reenactment on the weekend
closest to October 8. At that time, the camp is filled with hundreds of reenactors, reliving the military life of the Civil War
with friends and family. During other times of the year, the park
provides a great place for living history groups who come out and
recreate for visitors what life was like during the Civil War era.
The battlefield has over twelve miles of interpretive trails where
points of interest are signed. The management also offers the

award-winning School of the Soldiers for elementary children to
learn how the soldiers had to prepare for battle. They are enlisted
into the OVI (Ohio Volunteer Infantry) where they are taught the
drills, how to march, and how to use a musket. This program
won the 2006 Kentucky History Award.

Three times a year the Perryville Battlefield park also offers
a ghost seminar and a ghosthunt for visitors. Our group, which
includes Jeff Waldridge and Jennifer and Lee Kirkland, has been
given the honor of hosting these events during the upcoming
years. I asked Joan if she had had any experiences with ghosts
at Perryville. She laughed and said, "Yes, I have a few that I can
tell you." She described books flying off the shelves for no apparent reason, lights going on and off, doors slamming when the
doors were not opened, and other things that you might hear
when you work in a haunted place. She told me one particular
incident she experienced: "One morning around 7:00, I came
into the office and started to work on my computer. I was deep
in thought when I heard someone call me, 'Joani.'" I asked her,
"Do you go by Joani?" She said, "Here at work I do, so I thought
it was one of the employees. I turned and didn't see anyone so I
stepped out of my office into the museum, but there was no one
there. I thought that maybe the guys were trying to spook me,
so I opened the front door to see who was outside, but there was
no one there either."

I told her that I liked that story because a lot of times, especially on ghost investigations, I will not only hear a spirit call
my name, but I often record them saying my name on my audio
recorders. This phenomenon seems to be common with a lot
of ghosthunters. I asked her if she had another story, and she
thought for a moment and said, "My husband, Chad, and I
were dealing with some reenactor issues and trying to come
to an agreement while disagreeing. We became very adamant
about what each of us was wanting, and our voices were quickly

A vortex captured at the Confederate Monument taken by a member of S.H.O.C.K.

gaining volume. Just as our voices were about over the top, we were interrupted by a loud voice that shouted 'Chad!' We looked at each other, and Chad headed out of my office and into the museum to see if it was one of the guys butting into his business. There was no one to be found. As he looked back at me, I told him that I didn't think the soldiers liked the way he was talking to me. We laughed and agreed that we might not want to talk like that again."

My next question to Joan was, "What is the most common story that you have heard about the ghosts of Perryville?" Joan replied, "The one about Patrick Cleburne's horse. During the battle the Brigadier General was charging the enemy when his horse was killed by being shot out from under him. Soon after the battle the locals would report hearing a horse galloping by or near them, but when they would look for the horse there was never one around." "Have you ever heard the horse?" I asked.

She smiled and said, "Oh, yes, I have. One late night while I was camping out with some of the reenactors we heard the sound of a horse's hooves running on the pavement near the camp. We thought that maybe one of the horses in the camp had gotten loose, so we set out to find it. We aimed our flashlights out into the darkness but didn't see a horse. We went back to the enclosure and counted the horses, and they were all there. None were missing. It was at that moment I realized that we had heard Patrick's ghost horse."

While we were talking, Joan remembered another story that had happened while camping during an reenactment. She said that two of the reenactors were noted historians, and they told her a great story about being visited by a Civil War ghost. The men were asleep in their tent when they were awakened by what they thought was another reenactor. He barged into the tent and demanded to know the whereabouts of one of his soldiers. They looked at him and didn't recognize him as part of their group. He called his soldier's name over and over as he walked around in the tent looking for him. One of the men asked him who he was, and the intruder stated his name and rank. He then turned and stormed out of the tent. The two men got up and followed him as he went to the tent next door. When they got to the other tent he was gone and wasn't seen or heard of again. The two historians decided to investigate, so they looked up the names that this stranger had given them. To their amazement they found that both names were listed as two of the men killed at Perryville.

After my meeting with Joan, I wanted to do an actual investigation myself to see if I would be able to get anything that would be good evidence to share during the ghost seminar that we had scheduled. I talked to Jeff Waldridge, our Location Scout for Ghost CIA (Ghost Chasers in Action), to see if we could go one evening to do a ghost investigation. He agreed and we decided to invite another group called SHOCK (Spirit Hunters of Central Kentucky) founded by Lee and Jennifer Kirkland. They were also graduates of my ghosthunter certification classes. It just so happened that when it came time to go on this investigation I was unable to attend, so the group headed out without me.

When I talked to Jennifer to see how the investigation went, she told me they had gotten some amazing evidence. She said the first picture Lee took was of the area around the Confederate Soldiers Monument. They were thrilled to see a huge vortex and shadow that had been captured in the photo. A vortex is an anomaly that resembles a white tornado and is believed by most ghosthunters to be a form of energy created by ghosts and spirits. Jennifer said, "I felt like they were welcoming us." Lee continued to take more pictures and soon he captured a misty form just beyond the area where he got the vortex.

I asked Jennifer, "Were you able to get any EVPs?" "Yes, we were out behind the cornfield, and as we were walking we captured a deep male voice that said, 'Get out of the way.' We thought that was pretty wild since we were probably walking where the soldiers would have been shooting at each other. It would make sense that we would have been in the way."

As they were leaving the area, Jeff started to whistle *When Johnny Comes Marching Home,* and when he stopped in the middle of the tune, they heard an eerie whistle in the distance finish the tune. "It was really a creepy sound," Jennifer said. I was pretty excited about the last piece of evidence Jennifer told me about. She said that as they were walking back from the cornfield, they heard the sound of a horse's hooves running up to them as close as ten yards away, but couldn't see anything in the distance that would cause such a sound. They did not know the story about the ghost of Cleburne's horse; this was a great validation of Joan's story.

The day of the seminar arrived and I made my presentation before a soldout crowd. They seemed to enjoy the PowerPoint about the ghosts and history that I had presented before them. Afterwards, everyone set out for our ghosthunt. Since there were so many people, the ghosthunters divided the participants up into three groups. Jennifer conducted an EVP session where she asked the ghosts questions to see if they would answer into the audio device. Her question was, "How did you die?" Within a few seconds after her question was asked, they all heard the sound of a gunshot. The crowd was amazed and a little freaked out over the results. I told Jennifer that I had heard from others that sometimes you can even hear cannon blasts when no cannons are actually in use.

It's hard to believe that this pristine and peaceful paradise, filled with deer, beavers, turkeys, and other birds, and bordered by miles of nineteenth-century stone fences was once the site of so much death and destruction. But it was. One can only hope that the ghosts of Perryville will eventually find the peace that now surrounds them.

CHAPTER 17

Planter's Row Golf Course Clubhouse

NICHOLASVILLE, JESSAMINE COUNTY

AFTER ONE OF MY GHOSTHUNTING CLASSES, I met with the Coordinator of Community Education at the Lexington Community College. He told me that he had found another place for me to take the students for a ghost investigation. He explained that he had a friend who was the manager of a golf course in Nicholasville. His friend had told him about the ghostly activity going on at the clubhouse and that he would welcome an investigation. I jumped at the chance to go there.

I called the manager the next day and we set a date for me to bring my students to investigate the clubhouse at Planters Row

Golf Course. While I was on the phone I asked him if he could tell me about some of the things that were happening at the clubhouse. He told me that sometimes, while he was upstairs in his office, he would hear a strange noise. He said, "I'll stop my work and notice that it sounds like a bouncing rubber ball. It reminds me of a child playing with a small ball, bouncing it off the floor. Sometimes it goes on for a while. One day I decided to find out what was making this sound. I stepped out of my office and followed the sound. It led me down the hall and to the storage room. This door stays locked so I reached for my keys, unlocked the door, and went inside. Just as I entered the room the bouncing stopped. There is a window in the storage room so I had plenty of light to look around. There were a few chairs and some boxes in the room, but no signs of a ball or anything that would make the bouncing sound." I asked, "Is there a certain time of the day that this takes place?" He responded, "No, not really. It seems to be random, and sometimes I'll go a few days or even a week or more before I hear it again. For the life of me, I can't figure it out." "Has anyone ever seen anything unusual?" I asked. "I have heard a few stories from the other employees. They have seen a woman walking up the stairs in a long gown, and others have heard children laughing when there are no children in the building."

He told me that the elegant 9,500-square-foot clubhouse was once a Southern-style mansion built in the middle 1800s. Because of that, the eighteen-hole private course sits on fifty-five acres of beautiful farmland. I wanted to arrive a few minutes before my students got there. We live about eleven miles from Nicholasville, so I gave myself twenty minutes to get there in plenty of time. When we arrived at the turn-off to the golf course I was delighted to see the long narrow road leading down to a beautiful four-column white plantation. I could imagine a horse and buggy trotting down this same path in years gone by. The trees that were planted in a single row along the drive provided shade for us as we continued on our path to the parking lot.

Since my car has a magnetic sign on the door that reads "Ghost Chasers International, Inc.," many people will walk up to the car and question us about our profession. That was the case when we got out of the car at Planter's Row. A lady golfer walked up to us and asked, "Excuse me, but are you here to investigate the clubhouse?" I smiled and answered, "Yes, we are." "I knew it!" she said. "I believe that the clubhouse is haunted. Every time I go into the building I get this eerie feeling that I'm being watched. Once I thought someone called my name, but when I turned around there was no one there." She pointed to a second floor window to the right and asked, "Do you see that window right there?" I shook my head yes and she continued, "Once I was getting out of my car, and when I glanced up I saw a woman in a period dress looking back at me. She had her hand on the curtain as she pulled it back to get a clear view of me. When I started to walk towards the building, still looking at her, she and the curtain disappeared. Oh, by the way, my name is Paula Lewis, and I am a member here." After we shared contact information, Paula left to play a round of golf while we continued inside the mansion to start our investigation.

About three weeks later Paula attended my intro ghosthunter class at Lexington Community College. She was quick to also sign up for the advanced class and became one of my certified ghosthunter members of GCI. Paula was a physical education teacher at Lafayette High School, a golf coach, a midwife, and an EMT professional who worked in the hospital emergency room. She won Teacher of the Year Award and made it into the *Who's Who Among America's Teachers*. Later she became one of the finalists to appear on the TV show, *Survivor*. A year later Paula went with me on my second investigation of the Planter's Row Golf Clubhouse.

Since this was the clubhouse's first ghost investigation, several of the employees wanted to join us to observe what we were going to do. I listened to many stories and concerns of the employees. When I walked into the snack area I met a four-year-old girl who was the daughter of one of the employees. Just before she left to go home, the little girl asked me, "Are ghosts good or bad?" I told her that most of the ones that I had met were good ghosts. She pointed upstairs and said, "I was up there when the little girl kissed me." She took her finger and placed it on her cheek and said, "She kissed me right here."

By now more of my team had arrived, and it was time to start the investigation. I thought since most of the activity had been noticed upstairs, we would start there. We put an audio recorder in the storage room in hopes of capturing the sound of the bouncing ball as heard by the manager. Then I went into the other rooms to see what type of readings we would get with our EMF meters and infrared thermometers. We did a clean sweep with nothing to report. I walked down the hall, and while I was talking to one of my students, I picked up a blast of static on my cassette recorder. After the static, I recorded the sound of two little girls laughing. It was the cutest EVP I have ever captured. It sounded as if they were hiding and giggled as we passed by. I thought it was a wonderful piece of evidence since the little girl I met downstairs told me about the ghost child who kissed her on the cheek.

After about half an hour we went back into the storage room to listen to the recorder to see if we were lucky enough to get an EVP. When I played the recorder back I heard a sound like a ball bouncing on the floor. We searched the room looking for a source that might have caused this sound but could not find anything. None of us heard that sound of a bouncing ball while we were setting up our equipment upstairs, so I was glad that I had captured it on the recorder. This evidence would validate what the manager had heard over the last few weeks.

We went downstairs to check out the basement. The steep wooden stairs had loose boards and appeared to be a little unsteady, so I cautioned everyone to watch their step on the way down. There were two separate rooms below. During our search we found iron shackles screwed into the stone wall way back out of sight. I walked over to check them out and was amazed that we had found something that had been left behind from a more cruel time. At that moment I felt like a CSI agent who had found a clue to a heinous offense at a crime scene. We decided to set up our infrared camcorders in that area to see if we could capture any anomalies or sounds in our video. Later, while examining the results from our camcorder, I was excited to see that we did capture something down in the area where the shackles were. About half an hour into the recording we captured a misty form moving in the area of the shackles. There was a huge hole in the stone wall, and the misty form disappeared into the hole. We valued this as a great piece of evidence of a possible haunting.

We finished our session in the basement and moved to the first floor where we took several pictures and captured more strange shapes and shadows in our camera shots. I took my dowsing rods and was led into the snack bar. I asked if the energy coming through was a male and got a movement that indicated a yes response. I continued to ask yes and no questions and learned that I was communicating with a black male slave. He was in his thirties and was happy when he was working on the farm. After I go through a dowsing session, I get really thirsty so I went to the counter and asked for apple juice. The lady behind the counter wanted to know if I wanted it in a cup instead of the can, and I didn't answer her but shook my head no. When I reviewed my audio tape later that evening I found I had captured a male EVP that said, "Sure nuff." As if it were answering for me.

I took my drink and decided to take a break from the investigation. I went outside to sit while gazing out across the beautiful golf course. For a moment I thought I saw a tall black man dressed in a long-sleeved muslin shirt and overalls. He didn't remain in my sight for long, but he was definitely looking back at me. A thought occurred to me that he might be the slave with whom I had just communicated.

I went back into the clubhouse and concluded the investigation. I was anxious to find out about the history of this old house and the land surrounding it. I went home and for days I looked online and called many people, but couldn't find any stories about the lives of the people who had once lived in the Planter's Row home. About two years later I had another chance to go back and follow up with another investigation. This time Paula Lewis, who was still a member of the golf course, joined us. She wanted us to go upstairs into the room where she had witnessed an apparition looking down at her from the upstairs window two years ago. We took many pictures and did a couple of EVP sessions but were unable to record any evidence.

While we were upstairs Paula noticed a door that led to the attic, and we decided to go inside to see what we could find. She pulled on the doorknob but the door would not open. A staff member walked by as she was pulling on the door and said, "That door is so hard to open that we have stopped going into the attic. You can pull all you want, but it will not open." Paula looked at me and whispered, "I really want to go in there. I feel that we might have a better chance at getting some good evidence." She put her hand on the doorknob and gave it a pull, and the door opened almost effortlessly. Paula looked back at me, her eyes wide in disbelief that she had opened the door. We walked up the stairs to an empty attic, and I warned everyone not to disturb the insulation to avoid causing dust orbs to appear in our photos. We turned our recorders on and during an EVP session I asked the spirit, "Can you speak to me?" When I played the recorder back I got a female EVP that said, "All right." Paula was thrilled that her hunch had been right and that we got some good evidence. Maybe the words, "all right," were spoken by the lady Paula had seen in the window.

We left the attic and went down into the basement. Since I had a new group of students I wanted to share with them the shackles that we had found on our previous ghost investigation. After our descent into the cold, dark underground chamber with our flashlights in hand, we found the wall where the shackles had been, but to our dismay, the shackles were gone. Someone had taken them. When I asked the employees about them, no one knew what had happened to them. One of the employees noticed that they had disappeared shortly after our first investigation. Did they disappear because of a paranormal nature or because someone wanted to take them for a keepsake? We may never know the answer to that question.

Of all the places I have investigated, Planter's Row held the most mysteries. Since I could not find any history about the grand old house, Paula went to the county clerk's office and found a list of owners. The earliest date she could find on the house was when it sold in 1872 to Thomas and Kittie Johnson. Most old homes like this end up belonging to the state or are listed with the historical society, but this ol' gal proudly remains in service as an elegant clubhouse for Planter's Row Golf Course while remaining gently haunted.

CHAPTER 18

Rohs Opera House
CYNTHIANA, HARRISON COUNTY

AS A GHOSTHUNTER, I think the one thing I enjoy most is teaching the craft of ghosthunting to others. What makes this involvement so enjoyable is all the amazing and talented people I meet. I learn so much from each and every one of them. That being said, I had a wonderful conversation with one of my students, Stephen Platt, after class one day. He was excited to share with me some of his experiences about being a new ghosthunter. Stephen told me that he had already formed a group of ghosthunters called K5 Paranormal Investigators. Stephen held an analog tape recorder in his hand and was anxious to play me an EVP that he had captured.

"Where did you conduct the investigation?" I asked. "In an old building called the Rohs Theater in Cynthiana," Stephen said. "The building is pretty big, with three floors and two basements. I was told that most of the activity had been experienced upstairs in the second theater, the basement that extends under other neighboring buildings, the main theater, and the balcony. I had heard that the theater was haunted and was known to produce many apparitions and EVPs for other ghosthunter groups. Once our team had arrived at the theater and started to use our equipment to investigate, we got quick responses and this EVP was one of them," he said. "Did you capture the EVP with a question or did you get it randomly?" "I thought I would try a direct question. I asked the spirits in the room if they wanted something from us. We did not hear anything, but as soon as I rewound the recording, we heard a male voice respond, 'I want nothing.' He didn't sound very happy either," Stephen said.

I leaned over and placed my ear close the recorder to listen to the EVP and was amazed at the clarity of the words as I heard the voice say distinctly, "I want nothing." I would rate it as an "A" EVP. According to EVP experts, certain classes are assigned to the quality of EVPs. Class "A" means the EVP was so clear that everyone listening to the words would agree on what was said. If it had been a "B" EVP, it would have meant that it was questionable, and there would be different interpretations of what was actually said. If it had been a "C" EVP, it would have sounded like a human voice, but it would be very difficult to understand what words were spoken.

Stephen wanted to play me another EVP of a sound in response to a question. "While I was standing near the wall, in one of the upstairs rooms, I asked the spirits to listen to my taps on the wall. I tapped out the beat to a familiar ditty: 'Shave and a haircut, two bits.' I asked the spirits to finish my next taps. I began again, and left off the last two taps. We were shocked when we heard the two tapping sounds come from the other side of the wall. My entire crew was with me, and there was no one else in the building that could have caused the knocking," Stephen explained. I also heard the two taps on Stephen's tape, but then I heard something else that Stephen had missed. Shortly after the two taps, I heard a male voice say in a whisper, "Stop that tapping." This made Stephen happy—he now had another EVP to add to his evidence collected at the Rohs Opera House. After Stephen had captured the two knocks, he wanted to try it again to see if he could get the spirits to respond yet again. This time, before the recording session began, the recorder started to malfunction causing the team to think that something unnatural was affecting their equipment. When it started to work again, they got an EVP that said, "Don't be scared, we're having fun. Do you wanna have fun too?" Again, Stephen and his crew had captured another "A" EVP.

As Stephen and another ghosthunter, Marlene Miller, were finishing up the investigation, Marlene's camera turned off on its own. Stephen explained to her that it might be due to an automatic turn-off mode once the camera has been inactive for a few minutes. After Stephen made this statement, a male voice came through and said, "What's that you're saying?" Again, when I listened to this EVP it was another class "A" recording.

Stephen told me that several ghosthunting groups were getting great EVPs from a male ghost, and he was hoping to find out who this entity might be. Stephen planned to do some historical research to see if an incident took place in the opera house that might explain who this ghost could be.

After my class, I asked Stephen if he could make arrangements for me to meet the owners of the old opera house so that I might include the theater as one of the chapters for my next

A spirit orb was captured as Patti asked the ghost to show itself near Stephen Platt's hand.

book. He contacted Rodger Slade, one of the owners of the Rohs Opera House, to set up a time that I might talk with him and visit the theater. Roger was quick to agree and scheduled a time for us to conduct a ghost investigation. We met Roger and one of his partners, James Smith, when we arrived at the Rohs Opera House for the ghosthunt.

The Rohs Opera House is owned and operated by three partners: Roger Slade, James Smith, and Phillip Nickerson. Roger is a second grade school teacher at Eastside Elementary School in Harrison County. He is married and has two kids who love the fact their daddy is a ghosthunter. James is a pastor of the Mt. Carmel Christian Church, and Phillip has been an employee of Toyota for many years. All three of these men have a great love for the old theater and made a pact to keep it going by continuing to bring good, wholesome entertainment to the community.

Roger also hosts a ghost walk that starts and ends at the Rohs Opera House. He told me that the maintenance of the building was subsidized by the ghost walks and overnight investigations for ghosthunter groups.

The first thing Roger wanted to do was to show me a video clip he had captured one evening while he was alone in the theater. "I had borrowed a video camera from a friend and decided to set it up in the seating area of the theater," Roger said. "I placed it where it could record me as I walked around talking to the ghosts. I left the lights off so the EMF meter would not be affected by that energy. As the camcorder documented my moves with the EMF meter in my hand, the meter spiked slightly, and at about that time, the camcorder caught a full apparition. When I went back to review the film, I was stunned to see a man walk out of the wall and turn to follow me about the time the EMF meter spiked. He was only visible for a few seconds, and then he disappeared. Boy, now that was a shocking experience!"

I told Roger that I would love to see the video. I was shocked to see the clear form of a man that walked out of the wall and followed Roger. I had to rewind it right away to see it again and again. You could tell that the image was not a physical person because you could see though it. The outline of the body was distinct but his color was all gray. I told Roger that in all my years as a ghosthunter, this clip was the most amazing capture of an apparition that I had ever seen on film.

Now it was time to suit up with our ghosthunting gear and start our investigation. Roger wanted to show us around the opera house and explain the history to give us an idea about why this place might be haunted. He told us that the Rohs (pronounced Ross) Opera House was built in 1871, but at that time was known as the Aeolian Hall. It was located on the second floor of the building; a jewelry store was on the first floor. The jewelry store was owned and operated by a leading retail merchant, Herman

Rohs, whose father, Herman Rohs, Sr., had owned the business since 1895. There had been many renovations since the beginning of the combined businesses, as Roger explained, "It was like they took two buildings and squeezed them together back in the 1930s to form a new business called the Rohs Opera House. It was open to the public until 1941."

Before moving on through the theater with Roger, Stephen handed me a newspaper clipping from 1997. The story told of a man who lay dying on the sidewalk in the doorway of Marsh's Law Office next door to the Rohs Opera House. A passerby saw the man with blood on his hands; his shirt was pulled over his face. The passerby ran into the Rohs Opera House and called the police. The injured man was identified as Edward Whitaker, an alleged drug offender. He had received a gunshot wound to the face and was pronounced DOA at the hospital. Law officers suspected that Whitaker had been shot in the law office, which at one time had been part of the Rohs Opera House. Stephen thought that this information might explain the identity of the male EVPs voice.

During another one of Stephen's investigations at the opera house, he started to bait the ghosts by calling out to them and challenging them to come forth. He made a rude remark, and after that he got an EVP that sounded like a male who said, "There are boys here, bitch."

As we started upstairs to the second floor of the opera house, Roger told us that a maintenance man had seen a lady in white period clothing walking down the stairs. One evening while he was mopping the lobby floor, he saw a white figure out of the corner of his eye. When he turned and looked up the stairs, he saw a woman walking down. In seconds, she disappeared. He stopped mopping, grabbed his coat and hat, and left the building. He quit his job that night. When we reached the second floor, Roger took us in a room where the old balcony used to be. He had witnessed some strange paranormal activity in that room. While he and a few of his friends were walking around with an infrared camera during one of his ghost investigations, a coat rack in the corner of the room started to roll. They turned quickly and caught the whole incident on film as the rack rolled on its own at a slow speed until it reached the other side of the room. Roger said, "It appeared that the rack was being guided by someone invisible to us."

By now, we decided it would be a good time to sit down and try to coach the ghosts to speak to us. As we set up our audio recorders, I started to think of a name. I walked to the top of the stairs and looked down and thought of the name "Elizabeth." I asked Roger and the others if that name meant anything to anyone but no one could think of any references to that name. A few days later, Stephen found an article about the death of the senior Herman Rohs's daughter. She was born on January 15, 1860, and died November 4, 1932. Her name was Elizabeth Rohs Huerkamp. Since her family owned that building during her lifetime, I would expect she may have spent some happy times there. Roger was pleased when I shared this information with him.

"Maybe she is our lady in white," he said. I asked Roger if there was a common occurrence that took place at the theater, and he quickly answered, "A lot of men get freaked out when they go into the men's restroom. While they are standing at the urinals, they notice that someone has walked up behind them, so they say something like, 'Excuse me,' or 'Give me a minute, pal.' When they don't get a reply, they turn around to see who is behind them. They are shocked that no one is there. After one of our ghost walks, a police officer on the tour went into the restroom and had the same thing happen to him. When he came out of the restroom, he was a bit shaken and he was not amused." Roger told me about the most recent poltergeist activity that had happened in the theater. Poltergeist comes from a German word meaning "noisy ghosts." He told me that he was showing a presentation of paranormal evidence in one of the rooms upstairs, and while he was talking he heard something crash behind him. He jumped and noticed that the candle in a hurricane lantern had flown off the shelf behind him. The crowd was shocked and thrilled to have witnessed such spooky activity.

Our investigation of the Rohs Opera House was a great success, as we collected various data from each location in the building. At one point during the investigation, Stephen was touched on the leg and turned to see who it was, but no one was behind him. The Ovilus was silent until Roger joined us upstairs. He was walking up the stairs towards us as the Ovilus said "Roger," and then it said it again later in the investigation. We were pleased with the results, considering the name Roger is not one of the 512 words in the dictionary of the Ovilus.

We packed up our gear and thanked Roger for staying with us during our stay. He shared a wealth of knowledge about the place and was eager to have us come back again. We made some new friends that night, and that's the best part of ghosthunting—meeting so many amazing and talented people.

CHAPTER 19

Springhill Winery and Plantation Bed-and-Breakfast

BLOOMFIELD, NELSON COUNTY

EVEN THOUGH TOBACCO REMAINS the top crop of Kentucky, over the years I have noticed more grapes being grown for wine production. It seems that people are getting into the art and science of wine making throughout Kentucky these days. I decided to look into the history of commercial vineyards and was surprised to find that as early as 1798, the nation's first commercial vineyard was planted in Nicholasville, Kentucky. Within sixty-two years, Kentucky was the nation's third-largest producer of wine. The industry ended abruptly, however, once Prohibition came to the state. In recent times the popularity of wine among American consumers has grown again, and that has stimulated the growth of vineyards and wineries in Kentucky. Being an entrepreneur myself, I support products and materials that are produced here in Kentucky. I decided to check out some of these local wineries to see how they compared with the more established companies. Chuck and I occasionally love a good glass of wine with our dinner, and our favorite Cabernet, Merlot, and Chardonnay come from California. I thought it would be nice to find these wines right here in Kentucky, so we decided to take a trip to some of these local wineries to see how good they were.

I got online and googled "wineries in Kentucky," and out of the top ten that appeared I found one that was just off the Bluegrass Highway, not far from our home. Shortly after that, Chuck and I were on our way to visit the Springhill Winery. As we approached the area we could see the plantation off in the distance to the left. I looked at Chuck and said, "Now this place looks like the perfect home for ghosts." We pulled up the gravel driveway, and my entire body started to tingle with a strange energy—the kind of feeling I often get when I'm arriving at a haunted place to do a ghost investigation. I gazed up at this plantation that had such Southern charm it took my thoughts back to the early nineteenth century. "Remember, we are here to check out the wine and not to go on a ghosthunt. Stay focused on our mission at hand," Chuck said with a chuckle. Even though it was late August, the sun was still warm on our backs as we walked over to a smaller outbuilding that housed the winery's gift shop. The little bell at the top of the door rang out as we entered the pristine shop. The decor of the store had an Old World vineyard flavor. The colors were rich purples, gold, and greens with tattered grapevines twisted around different displays of wine and accessories. We walked to the back of the room where we found a small bar for sampling the wines. The only problem was, there was no one there. "Hello, is there anyone here?" I said. Within a few seconds a head popped out from a door on the other side of the bar. "Oh, hello, I'm running my copier and I didn't hear you come in." This tanned, attractive man with his polo shirt sporting his winery's logo came over to the bar to introduce himself with his hand outstretched. "So glad to meet you. My name is Eddie O'Daniel, and I want to welcome you to Springhill Winery." "Nice to meet you, Eddie. My name is Patti Starr and this is my husband, Chuck. We decided to check out the local wineries, and your place was the first one on our list."

Eddie asked us if we had any favorite type of wine that we would like to try. We started out with our favorites and then finished with some of Eddie's favorites. I must say they were pretty good. My favorite taste was a wine he called Plantation White. Eddie described it as a sweet white blend of French hybrids that has a light body . . . . Right in the middle of his sentence I blurted out, "Do you have any ghosts in the plantation?" I think I must have startled him because it took him a few moments to answer me. "I haven't heard any ghost stories about the plantation, but I have had some curious things happen to me."

I was delighted to know that he seemed to be interested in my question. I asked him if he would share some of his experiences. He told me there were times when he and his wife would hear footsteps upstairs when there was no one else in the house. He added that members of the family talked about hearing the sounds of children playing upstairs. The most bizarre experience was the time he returned from church and found all the bentwood kitchen chairs placed in a circle outside on the porch. After checking with the family, he learned that no one had moved the chairs out of the kitchen onto the porch. My curiosity was really up, so I asked Eddie if he had time to tell us about the history of this place. He agreed and told us that the house was built in the middle 1850s by John R. Jones and his sons. He lived on the land with his family, forty slaves, and nine slaves who took care of the house. During the Civil War some Confederate guerillas came to the house to collect food and horses. The captain spied a saddle and decided to take it as well. This act of thievery infuriated Jones so much that he pulled out his rifle and shot the captain. The other soldiers retaliated by setting the porch and balconies on fire before riding off. The captain was taken to a doctor, where his arm had to be amputated. This angered his men, and later that night they returned to the Jones place. They waited in the bushes, and when Jones came out to the well, they shot and killed him.

The killing didn't stop there. A few weeks later a Union troop came through town and heard the story about Jones's death. They went to Louisville and picked two Confederate prisoners and brought them back to Jones's place. The Union soldiers asked the sons of Jones what they wanted to do with these men to avenge their father's death. The prisoners were shot to death in the front yard. Shortly after this tragedy a doctor, James Hughes, offered the family a trade on their farm for his farm in Missouri. Once Dr. Hughes moved in, he started adding onto the house and bringing in imported ironwork from France. He finished off the inside with Greek and Egyptian influences.

Eddie told me that as a child he had heard stories that at one time Dr. Hughes abetted the Underground Railroad. During some renovation beyond the kitchen, Eddie found a hidden trap door that led down to the root cellar. He surmised that this passage at one time led to the cave system that opens out onto another plantation about a quarter of a mile down the road. This would have been a perfect place to start the slaves' journey to freedom.

I explained to him that I was a professional ghosthunter and that I would be interested in doing a ghost investigation of his plantation. Stacey Manning, a reporter from the *Kentucky*

**The trap door that lead down into a cellar where the slaves
would hide during the Underground Railroad era**

Standard newspaper, had been writing articles about my ghosthunting in local places around Halloween every year for the last
five years. I thought this would be a great place to bring her to
do our next story. Eddie was excited about the opportunity to see
what a ghosthunter might find in the house, so he agreed.

I do most of my ghost investigations during the day between
1 and 4 P.M. I am an early-to-bed person, so I don't really enjoy
staying out late and ghosthunting at midnight and beyond. I
find that if a place is haunted, you will get great results no matter what time of day you do your investigation. I called Stacey
and we went back to Springhill Winery the following Tuesday at
2:30 P.M. for our ghosthunt and her story. With our ghosthunter
vests fully loaded with cameras, audio recorders, EMF meters,
infrared thermometers, batteries, film, and more, we started
our investigation on the first floor in the kitchen. Stacey was
following close by with steno pad in hand, and every once in a
while she would take a camera shot of me using a piece of equip-

ment. We walked from room to room with no apparent activity, so we went upstairs. We continued our search, speaking softly to the spirits, asking them to please show themselves. Our meters were quiet, my senses were dull, and it seemed to me that we had failed to capture any evidence of spirits.

Just about the time I was going to leave the upstairs bedroom and call it quits, I noticed a sunporch and asked Eddie, "Is it safe for us to walk out on the porch?" He nodded and opened the door. Once we were out on the sunporch I noticed that it led into another part of the house that was unfinished. I asked, "Will you be finishing this part of the house?" Eddie explained, "At one time this porch and those rooms were exposed to the weather, and that's why the floors are so warped. These two rooms were once the slaves' quarters. One room was for the men, and the other one was for the women. Years later they cut out a door between the two rooms, and that door is almost impossible to open." Eddie walked over to the door to show me how difficult it was to open. He put his foot against the casing and pulled really hard until he finally got it opened. "Often times we will close the door, and when we return to this room the door will be open," he said, just as I let out a squeal.

I was video recording him from the other side of the room. As the door opened, it looked like hundreds of orbs came racing out from the room on the other side of the door. They were gathered and hovering around Eddie. I asked him, "Can you feel them? They are all over you!" He said, "I don't know if I can or not, but I've got goose bumps, and the hair on my body is standing on end." I decided this would be a great time to set our infrared recorder in the corner of the room to see if we could get any other evidence. While the camcorder was running, we turned to leave the room, and Chuck asked for that cup of coffee that he had been offered earlier. When we played the camcorder back to review our evidence, we got a spirit orb that circled the room and repeated Chuck's last words, "coffee, coffee," in a deep whisper. It sounded as if they were longing for that satisfying taste of coffee once again. When we returned to the sun porch I decided to pull out my dowsing rods to dowse for ghosts. I made contact right away with an older lady but it was a short visit. Then a little girl named Hanna came through and told me that she was the daughter of one of the builders of the manor. She became sad as she told me of her death. Hanna said she had been playing on the open sunporch when she fell from the edge to her death. She wanted Eddie to close in the porch so that no one else would fall off. Shortly after speaking with Hanna, another little girl named Laura came through. We actually got an EVP that said, "My name is Laura," which helped validate her presence. Stacey was pleased that she would be able to write a good, solid story about our ghost adventure. Eddie was pleased since the story brought lots of people to his Halloween Festival. I was pleased when I got a call from Eddie, validating the presences of the little girls from a psychic named Michael, who had attended the Halloween Festival. When the festival was about to end, Eddie asked Michael if he would go upstairs to the slaves' quarters to see if he thought any spirits were there. At first Michael was able to communicate with an older male slave, but when he lost communication with him, he soon discovered the little girls. He told Eddie that they were very playful because one had just goosed him. The little girls began to communicate with Michael, revealing their ages and how they died. Eddie told me he was excited to learn from another psychic about the little girls. I thanked Eddie for sharing his story because it made me happy to have my discovery of the little girls validated.

A couple of years later I was able to visit with Eddie again, and he told me another story about the little girls. He said he had been working on the house and went to the downstairs bathroom to wash up. As he turned the doorknob, the door bucked

A spirit orb was captured over the head of Eddie O'Daniel while he was telling Patti about the ghostly activity he'd witnessed in his bed-and-breakfast.

off its hinges and almost knocked him to the floor. He grabbed hold of the falling door with both hands to balance it. Just as he moved the door back to the hinges, he noticed that the pins were suspended up at the top. Then as he pushed the door against the hinges, the pins dropped down in place, and the door was secured once again. He said that it was at that moment he thought of the little girls and how they like to tease and cause mischief. While we were talking he remembered another incident that he wanted to share. One afternoon a lady came into the winery shop and introduced herself as Nancy, the great-granddaughter of Dr. James Hughes, who was the second owner of the home. After telling him a little bit about her family's history, she asked if Eddie would give her a tour. She wanted very much to see the room where her mother was born.

As they were walking through the house and Nancy was remembering old family tales, she turned and asked Eddie if he had heard of any ghost stories. She proceeded to tell him about the little girls. This was a ghost story that had been passed down from her family for a hundred years. She told Eddie that when she was young she would come there to have dinner with her grandparents. Many times during their evening meal they would hear the laughter of the little girls along with the sound of their footsteps upstairs. Nancy said the girls were always full of mischief and playing tricks on them. Again, the spirits of the little girls were verified by another person. Nancy even showed Eddie a picture of four little girls she found in an old box of family photos. She said that she couldn't get anyone to identify them, so she thinks they might be the pictures of the little girls who are haunting Springhill Winery.

The popularity of Springhill Winery is growing by leaps and bounds. Guests are gathering there for the fermented spirits and the ghostly spirits that harmonize to make this a wonderful place to stay for a weekend full of fun and thrills.

CHAPTER 20

Tent Girl

Georgetown Cemetery,
Georgetown, Scott County

I GET UP VERY EARLY every morning between 3:00 and 4:00 A.M. For me, this time of day is quiet and soothing, which helps me focus as I answer e-mails without being disturbed by phone calls or knocks at my door. One morning I received an e-mail from a young man in Tennessee named Todd Mathews. Todd found my Web site during one of his all-night sessions searching the Web to find information on a Jane Doe case, known as the Tent Girl. He wrote to me about ghostly activity he had been experiencing, which he suspected might be related to a cold case he was involved in. We set up a phone interview and he explained to me that he had started a couple of different agencies that were designed to help law enforcement officials find Jane and John Doe missing persons. He wanted to speak to me about the psychic impressions he was receiving and how his intuition was helping him to solve these mysteries.

"When did all of this start?" I asked him. He explained that it all started one morning while he was shaving. He saw in the mirror a shadowy person walk up the hall and come toward the bathroom. He stood there frozen, afraid to move, not knowing what it would do if he tried to turn and face it. In just a few seconds he finally turned and it was gone. Another time, he was sitting in his chair in the living room, and he heard voices in the kitchen, as if two people were having a conversation. He couldn't identify the voices, and when he got up to see who was there, the voices stopped; there was no one there. He also heard a door slamming for no apparent reason, footsteps in the hall when he was home alone, and the sound of chairs sliding across the floor when in fact they had not moved. His wife, Lori, began to witness these bizarre incidences as well, so Todd knew there was more to them than just his imagination.

As I started to ask him more questions, I discovered that Todd had been working on one particular case since before he and Lori were married. He chuckled as he said, "The ghost seemed to get most active when I wasn't working on her case and trying to rest and enjoy my family. After a while I would even start to feel guilty if I was not on the computer searching for her identity." He told me how she would come to him in his dreams and reveal little hints and clues that he would follow up on, and sometimes it would bring him closer to finding her identity. At other times it would lead him on a wild goose chase. This was why he had called me. He was hoping that I could help him make more sense of it all.

By now my curiosity was about to get the best of me. I wanted to know all about this missing person and what had happened to her that caused Todd to be so drawn to solving such an old case. He told me that she was buried in a cemetery in Georgetown, Kentucky, and that he would like for us to meet at her grave. He felt that if we met there we might be able to feel her presence, and he wanted to have some closure himself. I was excited about this opportunity to meet him and to learn more about this woman and her restless spirit that continued to haunt him. When Chuck and I arrived, Todd was waiting in his car and got out before we were parked. As he ambled over to our car, I couldn't help but notice how his dark hair curled around the edges of his baseball cap while the rest cascaded down the back of his neck. It was a cold day in March, and a light rain was starting to fall. The sky was gray and the wind gently gusted over us as we stood by the cars introducing ourselves and shaking hands. I asked Todd if I had his permission to record our interview, and as soon as he agreed I pulled out my cassette recorder and turned it on.

He took a deep breath and said, "One day, in 1968, Wilbur Riddle, who became my father-in-law twenty years later, was walking along a rural Kentucky highway near Eagle Creek, just off Interstate 75. He was picking up glass power line insulators that had been discarded by the linemen working for the electric company. He liked to collect them to sell as paperweights. As he ventured down an embankment to pick up another insulator, he saw an old green tarp wrapped and tied around something. He walked closer to it and noticed a horrible smell. He pushed it with his foot, which knocked it loose and it started to roll down the hill, exposing the dead body of a woman inside. In total shock, Wilbur ran back to his truck, drove to the nearest pay phone and called the police." At this point, Todd stopped talking, reached into his jean jacket pocket and pulled out a glass, domed-shaped object, which he handed to me. He said it was one of the insulators that his father-in-law had picked up when he found the

Tent Girl. He wanted me to have one to show his appreciation for our friendship. I thanked him and gave him a big hug for his special gift. As we resumed our journey to the Tent Girl's grave, he continued, "Her body was taken to St. Joseph's Hospital in Lexington for an autopsy. As they peeled away the tarp, they noticed that her hands were still grasping the material, as if she had tried to rip herself free from her cloth coffin. Since there was no means to identify her, she was described as a white female, five feet one inch, between sixteen to nineteen years old, with short, reddish-brown hair." Todd told us that the coroner's report concluded that she had been struck on the head, wrapped and tied up in the tarp, and thrown down the gully where she slowly suffocated. She was later named the Tent Girl because of the way she was wrapped in the canvas tarp.

A composite sketch was sent out to other regional newspapers in hopes that someone would come forth and identify her. There were many leads but none of them turned out to be this girl. Meanwhile, the Tent Girl was buried in a cemetery in Georgetown, Kentucky, under a marker with "No. 90" on it. Later that year, some of the local residents came together and donated a headstone with a sketch of her face and these words inscribed on the new headstone:

> TENT GIRL
> Found May 17, 1968 on U.S. Highway 25 N
> Died about April 26–May 3, 1968
> Age about 16–19 years
> Height 5 feet 1 inch
> Weight 110 to 115 lbs.
> Reddish Brown hair
> Unidentified

Just as Todd finished his story, we arrived at the Tent Girl's grave. The rain was coming down a little harder so I opened my umbrella. We were quiet as we read the inscription. Todd turned to me and said, "Even though the case is solved, I still feel she is with me, and my wife has felt her as well. During my search for her identity, I would travel from Tennessee to stand at this grave. While I was here I seemed to connect even stronger with her when I would ask for help. I would gently probe with questions, hoping for more answers as I stood at her grave. Sometimes it felt as if she were whispering in my ear as I closed my eyes to receive her messages."

"Todd, how did you solve this mystery?" I asked him. "Did the ghost of this young woman give you clues in her messages?" A slight smile curled beneath his dark mustache as he looked up from her grave and said, "Yes, but at first I was a little freaked out and didn't listen, and sometimes I didn't pay attention until I started to allow myself to pay attention. After I got used to her coming to me and not feeling the fear so much, I started to notice the way she was standing, or the way I felt, or a thought that would just come to me. She would also come to me in my dreams, but while I was dreaming it would seem as if it were really happening, not like regular dreams."

"What was one of the most memorable experiences you had with her?" I asked. "I had been working late nights and then staying up searching the Web until I was so exhausted I had to quit to get some sleep." He looked at me and asked, "Have you ever been so exhausted that when you lay down to finally close your eyes, you find yourself so wide awake that sleep just won't come?" I nodded. Looking back down at her headstone, he continued, "One morning, when I couldn't stay up any longer, I fell into bed with the hope that sleep would bring me some relief. I was staring up at the ceiling when I heard a thump and then another thump coming from the kitchen. Since there was no one else in the house, my wife being at work and the kids in school, the noise stirred my curiosity, and I got up to check it out. As I walked down the hall and entered the kitchen and living room area, I saw standing in front of me the Tent Girl. The tarp was still wrapped around her, secured by the ropes, revealing only the shape of her body inside." Todd got quiet for a moment as if he had been taken back to that very moment. I asked him, "Did she disappear?" He took a deep breath, as if my question had jolted him back to me and said, "No, she didn't. I asked her who she was, and she replied, 'Get me out of this bag and you will know.' I slowly walked over to one of the cabinet drawers and pulled out a knife as she remained standing, not moving from her post. I walked over to her small frame and lifted her into my arms. She was ever so light, and I rushed her over to the couch to put her down. I took the knife and started to cut into the canvas. I'll never forget the vibration I felt in my hands as I sawed back and forth to set her free. I laid the knife down on the arm of the couch and took the hole I had created and started to rip it open. The sound of the canvas as it tore sounded unusually loud. I bent down to take a better look inside. and as I lowered my head she quickly popped her decayed face out at me. I jerked backward, falling over the coffee table, struggling to get away."

At this point in his story I started to feel the hairs on the back of my neck stand straight up and goose bumps travel down my arms. I wasn't sure if it was his story or maybe she was about to present herself to us. He paused for a moment, looked over at me and said, "The fall woke me up, and like so many times before, I realized it had all been a dream that felt so real. I got up from my bed and went back into the kitchen to look around, but nothing was out of place. I walked into the living room as I retraced my steps, and there on the arm of the couch was the knife, laying in the same position where I had put it down after cutting into the tarp. I gasped as my heart felt like it took a leap out of my chest. So many questions were racing through my mind. Did I just have a nightmare? Was I sleepwalking through the dream and acted it out by the couch and then returned to bed? I had so many unanswered questions that morning."

I asked him if she had tried to communicate with him in other ways. He said that sometimes he would wake up in the middle of the night and find himself working at his computer. The computer would always be on a site that he would frequent when trying to find out about her identity. Once he was fully awake, he would be shocked to realize that he must have walked to his computer in his sleep. What was so amazing is that the Web page he was on when he woke up would deliver yet another clue.

By now the rain was really coming down, and the wind had picked up, so we decided to leave the grave to get something to eat at a local restaurant. This would also give me more time to find out how Todd was able to discover who she was. After ordering our food, I pulled out the tape recorder once again to continue my interview with Todd. As he lifted his cup of coffee for a sip, I asked, "Todd, how did you first find out about the Tent Girl?" Looking as if he had just tasted the best coffee ever he answered, "When I was seventeen and dating my wife, Lori, her father, Wilbur, told me his story about how he found this young woman on the side of the road, twenty years ago. While listening to Wilbur's story I began to feel a strong connection with her. Then the feeling turned to a sense of duty—as if I had to find out who she was even though all of this took place before I was born. Wilbur gave me a copy of the 1969 *Master Detective* magazine that had featured her story, and I was captivated by the sketch of her. I'm sure this was the day that started my obsession of the Tent Girl's identity."

I asked, "Once you had the full story about the Tent Girl, how soon did you realize that she was trying to get your attention?" Placing his cup back down on the table, he rolled his eyes upward in an attempt to retrieve his earliest memory and stated,

"I was riding in my truck with my buddy on Halloween night and decided to take him by my girlfriend's house to show him where she lived. Once we passed her house and continued our drive, I told my friend the story of the Tent Girl. Just as I was finishing my story and turning around a bend, I had to slam on the brakes to keep from hitting this cloaked person standing in the middle of the road. I swerved, which caused me to lose control of my truck. We flew over an embankment and landed on a short ledge. Since it was Halloween, I thought it was someone dressed up in a sheet for the occasion. I didn't make the connection until later that what I saw was the Tent Girl standing there all tied up in the tarp. After this incident she began to show herself to me more frequently in the same image, which helped me to realize it was her in the middle of the road that Halloween night."

"Were you able to connect with her on any other level?" I asked. "Yes," he said. "In 1995 I had a strong urge to sit down to write, but as soon as I got my paper and pencil in hand, I started to draw instead of write. I had a clear vision of her in my mind and drew the face of the Tent Girl that turned out to be different from the previous police sketch of her. It wasn't until after I had found her family that I could compare my sketch with her picture. It was amazing how similar my sketch was to her photo."

Todd also expressed to me that he had impressions that the Tent Girl was older than her profile suggested and felt that she was probably a mother. He even went so far as to request that her body be exhumed to check her pelvic area to see if she had delivered a child. The authorities denied his request.

Todd drove two hundred miles from Tennessee to Kentucky as he researched old newspaper articles, talked with the locals, met with the undertaker who had handled the girl's burial, seeking answers or leads to help with the identity of the Tent Girl. Todd eventually set up a Web site devoted to the Tent Girl in hopes of getting others to assist him in identifying her. Many months passed, and one night in 1998 after surfing through over four hundred descriptions of missing persons, he came across three words that seemed to leap out at him —"Lexington . . . 1967 . . . Missing." It was posted by Rosemary Westbrook, and the details listed were about her missing sister, Barbara Ann Hackmann-Taylor, born December 1943. The post read:

> My sister Barbara has been missing from our family since the latter part of 1967. She has brown hair, brown eyes, is about five feet two inches tall and was last seen in the Lexington, Kentucky, area. If you have any information, Please contact me at the address posted.

Todd said that for some reason, this information felt absolutely perfect and that he had found her. There was no doubt that this would be his final lead to her. He contacted Rosemary right away, and she told him that her sister was twenty-four years old and had a little girl when she went missing. This validated what Todd had felt all along about her age and being a mother. She had been working at a restaurant in Lexington while married to George Earl Taylor, a carnival worker. Her husband claimed that Barbara had run off with another man. After Todd shared his information about the Tent Girl with Rosemary, they felt that there were enough similarities to warrant further investigation. Todd contacted the officials, and on March 2, 1998, the Tent Girl was exhumed and her remains were sent to a laboratory in Frankfort, Kentucky. The state medical examiner concluded that the Tent Girl was between twenty and thirty years old. A cheek swab from Rosemary and pulp from a tooth of the Tent Girl for DNA testing matched genetically. The Tent Girl was indeed Barbara Ann Hackmann-Taylor.

Todd Matthews believes that George Earl Taylor was responsible for Barbara's death. He felt that the story Taylor told about his wife leaving him for another man was to cover up his crime.

However, it was not possible to question George Earl Taylor since he had died of cancer in October of 1987.

My final question to Todd was, "When you look back on all of this, what have you learned from your experience?" He replied, "The tragic death of Barbara Ann Hackmann, the Tent Girl, inspired me to work in the field of missing persons. Over the years I have developed several Web sites to help find these John and Jane Doe identities. By using these Web sites we have been able to assist the police and other authorities in finding missing persons throughout the U.S. I'm sure that Barbara Ann would be proud to know that something good came from her untimely death."

The Georgetown Cemetery was established in 1850 and is the final resting place for notables such as two Kentucky governors, an equine artist, and Tent Girl. The citizens of Georgetown buried her there and visited her grave for over thirty years as she remained unknown. When she was identified, her relatives came to Georgetown to visit her gravesite. They decided not to move her but to leave her there with the people who had taken care of her for so long.

Even though it is a four-hour drive from Tennessee, Todd still visits Barbara Ann's grave in Georgetown. He sits and talks to her on his visits. Todd feels that when he goes there, she comes in spirit to be with him. Her story has ended, but the quest to find others lives on.

CHAPTER 21

Thoroughbred Community Theater

MIDWAY, WOODFORD COUNTY

ONE AFTERNOON, while going through some old ghost-hunting cases, I received a phone call from Tony Marino, the owner of the Thoroughbred Theater. He told me that a University of Kentucky student who was studying TV media was going to do a story about the haunted theater. My group, Ghost Chasers International, Inc. (GCI), did an investigation at the theater a couple of years ago, so I knew that the student, Lindsey Ashcroft, had chosen a great place to do a news report about a haunting.

Midway is a small rural town of about 1,800 people. Founded in 1835, the town has an interesting history. I was thrilled when Tony told me that Jesse James's mom, Zerelda Cole, was born in Midway at the Lee-Cole Tavern, today known as the Black Horse Inn, only a mile down the road from the theater. Her father operated a tavern from the inn.

Midway, formally named Middle Way, became Kentucky's first railroad town in 1835 because it was equidistant from Lexington, Frankfort, Versailles, and Georgetown. Some of the major streets in town are named in honor of the first railroad officials. When our group investigated the theater, we stepped outside and went across the street. We walked over to the single railroad tracks that ran through the center of town. We liked the high EMF reading that we got at the tracks and decided to come back another day to investigate it for spirit activity.

While standing with Tony in the theater, I asked him, "Can you share some of the history about Midway?" He smiled and answered, "I bet you didn't know that the porterhouse steak originated right here in Midway." I replied, "You are right. I didn't know that. For some reason, when I think of steaks, I think of Texas. Where did this all take place?" Tony answered, "The Porter House, which still stands on Winter Street." Midway is also the home of a major Thoroughbred farm, Three Chimneys Farm. If you walk down the street a ways and turn to the left, you will see the Weisenberger Mill. It is the oldest operating mill in Kentucky. There are also two large Indian mounds, plus several smaller ones, located throughout Midway." Listening to Tony boast about his town, I could see how proud he was to be a part of its rich history.

"What can you tell me about the theater? When was it built and has it always been a theater?" I asked. Tony said, "There was another building on this spot in the 1880s but it caught fire in 1914 and burned down. The new playhouse, Amusu Theater, was built in 1916, and the newspaper reported that it surpassed any house of its kind in central Kentucky. It remained open until the 1950s. Over the next few years there were other business here, including a hardware store. I bought the building in 2003 and started a huge renovation to bring it back to a grand theater. I wanted to bring the history of the horse industry into the décor, hence the name Thoroughbred Theater. To enhance the theme I brought in barn doors from Faraway Farms, home of the famous Thoroughbreds, Man o' War and War Admiral. I was excited to find stall doors from Hamburg Place and ballroom doors from the Hopewell Farm to install in the main room of the theater." "So, during renovation did you experience any type of paranormal activity?" I asked. Tony, who did not want to fully admit that there might be ghosts in the theater, chuckled and said, "I heard many stories from the construction crew. At first it was little things, like tools missing and then being found later in the most unusual places. They complained of hearing whispers while working on stage but when they would check it out to see if someone else was in the room, there was no one there. Sometimes, while working in the basement, the workers said they would see a shadow person in the corner of their vision. They would be bent down working and think someone had walked up to them, and when they would turn their heads to see who walked up the stairs, no one would be there. After a while we lost a few of the crew because of the spooky things that were happening."

I asked Tony if he had experienced anything himself. He replied that once or twice while working upstairs in the office he thought he heard someone open the front door downstairs and start walking up the steps. The footsteps would stop and he would wait for someone to come into his office, but there would be no one there. When he got up from his desk to go and check, he found the stairs empty.

Shortly after Tony, Chuck, and I arrived at the theater, Lindsey got there with her camera crew and other paraphernalia. Once introductions were finished I put on my ghosthunting gear and filled my pockets with all my gadgets and instruments to aid with the ghost investigation. Lindsey wanted to interview me before we got started so that I could explain what we were going to do. The camera was rolling as I was talking about our mission for the night, when my meter went off and surprised all of us. It started by blinking the red light while beeping at the same time. I couldn't help myself and started to laugh and said, "This has never happened." I glanced over to my left side where the meter was going off and said, "Be patient," and the meter stopped beeping.

We started our investigation upstairs in the balcony. The first thing I wanted to do was an EMF sweep, in which I use my EMF meter to scan the walls, floor, and the ceiling as high as I could reach. I did not get any false positives, meaning that I didn't pick up any readings from wiring, cable, or other explainable

During a dowsing session, Patti contacted a woman who haunts the theater.

interferences. The meter was quiet. I did get a different reaction when I pulled out my infrared thermometer. While standing in about the third row, the temperature started to drop. It went from seventy-eight degrees to sixty-one degrees in a matter of seconds, a significant drop in temperature.

I figured this would be a good time to conduct an EVP session that I refer to as an "absolute." This is where I ask everyone to remain perfectly still and absolutely quiet for thirty seconds to see if we can get a voice or a noise to come through for us on the recorder. After the thirty seconds I play back the recording to see if we captured anything. We did not get a voice, but we did get a distinctive and eerie scratching sound that seemed to come from the floor below us.

I was anxious to go back downstairs to check out the auditorium where the construction workers claimed they had heard whispering. I thought maybe I would be lucky enough to get a voice to come through for us. That would be super evidence of a haunting, especially since this shoot might be airing on TV. I pulled out my dowsing rods and started to ask questions to see if I could identify who was there. Dowsing is a method I use to tap into the energy of the universe when asking questions of the higher self. The dowsing rods, made from one-eighth-inch brass rods, respond to the questions I ask with distinctive movements. After several questions I was able to reveal a female spirit who was in her late twenties. She loved being in the theater because of the people who gathered there during events. As I was talking to her I looked up and saw a faint figure of a woman standing beside Lindsey's assistant. I put my rods away and grabbed my camera. I asked the sweet spirit if she would show herself beside Lindsey's assistant, and when I snapped my camera, I got an orb, the first and only one for the entire evening. After the investigation was over, and Lindsey was back at her studio, she discovered that she had caught some evidence on her camcorder. While I had been talking to the spirit, I asked her where she was standing. Instantly, the TV camera picked up a woman's voice that said, "I'm over here." After that I asked the spirit to show herself, and I got the orb hovering over the assistance's shoulder. All of this happening at the same time was great evidence for me and for the TV special.

When I finished in the auditorium, we headed for the basement. This is where some of the construction workers had seen the spooky shadows. I checked to make sure that my recorder had plenty of tape and began to ask questions. I felt a light touch on my back, and I made note of that aloud. When I rewound the recorder I heard a voice say "my back" just as I finished saying that I had felt a touch on my back. Many times I have recorded EVPs that mock or repeat what I say. I feel this is good evidence that we had an intelligent spirit present, one that was communicating with us as we talked. As I continued to walk around, my EMF meter registered a disturbance in an area where I had already completed an EMF sweep. It had been a clean area, meaning I found no disturbances. Now my meter was sounding, but only a few beeps at a time. This is a good indication that I can communicate with the spirits by asking "yes" and" no" questions. I instruct the spirits to come close enough to make the meter beep for "yes" and do nothing for "no." Sure enough, I started to get responses to my questions. The session was brief, and I was only able to identify a male presence with me.

We returned upstairs to the auditorium to pack up and go home. I felt the investigation had been a success, and I could hardly wait to see the finished media product. In a few days, Lindsey came by the Ghost Hunter Shop and gave me a copy of her feature story. She was so excited about capturing the EVP during my dowsing session. She felt that her clip might win her some acclaim as a TV reporter. I was delighted when I found out later that Lindsey did win a few placements in her field and used the clip as part of an interview when she tried out for a reporter position for a TV station in Lubbock, Texas. She was so kind in telling me that I helped her land the job by doing such a great job on the ghost investigation. If you want to see the clip of the investigation at the Thoroughbred Theater just go to www. youtube.com and type in Lindsey Ashcraft ghosthunter, and the video will come up for you to view.

Since my last investigation at the Thoroughbred Theater, Tony has left Lexington and has leased the theater to the McDaniel brothers, Jim and John. The ironic part of this story is that the brothers at one time owned the theater and sold it to Tony in 2003. They loved what Tony had done to the place and agreed to keep the theater opened while Tony was away. Jim and John are going to continue to bring good entertainment to the Thoroughbred Theater to enrich and educate the community through the arts. I asked them if they had seen or felt the paranormal activity that had been reported while Tony was there, and they agreed that there had been a few things still happening. They love the fact that the ghosts find their theater a perfect place to haunt.

CHAPTER 22

Waverly Hills Sanatorium
LOUISVILLE, JEFFERSON COUNTY

"ARE YOU SERIOUS? The ball had rolled down the hall and was resting at the bottom of the stairs? What happened next?" "We walked over to the ball to make sure that no one else was there. Standing at the bottom of the stairs, I called out to Timmy in hopes that he would answer us, 'Timmy is that you?' I picked up the ball, which was wet from rolling in the water puddles on its journey to the stairs. Since there was no one else with us, we were amazed how Timmy had moved the ball as we had asked him to do so."

"Who is Timmy and what about the ball?" you might be asking yourself. Timmy is one of many ghosts that haunt the building that was once a tuberculosis hospital. If you go there, you

This is the ball that the little boy ghost, Timmy, likes to play with.

will find a ball that has been left as a toy for Timmy to play with in the deserted hallways.

Many ghosthunters have taken the opportunity to communicate with Timmy by asking him to move the ball. They instruct the child to play with the ball in hopes that they will be able to record its movement on their camcorders. Sometimes the ball would start to roll back and forth right in front of them. Other times it would be placed at one end of the hall, and Timmy would be asked to move it. The ghosthunters would leave the area and come back to find the ball missing. As they searched for the missing ball, they would be shocked to find it at the other end of the hallway or on another floor.

Being the true ghosthunter that I am, one of my favorite places to go, whether it is for a ghosthunt, ghost tour, or a Halloween event, is this old TB hospital. You may have heard of it. Waverly Hills Sanatorium in Louisville, Kentucky. It has been featured on many television shows including ABC's *Scariest Places on Earth*, VH1's *Celebrity Paranormal Project*, the TV show *Most Haunted* as well as one of the most popular sci-fi shows *Ghost Hunters*. In one of the *Ghost Hunter's* episodes, Jason and Grant, using a high-tech thermal camcorder, captured something crawling down one of the halls. It was truly amazing and disturbing.

When you drive up the decaying road to Waverly, it sets the mood for what you will eventually see as you come to the top of the hill. Even during the day, Waverly Hills Hospital looks forebodingly doomed. There are signs posted at the gate, warning that trespassers will be prosecuted, and security cameras are attached to the outside of the building to record any trespassers or vandals. It's easy to see how this place has lured teens, thrill seekers, and vagrants to break into the property. It would make a perfect refuge in which to party, get high on drugs, or search for ghosts. There were also rumors of satanic rituals held throughout the building.

In its prime this hospital provided a place to treat people suffering with tuberculosis. In the 1900s Louisville had the highest tuberculosis death rate in the United States. Waverly Hills Sanatorium was considered a superior facility for treating this disease, which was sometimes call the "white plague." Before advanced medicine, simple remedies were used to treat the disease. It was understood throughout the medical community that these patients needed to receive good nutrition. Their diets included lots of protein to boost their immune system. Fresh fruits and vegetables along with milk, butter, and cheese were added to give them a complete balanced diet. Another important factor in the healing process was to get plenty of fresh air. That is why Waverly was built with a surrounding solarium on each floor. The sun's ultraviolet rays, which helped the body to produce vitamin D, were also another important factor in the healing process. Each patient was scheduled to get plenty of sunshine and fresh air every day. Even in the cold winter months, the staff would roll the beds out onto the solarium. The patients were tucked in their beds while covered with electric blankets so they could continue to get the fresh air and the sunshine their bodies needed.

Even though suffering and dying was commonplace, the patients were kept in high spirits with lots of fun activities to keep their minds off their disease. The patients were offered craft classes; they were shown movies; and they could listen to their favorite radio show from headphones. Some of the healthier ones could enjoy horseback riding. At Christmas the children were entertained by watching Santa with his reindeer riding his sleigh around the Waverly grounds.

I remember the first time I met the owners of Waverly, Tina and Charlie, in 2002. I had acquired permission to bring my Ghost Chasers International members there for a ghost investigation. The evening we arrived, Tina, a petite yet commanding lady, joined us as our group was preparing to start our prayer of protection. She wanted to lay out the ground rules so that no one would get hurt during our investigation. Before starting the investigation, she suggested that we meet in an outbuilding down from the sanatorium to learn more about the property. While we met there, Tina and Charlie told us about the history and the different hauntings reported in the hospital.

The Waverly Hills Sanatorium was described as having five stories including a morgue and a "body chute." Actually, the body chute (or the death tunnel, as it has been labeled) is part of the exaggerated horror history of Waverly. The five-hundred-foot tunnel was originally used as a passage way for the staff to walk up the hill during bad weather and to transport supplies. The tunnel was also constructed with a heating system, pipes that ran up to the building. It wasn't until the death toll rose unusually high during the 1940s that the tunnel was used to transport the bodies to the hearses below. This action was taken to protect the patients' morale from dropping by shielding them from seeing so many patients being transported to the mortuary. It was never used as a slide to dump dead bodies so they would roll down to the bottom of the hill.

A small hospital was built on the property in the early 1900s to house patients suffering from an outbreak of tuberculosis in Louisville. As the number of patients grew, so did the need for a larger hospital. In 1926 the door to Waverly Hills Sanatorium was opened to fulfill this need. For many years the four-hundred-bed facility was filled with patients until the 1943 discovery of streptomycin. The cases began to diminish, and in 1961 Waverly Hills closed its doors forever.

In 1962 the building was renamed Woodhaven Geriatrics Center and opened to take care of the aging. Over the years there were rumors that this institute was not giving the proper care to the elderly, and there were reports of physical abuse. In 1980 the center was closed due to inappropriate patient care.

For over a decade this building was considered for other business opportunities, such as a prison and later a worship center. The approval or funding for these enterprises did not go through, so the old Waverly building remained abandoned. In 2001, Charlie and Tina Mattingly bought Waverly in hopes of restoring the old building to preserve its history for future generations to enjoy. Waverly meant something special to them since they each had relatives who were treated for tuberculosis at the Sanatorium.

Charlie admitted that he knew about the haunted history but didn't give it much credence. That is until he started to hear disembodied voices and to see weird images down the hall. When he shared what had happened to him with Tina, she agreed that similar things were happening to her. He decided to bring

The death tunnel at Waverly Hills

his camcorder into the building and was amazed at the many anomalies he captured on film. Some of the images were balls of lights moving down the halls at incredible speed. Once he captured what looked like a shadow person walking around in one of the rooms. He also caught misty forms and vortexes as he walked down the halls with his camcorder.

Soon after the Mattinglys bought Waverly, the vast efforts to clean the building became a reality with the help of friends and local ghosthunting groups. The strange and bizarre activity continued to happen to the volunteers. The Mattinglys started to allow outside ghosthunting groups to enter the property to investigate for ghostly activity and to collect paranormal evidence. Because of so much interest in Waverly, Tina and Charlie realized that they could raise money to restore this building by scheduling overnight ghost investigations, historical tours, and an annual Halloween attraction. Tina is also the head of the non-profit Waverly Hills Historical Society.

Once the orientation with the Mattinglys was over, it was time for our group to start the investigation of Waverly. We followed Charlie down a hallway connected to the main Waverly Hills Hospital. We had four hours to walk through the halls and rooms with a volunteer security guard for our safety. We took many photos, recorded a few EVPs , and set up our camcorders. One of my favorite experiences at Waverly is to stand at one end of a long hallway, and as my eyes adjust to the dark, I can see dark, human-like images walk in and out of the rooms. Even the other ghosthunters who are standing against the walls see them as well. Another experiment that we did was to have two of our ghosthunters walk down the hall, and when they got almost to the end, they separated. In their path we saw two dark shadows that continued to walk down the hall as if they had been following behind the ghosthunters. Each time we return to Waverly and do this experiment, the sight of this phenomenon always makes the hair on the back of my neck stand straight up.

While we were in the cafeteria area, Chuck took the camcorder and switched it to the infrared setting. As soon as he turned it on, he captured a vertical vortex that streaked across the view of the camcorder. We believed that we had caught evidence of spirit activity.

Not far from where we were recording, Walli Scott, one of our investigators, called me over to take a look at what she had just shot in her infrared camera. She had an image of a partial apparition of a headless man walking past her as she was shooting. He was a hefty size and was wearing a white uniform. When we asked our guide about the apparition he started to tell us stories associated with the cafeteria. Volunteers and workers reported seeing an apparition of a heavyset man wearing a white jacket, walking back and forth in the cafeteria. This was the same area where Walli had captured the apparition and where Chuck had captured the vortex. The guide continued telling us about other reports, including the scent of food cooking, especially the smell of bread, that would waft through the room. The sound of doors slamming shut and footsteps walking nearby were also reported. We were extremely pleased that our evidence seemed to be related to these other sightings.

We left this area and continued our investigation by going to the fifth floor. The most famous Waverly tale is about the suicide of a nurse, who had hanged herself outside of Room 502 in the middle 1920s. Our guide told us that sometimes pregnant women on the tour would complain about being nauseated or dizzy when stopping in front of Room 502. Others have reported hearing voices coming from Room 502. "Get out of here" has been heard more than once. Some have seen shadows walking around inside the room as they pass by. When they stop and go back for a better look, there is no one there.

Professional photographer and ghosthunter Tom Halstead captured one of the most stunning photos I have ever seen of a female full-bodied apparition. He captured this image while shooting down the fourth floor hallway at Waverly with his Pentax K1000 35mm film camera. It would make sense to capture her ghostly image on another floor since her duties would not limit her to the fifth floor. The tour guide told us that the nurse had become pregnant by one of the doctors at the hospital. She went into room 502 and gave herself an abortion. Afterwards, she walked out of the room and into the hall where she then hanged herself. The guard said she had hanged herself on the water pipes that lined the ceiling.

I asked Tom what was going on at the time he captured the

**This photographic negative shows a full-bodied appa-
rition on the fourth floor of the Waverly Sanitorium.**

image. "When our group, Paranormal Task Force, arrived at
Waverly," Tom said, "we started on the first floor and decided
to work our way to the roof. At first, it was quiet and nonevent-
ful until we made it to the third floor. I heard a faint sound of
a woman screaming, and so did several other members in our
group. We agreed that the screams sounded as if they were coming from upstairs, so we decided to go to the fourth floor and
check it out. As we were walking towards the stairs, several pieces
of plaster fell off the wall and came flying across the room. Some
of the pieces hit my leg and also hit a couple of the others. As we
reached the fourth floor, we heard footsteps, and then it sounded
like someone was being dragged across the floor. When I looked
down the hall, in the dark I could see a misty light moving near
one of the rooms. I looked into my viewfinder on my camera
and saw the same misty light. I took several shots but did not
capture anything—or so I thought. It wasn't until I returned
home and reviewed my photos when I noticed the apparition of
a young woman. At first I thought that I might be matrixing or

just wanting to believe that it was a ghost. I pulled out the negatives of that roll of film to see if the apparition could be seen in the negative, and there she was. After finding it in the negative and then enlarging the photo, I knew the female apparition was real, and I had captured a ghost on film."

After hearing so many stories and getting some pretty good evidence in photos and video, I couldn't wait to start my history research on Waverly. While searching newspaper articles, the Internet, and other resources, I couldn't find anything that supported the story about the nurse committing suicide in room 502. Some information written about the nurse said that she couldn't have hanged herself from the water pipes. Records show that they were not installed in the building until 1972, when they added the sprinkler system to the hospital. The more I searched, the more I could see that the story of the nurse and room 502 must be another myth.

As I was gathering my information to write this story I decided to visit with Charlie Mattingly and ask him if he had any luck finding evidence about the nurse and room 502. He perked up and gladly told me what he had discovered. One afternoon, while Charlie was finishing a project outside the building, an old truck came up the hill to Waverly. The truck stopped a few feet from Charlie, and an elderly man got out and walked over to him. The stranger extended his hand and introduced himself as John Thornberry. Charlie introduced himself and then asked, "Are you related to the Thornberrys who are connected to this place?" "Why, yes, I am," he said. "My father was hired as head of maintenance when Waverly first opened. I also started to work here when I turned seventeen to help my father. Eventually, most of my family got jobs here and lived in the housing that was provided by Waverly until the hospital closed." Charlie told John that one day he had found an old filing cabinet, and there was a bank deposit book with the name

John Thornberry on it. John claimed that book belonged to his father. This amused Charlie to find someone else with close ties to the old hospital. As they continued their conversation Charlie thought about the story of the nurse and room 502. He asked, "John, do you know anything about a nurse who committed suicide after aborting a baby here at Waverly?" John replied without hesitation, "Yes, sir, I do. My father and I were called to the fifth floor to assist as they cut the hanging nurse down. At first we couldn't understand where all the blood was coming from until we followed the blood trail to room 502, which was a washroom. There was blood all over the floor and commode so we figured that she had performed an abortion."

Charlie asked, "Did you find the baby?" "My father and I left the building and went down the hill to the cistern. We lifted the cover but didn't see anything big enough to be the body of a baby. My father sent me back up to the building into room 502 and had me flush the commode over and over until it finally forced the baby's remains down to the cistern. My father retrieved the baby's body, and later it was given a proper burial," said Thornberry.

When I asked Charlie, "How did John explain about her hanging from the pipes when they were not installed until the 1970s?" Charlie said he asked John if the nurse was hanging from the pipes. John said that there was a pulley in the ceiling that was used to raise and lower the elevator, and she used the hook from that to hang herself. "Why wasn't this in the newspaper? How could something like this happen and there are no records to support it?" I asked. Charlie agreed with me and said he asked John about that. John said that in those days abortion was such a disgrace that an act like that would be covered up and kept a secret. The hospital staff made sure that no one talked about the incident to avoid the story getting out to the public. That kind of publicity would ruin the reputation of the doctors.

It would not have benefited the patients, and it would have damaged their trust and morale. Keeping a high and happy morale, in spite of so much death among the patients, was an important element in the healing process.

After Charlie told me about John's experience, he suggested that I call one of his volunteers, Shirlene Edwards, and talk to her about the Thornberry family. I took his advice and called her the next day. She answered the phone in a youthful and cheery tone, "Hello, Waverly Hills Tours." I introduced myself and asked her if she knew the Thornberrys. She immediately answered, "Yes, I was born and raised close to the Thornberry families here on the Waverly property." I asked, "Where did you live once the hospital closed?" "We still live here. There were over six hundred acres, and the housing area was located down the hill from Waverly, where Bobby Nichols Golf Club is now located. The Thornberrys still live there too, and my family has been friends with them for many years. Waverly was a very loving and supportive community, and while it was in service, provided jobs and security for all of our families."

I asked, "What did your parents do at Waverly?" "My Grandfather, Claude Hawkins, helped build Waverly, and once it was opened, he remained there as a butcher in the kitchen. My Father, William Hawkins, was born on the property, and as soon as he turned fourteen, he started to work at Waverly. My Mother didn't work at Waverly because she was a stay-at-home mom." Her father was hired into maintenance at first. "When the death toll increased, he worked in the tunnel, where he escorted the bodies down to the hearses. He continued to work at Waverly until it closed," she said. Through my conversation with Shirlene, I realized that John's story made sense. I could see why he and his father, along with the staff of the hospital, chose to keep the nurse's tragic death a secret. How devastating it would have been for this close-knit community to know what had happened. Once I had all of my information verified, I was convinced that the story about the nurse and room 502 was no longer an urban legend. This heart-wrenching tale was a dark secret that remained hidden deep in the halls of Waverly as it continued to serve the community. Even though the incident happened many years ago, it's good to know the truth as John Thornberry revealed what he witnessed in room 502 on that tragic day.

I am convinced in knowing that folklore, legends, and documented ghost investigations continue to perpetuate the mystique of Waverly Hills Sanatorium.

CHAPTER 23

White Hall Historic House
RICHMOND, MADISON COUNTY

IN 2001, CHUCK AND I had to visit one of his clients in Richmond, Kentucky, and while on our way there I remembered that I had read an article about a place in Richmond called White Hall. It was the home of Cassius M. Clay, nineteenth-century emancipationist, politician, newspaper publisher, and ambassador to Russia. His father, Green Clay, was a Civil War general who built the mansion in 1789. I had a strong feeling that with its kind of history, there might be a chance the mansion would be haunted.

It was a cold, gray, and rainy November day so we didn't plan on being at White Hall for too long. Before getting out of the car I took a moment to gaze at this stately plantation frozen with the cold in time and history on top of a hill. For a brief moment I thought I saw someone looking back at me from one of the upstairs windows. I found out later that no one was in the house and was told that many times people would report seeing someone standing in a window. Maybe I had also witnessed one of the many ghosts that haunt White Hall.

When we entered the gift shop near the mansion, a member of the sales staff greeted us. She extended her hand and introduced herself as Judy. Dressed in slacks and wearing a gray sweater, she was chilled by the winter's cold as it seeped in through cracks in the bottom of the door. We told her that we were ghosthunters and wondered if she knew of any ghosts or ghostly activity at White Hall. Her face lit up and a big smile appeared as she began to tell us her accounts.

She took us over to the counter where there was a young lady sitting on a stool reading a magazine and asked her if she knew of any ghostly experiences at White Hall. She looked up from the article she was reading and said, "There is a lady who was a tour guide here, and she had many ghostly experiences happen to her. She is now the curator. Her name is Lashe Mullins. Her husband, Charles, is also a tour guide, and I've heard that he has also had some strange encounters." "Would it be possible for Chuck and me to schedule a ghost investigation in White Hall?" I asked. I could see that she was taken aback by my request and was hesitant to agree. She told us that there had never been paranormal investigators at the mansion before, but she would try to get permission for us to conduct an investigation.

Judy told us about the history of White Hall and shared some of the ghostly experiences she had witnessed there. Most of her experiences were common to hauntings: cold spots, hearing whispers, doors opening and slamming on their own, and glimpses of a figure in the corner of her vision, which quickly disappeared as she turned her head in its direction. She admitted that she wasn't convinced that all of the activity could be attributed to ghostly activity. Sometimes she just brushed them off as coincidence. Before we left, Judy gave me the contact information for the curator, Lashe Mullins, so we could contact her to get more information about the hauntings at White Hall. Judy offered to give us a tour of White Hall before we left, and we were glad to take her up on her offer. As we followed Judy up the walkway towards White Hall, it started to spit rain and sleet. Even the miserable weather couldn't dampen the beauty of this regal Italianate mansion with its four white columns gleaming down at us. Judy said that when the mansion was built in 1789, it was known as the Clermont. It started as a two-story Georgian brick home, quite different than what it is today. In the 1860s a new addition was built in the Italianate style, which included such modern comforts as central heat and indoor plumbing. After the addition was completed, the name was changed from Clermont to White Hall.

Once we were inside, Judy took us to a room that housed a few glass display counters where we could see old documents and original old pictures of the structure during its grand life and after it was forgotten and abandoned. After Cassius Clay's death in 1903, White Hall was rented out to tenet farmers until the 1960s. During this time the home began to fall into despair as the farmers had no regard for this once magnificent home. They even brought in bales of hay to store in the main living room and treated it as if it were a barn. The roof finally gave way to years of erosion as the rain poured through the cracks. It seemed that the house was doomed for destruction. As I was looking at these photos I noticed that one of them displayed a bright glowing vortex, a form that looks like a white tornado extending from one end of the photo to the other. It appeared in a photo taken in the late 1960s, just after the property had been donated to the state. When I pointed out the vortex to Judy, she said that she had never noticed it before. I explained to her that, as a ghosthunter, we look for this type of anomaly when taking photos of haunted locations. We believe that they represent the unseen energies of spirits or ghosts that are captured by the camera. At this point I felt that if we were permitted to do a ghost investigation, we would probably get lots of evidence with photos and possibly ghostly voices with our audio recorders, along with positive readings from our other ghosthunting instruments.

As soon as we returned home from our visit to White Hall, I got on the phone and called Lashe Mullins to see if she could tell me some of her experiences while a tour guide at White Hall. She was willing to share lots of stories with me, and we decided that if the state gave us permission to do the investigation, Lashe would come along with us. I also asked if her husband, Charles, would mind going, and he agreed to join us as well. I later found out that Charles had some very strange contacts with the spirits there and had even seen apparitions.

Within a matter of a few weeks I received a phone call from Judy with the permission to get into White Hall for our ghost investigation. At last we got to meet Lashe and Charles as they stood on the grand porch of White Hall. Lashe was a petite woman with long dark hair that complemented Charles's short dark hair. They were ready and anxious to get started with our tour and the investigation of the house and around the property. We started on the first floor, and as we moved from floor to floor and then later to the basement, Lashe filled us in on some of the activity that she had witnessed and also what some of the tour guides shared with her.

We set up our infrared camcorders on the second floor in hopes of capturing the apparition of the "Lady in Black," as Lashe referred to her. She said that one of the employees had seen what looked like the end of a hooped, black gown turn a corner and disappear down the small stairs to Green Clay's bedroom. Other tour guides said they had seen this apparition but noticed that her gown was blue, and others had seen her wearing other colors as well. Listening to Lashe explain how different people saw her in different colored gowns made me wonder if maybe she was seen in different colors because of the combination of energy or the light in the room, which may have altered the color.

Charles said that one time he was guiding a tour through the building and stopped the group to explain how the plumbing worked in the 1800s. It was rare for a home to have indoor plumbing back then and so was the copper bathtub that was installed in the bathroom. As he continued to talk about this special feature of the house, he happened to glance up and saw the form of a woman on the third floor landing. He could see her from her neck down, although the rest of her was obscured by the railing. She was solid enough that he could tell she had on a white blouse and navy blue hooped skirt. He knew at that moment that he was looking at a ghost instead of a guest because he could see right through her.

After Charles's tour was over, another guide came up to him and asked him, "What were you looking at when you were staring up at the third floor railing?" Charles said, "What do you mean?" The guide said, "Didn't you see me looking down at you?" Charles, a bit confused, replied, "No, I didn't see you." The guide said, "I saw you look up at the railing, and you were as white as a sheet." Jokingly he asked, "Did you see a ghost?" Charles realized that his attention was so absorbed by the apparition that he did not see the guide standing by the railing. Charles said, "You mean you didn't see her? She was standing right there beside you." The guide admitted that he did not see anyone or anything standing beside him when Charles was looking up at the railing.

Lashe said that the ghostly woman might be Mary Jane Warfield Clay. She was the mother of ten children and the wife of Cassius Marcellus Clay for forty-five years, until their divorce. While Cassius was away in Russia, Mary Jane managed the remodeling of Clermont all alone. After a long separation, Cassius Clay returned from his tour to an unhappy wife. Adding insult to injury, Clay also brought home a young boy he had adopted as his son. All of this led to the couple's divorce in 1878. I'm sure it was a sad day when Mary Jane had to leave her beloved White Hall, and maybe that is why she has decided to come back in spirit to oversee her home as she continues with her daily duties.

At age eighty-four, Cassius Clay remarried. His bride was a fifteen-year-old girl. This outraged the community and even made national headlines. The marriage was doomed from the beginning and only lasted for a few years. In later years, as his body aged and he developed the gout, Clay moved his bedroom downstairs to the first floor into the library at the back of the house. He had been tipped off that someone overheard a plan to rob his home. He sent a message to the local sheriff, hoping he would come to help him protect his property from these thieves. Cassius gathered an arsenal of guns and knives and placed them by his side and in his hands while he sat in his chair waiting in the dark for the attack. As he suspected, three men entered his home through the window of the library only to find a man in a rage determined to save and protect what was his. He shot the first man dead. Cassius turned as the second intruder jumped him, but Cassius managed to stab the culprit with a hunting knife before he pushed Cassius into the fireplace. The third offender turned and ran along with the wounded man. When the sheriff arrived he found the man that Clay had killed by the ice house. The only injury to Cassius, now eighty-nine years old, was a singed night shirt from getting too close to the fire in the fireplace during the attack.

A recent report of spirit activity involved a tour guide, Buffy Turner, and another guide who were playing around on the first floor before the tours started. Since they were both in period clothing, the other guide grabbed the bottom of Buffy's skirt and held it as if she were a bride about to ascend the stairs. Once they got to the top of the stairs, they both saw a man walk into the doorway of one of the bedrooms. The guide actually jerked the skirt as a reaction to the sight of this unexpected visitor. They watched as he stopped and looked at them and then walked past the doorway. They turned and hurried back downstairs to tell the other guides what they had just seen. They explained that the man was dressed as if he were one of the tour guides. As they were telling their stories everyone looked around to see if there were any guides missing. They were all accounted for, so

At Misti Dawn Covey's wedding, Jeff at Aaron Photo-
graphy, captured an apparition in this photo.

who was the man they saw in the upstairs bedroom? Buffy was
terrified. "I just about chewed all the skin off the tips of my fingers," she said.

A few years later, after my ghost investigation at White Hall,
I entered the waiting room of a local radio station. I introduced
myself to the receptionist and explained that I was going to be a
guest on the radio show to talk about ghosthunting. While I was
waiting, she introduced herself to me as Misti Dawn. She, as
so many of the people I meet, wanted to tell me about her para-

normal experience. She came around from behind the counter and asked me, "If I send you a picture of me and my husband, Tommy, at our wedding, would you mind looking at what we think to be an apparition in the photo. You see, I got married at White Hall, and I had heard it was a very haunted place, and I was hoping that I might have a ghost in my photo." I agreed for her to e-mail me the photo, and, sure enough, it contained a very convincing image of an apparition hovering over one of the windows just beyond where Misti and Tommy were standing when the picture was taken. I was quite excited to see that White Hall was still sporting ghostly activity, and this photo was great evidence to support my suspicions.

East

Ashland, Boyd County
Paramount Arts Center (formerly Paramount Theatre)

Prestonsburg, Floyd County
Jenny Wiley State Resort Park

Slade, Powell County
Natural Bridge State Resort Park

Van Lear, Johnson County
Coal Miners' Museum

CHAPTER 24

Coal Miners' Museum
VAN LEAR, JOHNSON COUNTY

THE FIRST TIME I HEARD ABOUT the movie *Coal Miner's Daughter,* featuring Loretta Lynn, I thought it would be a hit because it featured two of my favorite stars, Sissy Spacek and Tommy Lee Jones. Boy, was I surprised once I saw the movie in 1980. It was a great hit as I suspected. Not for the performances of these two superstars, even though Sissy Spacek won the Academy Award for Best Actress, but because of the subject matter it brought to life. The story focused on a young girl in the Appalachian Mountains who suffered an impoverished upbringing, which led to a troubled but committed marriage, a hectic pace of life, and many tragedies that became the subjects of the songs she wrote. The lyrics solidified her reputation as an advocate for the common woman, attuned to the lives of the blue-collar audience. Her words sang loud to the wives and mothers who weren't about to be pushed around by cheating or abusive husbands. Never in a million years did I think that one day I would be standing on the property of the home where Loretta Lynn, The First Lady of Country Music, was born and raised. How did I end up there? I was talking with one of my GCI members, Joe Clark, and he told me about a super place to do a ghosthunt called the Coal Miners' Museum in Van Lear, Kentucky. I asked him, "You mean where Loretta Lynn lived as a child?" "Yes," he said, "and Loretta's home is only three miles down the road from the museum."

Joe continued to tell me about the experiences that he and his group, Commonwealth Paranormal, had during their investigation at the Van Lear Coal Miners' Museum. Tina Webb, the museum director, joined a reporter, Shawna Howell, from the local newspaper, *The Big Sandy News,* who went along with Joe's ghosthunter group to observe and write an article about the investigation titled, "Haunted or Hoax?"

I asked Joe, "Did you get any solid evidence of a haunting?" "While upstairs in the museum, during a dowsing session, we discovered a twenty-two-year-old female spirit. She had worked at the bank that used to be in the building before it became the Coal Miners' Museum. We found out that she died of influenza. Sally, the name she revealed to us, hid in the vault upstairs to protect herself from evil ones." When Joe was telling me about the investigation, he said that one of his members, Tyler Holbrook, had his necklace torn off as they stood in front of the coal miners' mural that is painted on the wall where they were investigating. This rough act left a red welt around Tyler's neck."

Did you get any EVPs while you were there?" "No," Joe said, "but we did get some voices that came through the Hack Shack Ghost Box. They were ugly words and revealed a lot of anger. It was a male ghost and he said, 'Get out.' We also got some good responses with our EMF K-2 meter as well."

At our Ghost Chasers International, Inc. (GCI), Nightmare Before Christmas party, I saw Joe and asked him if he would be able to arrange for me to meet Tina so that I could include a story about the museum in *Ghosthunting Kentucky,* the book I was writing. He agreed and called me back in a couple of days with an appointment for an interview and a ghosthunt with Tina Webb. I was totally psyched.

While Chuck and I were planning our trip to Van Lear, I got a call from Dotti Kult, a member of GCI, and invited her to join us the next day for the investigation. I didn't know how much time we would have, so I decided to keep my group small, with only Chuck, Dotti, and I joining Tina for the ghosthunt. I don't think there is a place on earth as beautiful as Kentucky when you start to drive up into the hills and mountains. No matter what time of the year you decide to visit, the beauty of the countryside is so vivid. Since we had had snow for the past two weeks, it was truly a winter wonderland of snowy hills, frozen lakes, bright sunshine, and fresh, clean air. No words can adequately describe the exhilaration I felt being in this part of the world.

We met Tina at Shoney's in Paintsville, which is about ten minutes away from the museum. During lunch she told us the history of the museum and the town. Van Lear was incorporated in 1912 and named after the director of Consolidation Coal Company, Van Lear Black. Five coal mines were opened and operated in Van Lear from 1910 through 1946. Presently, Van Lear is an unincorporated community, which means the area is not a part of any municipality, city, or town with its own government. Most of the current working population is employed outside Van Lear in nearby cities. Loretta Lynn sings about the Van Lear mines in her hit songs *Coal Miner's Daughter* and *Van Lear Rose*. Coal mines and Loretta Lynn are synonymous in the town of Van Lear, with the small community of Butcher Holler about three miles down the road from the museum.

We agreed to follow Tina back to the museum. She laughed and said, "You won't find the museum by using your GPS. It's out in the country and off the grid." We followed her closely so not to get lost. We arrived at a huge, old wooden structure. Looking at the building, it was obvious that the second and third floors had been added on later. I learned from Tina that as the town grew, this building had to expand with new enterprises, and that was the reason for its piecemeal design. Tina called it the first mall. Tina unlocked the side door that led us into a novelty shop called Icky's. She began to tell us the history of the building by saying, "The building was built in 1913 and housed a cobbler's shop in the front and the jail cells in the back. In the 1940s, Richard (Icky) Wetzel opened a lunch counter and shop called, Kay's Novelty Shop, named for his niece. Since the schools didn't serve lunch, the students would come here to eat, along with some of the townspeople. Richard also cooked meals for the prisoners incarcerated in the jail cells. Later, he changed the name of his store to Icky's."

"Tina," I asked, "Why would he call a place where you can eat Icky's? That doesn't sound very appealing to me." Tina chuckled and said, "When Richard was little, he went with his siblings to watch the movie, *The Legend of Sleepy Hollow*. It scared him so bad that the other children teased him and started to call him Ichabod. Throughout the years, the nickname was shortened to Icky."

Tina continued the history lesson: "On the second floor, there was a post office, a bank, a doctor's office, a dentist's office, and a beauty shop. On the third floor was the map room with a dark room set up for the employees of the five mines to work on their maps."

After Tina led us around the first floor and showed us the rooms while telling us the history, I was able to ask her about the paranormal activity there. "Tina, what has happened to you since you've been here?" "So many times I've been sitting in my office and heard foot traffic above me. Even the volunteers will hear it with me and when we go upstairs there is no one there." Tina replied, and then pointed at her radio sitting on the corner of her desk. "Sometimes the radio will pop on and other times it will be on and the channels will change without me touching it. I was sitting at my desk with my head down working on a project and got a weird feeling that someone was watching me. When I looked up, I saw a shadow person pass by my door. I stepped out of my office to make sure I was still alone, and there

was no one else in the building with me. One time, I looked up
and saw a full shadow of a man looking back at me. I froze for
a moment, and then it disappeared. Even though it startled me,
I'm not afraid of what is here. I believe that it might be the spirits
of others looking out for me."

"Has anyone died in this building?" I asked. Tina replied,
"Yes, several people have died here. In 1984 a man by the name
of P.J. volunteered to stay here at night. He was acting security
because during renovation people were breaking in and stealing
supplies. One morning P.J. was found lying dead right in front
of my office door. He had died of an aneurism. I believe P.J.
showed himself to me one night. It was about 10:30, and I was
locking up the doors. I went to pull the door shut that led into
the room where they found P.J. I was standing behind the candy
counter when the door slammed in my face, knocking me into
the counter. This didn't scare me as much as it made me angry.
I shouted a few cruse words at P.J. and warned him not to ever
do that again. I believe that he is upset that he died alone. After
I was pushed by P.J., I thought if I gave him a job it would make
him happy to have something to do. I asked P.J. to look out for
me and protect me while I was here."

She turned in the direction of the front door and said, "The
door bell will ring while I'm sitting at my desk, and since my
office door is open, I can see who is coming in. I'll look up, but
there is no one there. In a matter of minutes, someone always
comes through the door. I think the reason the doorbell rings is
to let me know that P.J. is taking his job seriously, and he is letting me know when people are about to come in."

Tina was finished with her stories of the first floor and suggested that we go on upstairs to start our investigation there.
We left the shop and went back outside to go up to the second
floor from another side door. It was about forty-five degrees by
now, so it wasn't freezing cold until we walked into the second

floor. It was about thirty-nine degrees, so we pulled our scarves around our necks and waited for the heater that Tina turned on to heat us up. During that time we were joined by one of the high school volunteers, Brook Casey. She told us a few stories about a little boy who haunts the building. Tina pointed at the mailboxes that were left behind when this room used to be the post office."

"Remember when you asked me if anyone had died here?" she asked. "Yes. Why? Did someone die here?" Tina replied, "Dan Short died of a heart attack right here in front of these mail boxes. He used to work for the coal mines until they closed. He came here to work with his wife, Catherine Short, who was the postmaster at the time. We also had a gentleman die upstairs, but I'll tell you about him later."

We left the comfort of this warm room and ventured out into the cold of the other room that had no heat. As I went through the door, my EMF meter began to beep at a fast speed. Usually this means I'm picking up something electrical, so I pulled my probe and pointed to the floor and walls, and there was not a disturbance. The meter was quiet. I asked that if a spirit was making my meter go off to please do it again. At that moment my EMF meter started to beep furiously. "Okay, Okay," I said. "Please answer this question. Are you a little boy?" Again the meter beeped. I said, "Please stop the meter from beeping." It stopped. I asked if there were any other spirits, and there was no answer. Realizing that it was a child, Tina suggested I ask if friends or family were here with us, and I got a positive response to that question. I was thrilled to get the little boy, since Tina and Brook had told us about him being seen in the hall on the second floor. I asked the sweet spirit if he would stop making my meter go off so I could check out the other rooms, and the meter stopped and didn't go off until I asked the child to come back again when we went upstairs.

**Lakyn Blair's drawing of the little ghost boy that she and others
have seen on the second floor of the Coal Miners' Museum.**

We continued our walked into the room where Dr. Turner examined his patients. Tina pointed at the GYN table and told us that that is where Loretta Lynn was examined when she found out she was pregnant.

I pointed into the hall where people waited to see the doctor or dentist and asked Tina, "Is this the area where you think the footsteps come from when you are sitting at your desk below us?" "Yes," Tina answered. "It would make sense to me that I might be hearing the footsteps of so many people who paced up and down this hall while waiting for their appointments." I told her that she might be hearing a residual haunting in which their footsteps have left a memory of their energy behind. Tina led us over to the stairs leading to the next floor and said, "We have high school volunteers that come and work with us. One day three of the girls were sitting on this couch and looked up at the landing on the stairs. They could see a little boy peeking out at them from the railing. At first they weren't sure what they saw. Again, a little boy popped his head out and all three girls giggled with joy that they had seen the little boy. We have a ball that we keep upstairs for him to play with. I will put it in the schoolroom before I leave for the day and tell him he can play with it. When I come back the next day the ball is gone and sometimes we never find it, so I go out and buy a new ball. One of the girls drew a picture of the little boy."

Our next stop was a room on the third floor that was set up like a children's schoolroom that reflected an earlier time in history. When I stepped into the room, I was shocked at the drop in temperature. I realized the building was cold due to the weather and that it had no heat on the second or third floor, but this room had a huge drop in temperature. It was so cold we could see our breath as we talked to each other. Even with my long padded coat, scarf, hat, gloves, thermal underwear, blue jeans, and a pair of thick sweat pants I was still freezing. The longer we stayed in the room, the colder it got, so I had to hurry through my investigation while collecting data. I decided to get my thermometer out and see how cold it was; it registered eight degrees.

While we were in the schoolroom, Tina walked over to the left of the room and opened two heavy metal doors. I said, "Tina, what is that?" "This used to be the vault when the bank was here," she said. We stepped inside, and it was even colder in there. While I was standing inside the vault, I turned on the Ovilus and got the word "tragic." I turned to Tina and asked, "Has anyone been locked up in the vault or died here? We have felt that maybe something tragic happened in this room, but I've never found any history in my research to support that belief," she said.

We stepped back into the classroom to see what the Ovilus would report. I got the word, "base." I repeated the word and said, "This is our base for this investigation." Later, while listening to my audio recorder, I captured an EVP that repeated the word "base" after I said it. I also got the word "help" and then "help them" from the Ovilus. When I listened to my audio recorder, I got an EVP saying "help" after the Ovilus had said "help." At that point I said, "I will send you a prayer that will help you cross over." The Ovilus said, "All of them." I agreed and said, "Yes, a prayer for all of them." A couple more words came out of the Ovilus, but they were full of static, and we couldn't make out what it was saying. Then it clearly said "kitchen," and a second later it said "Richard." Dotti looked over and asked, "Did it just say 'Richard?' Isn't that Icky's name? Tina said he cooked for the lunch bar and prisoners. Isn't it strange that the Ovilus would say 'kitchen' and then 'Richard?'"

I walked over to the row of student desks and the Ovilus said "study." Then it said "Jane." I looked at Tina, but she did not recognize the name as someone she knew or was related to the museum. Then I realized that one of my first books in the first grade was a Dick and Jane reader. I loved the connection the Ovilus made: we were in a schoolroom and it said "study" and "Jane." The next word that came through the Ovilus was "ball," and I remembered Tina's story about the little boy playing with a ball, so I asked her if she had a ball. She walked behind me and gave me a ball. I placed it in the middle of the floor. I was hoping that the little boy would make it move for us, but by this time we were so cold that we decided not to stay in the room any longer. The batteries in my camera and my digital recorder went dead. The cold made my fingers feel dead, so I decided it was time to go. I said, "I'm freezing and need to leave this room." The Ovilus said "blanket." "Yes," I thought, "I need many blankets to get warm."

When we stepped out of this room, the rest of the building felt warm at thirty-nine degrees compared to the eight degrees we'd been in. We headed into the back of the third floor and found another wonderful museum feature. There was a huge, unfinished miniature layout of the town. It would eventually include a train that would travel around the town, disappear in a tunnel and come out on the other side.

Tina said, "Here is another story about someone dying in this building. Elmo Burke was raised in Van Lear but left for a career opportunity. When he retired he moved back to Van Lear to give of himself to a community that he loved as a child. His dream was to complete the miniature town and display it for the townspeople and tourists to enjoy. He gave hours of construction work on the project." Tina opened a door and took us into a small space behind the structure so we could see all the hidden components that would make the train work and the little street lights shine. It was amazing to see all the work that had gone into Elmo's design. Tina said, "One day, in 1989, Elmo was behind here working on the set. He started to experience pain in his chest and left the space through the door. As he passed through the door, he collapsed dead on the floor. It was a shock and a sad blow to the community to have lost him."

"Since Elmo loved being here, do you ever feel his presence?" I asked. "Late one night I was up on a ladder out in the hall in front of the schoolroom. I was painting the walls to get ready for a festival. As I was stroking the walls with my paint brush, I heard an assertive male voice say, 'Get down.' My cousin was downstairs putting up a string of lights, so I knew it wasn't him. I continued to paint and ignore the eerie command. A few minutes later I heard it again, 'Get down!' And this time it was even louder and more demanding. I got down off my ladder and went downstairs. I found my cousin and told him to come upstairs and spot me while I was on the ladder. I didn't want to fall or have an accident. I felt that it might have been Elmo concerned about me falling off the ladder. When I returned with my cousin to watch me while I was painting, I didn't hear the voice again. It came to mind that it might have been Elmo looking out for me."

All of Tina's information, history, and ghost stories along with the evidence that we gathered were going to make a super chapter on the Coal Miners' Museum. Even though we had less than an hour of investigative time, we were able to get great evidence with our recorders, EMF meters, infrared thermometer, and the Ovilus. I asked Tina if we could come back when we could do a full-scale ghost investigation, and she quickly agreed. I concluded that the Coal Miners' Museum revealed enough activity for a haunting.

CHAPTER 25

Jenny Wiley State Resort Park
PRESTONSBURG, FLOYD COUNTY

WHEN I'M INTERVIEWED BY THE PRESS, I'm often asked some of the same questions over and over. The two most popular questions are, "What have I learned from being a ghost-hunter?" and "What do I like the best about being a ghosthunter?" I usually answer the first one by saying, "I've learned more about life from the dead than I could ever learn from the living." The second question I answer, "I have met some of the most amazing, talented, and wonderful people who have all become friends to me. I am truly blessed to be so loved." I don't know of any other profession where I could have acquired these two major benefits.

One of these friends happens to be Serena Gordon. While shopping at Joseph-Beth Booksellers one afternoon, browsing my favorite section, New Age and Metaphysical, a petite young woman stepped up beside me and began to search the book shelf. She turned to glance at me as she reached across to retrieve a title that caught her eye. She said, "Excuse me, I'm going to reach . . . . Oh, my gosh! Are you Patti Starr?" "Yes I am." I said. "Have we met before?" She extended her hand and said, "No, we haven't. My name is Serena Gordon. I just read your book and it was fantastic."

I was honored to meet someone who was grateful for my work Before I could give her my gratitude, she started talking quickly about an incident that she was dealing with in her home. I gave her my card and told her to call me, and I would come to her place to see what I could do. She told me that the house was only three months old; she couldn't understand how a new house could be haunted. I explained to her that it could be due to several things. Maybe her home was built on a grave, or the ley lines beneath the ground could contain high energy, or it could be a binding to a recent purchase, or someone was trying to get in touch with her from the other side. I told her that we would try to help her figure out what was going on.

About three weeks later, Serena called me, and I went straight away to see how I could help her. She took me over to her computer. It would turn on by itself and go to the Internet. This was during the dialup days when you could hear the annoying sound as the computer connected with the phone line. She also had her clothes thrown from the bed, and a cap she wore would fly off her dresser. She felt the presence more in the basement while exercising on her stationary bike. So the basement was where we started the investigation. We discovered through dowsing that the ghostly activity was coming from a previous boyfriend who had died a suspicious death. While dowsing, we found out that he was killed by two people because of a drug deal that had gone bad. He wanted Serena to know that even though they broke up, he never stopped loving her. We did a crossover for him, and he never bothered her again.

About two years later I received a call from her once again. She told me that she was going to take my class and become a Certified Ghost Hunter. She had become more and more in tune with the spirit world and wanted to learn more about ghosthunting. About a year after she became a Certified Ghost Hunter, she called me to sign up her uncle, Randy Bentley, and a couple of his friends for the Certified Ghost Hunter Course. While Randy was taking my class, he had decided that the first place he was going to investigate was his work place at Jenny Wiley State Park. He had worked there for eleven years and had witnessed some strange activity. Now that he understood how to use the various instruments and equipment, he was excited about going back to work to see what evidence he would be able to record.

Three years later I got yet another call from Serena, telling me about all the fascinating results Randy continues to get while ghosthunting at Jenny Wiley State Park's lodge. She told me that he wanted me to come out to see what I would find that might support his findings. I was ready to take him up on his offer. I think my favorite places to investigate for paranormal activity are state park facilities. They give you the chance to go to locations rich in history of the early settlers. Some parks offer places where you can walk through previous battlefields of the Revolutionary or the Civil War. I've visited some parks that go back to the Pleistocene Era, where the wooly mammoths wandered over the land. I find history and ghosthunting go hand in hand.

Randy made arrangements for us to stay at the Jenny Wiley Lodge, since that was the location where he had gotten most of his results while investigating. After picking up our room card at the front desk, I noticed a flyer with a brief story about Jenny Wiley. I wanted to know as much as I could about her and the history of the park in case we collected evidence that would relate to any of the events of that time.

In 1789 a young pioneer mother, Jenny Wiley, was captured during an Indian raid. Struggling with her attackers, Jenny witnessed the massacre of three of her children and her younger brother as the Indians scalped them in front of her. Since she fought off her attackers while holding onto her two-year-old son when they kidnapped her, she was allowed to keep him. During their long journey back to the Indian village, Jenny was having difficulty keeping up. She was not only carrying her son but was also heavy with child. The Indians finally pulled the child from her arms and killed him so she could keep up with the others.

After a few months of moving from one camp to another, Jenny delivered a baby boy. When he was three months old, the Indians gave the infant a test of bravery. They tied him to a piece of wood and set him in a stream of water to see if he would cry. Of course, he screamed and they killed him as well. After that, the Indians sentenced Jenny to die, but at the last moment, an old chief bought her. She performed many chores including teaching the women of the tribe how to make cloth. After living with the old chief for several weeks, Jenny escaped into the night. She was determined to get back to her husband, Thomas. She followed the river, led by divine intervention through dreams and visions, until she found her way home. She had to swim across Big Sandy River, just as the Indians were about to catch up with her. She was reunited with Thomas in the fall of 1790. They continued their lives together and had five more children. Jenny lived to be seventy-one, and her grave is located north of Paintsville, in River, Kentucky.

Jenny Wiley Park, which opened in 1962, is located in a moist Appalachian environment enriched with maple, pawpaw, and tulip poplar trees. It lies amidst some of Kentucky's most beautiful scenery. You can take a walk on the Jenny Wiley Trail that marks the passage that she took to escape from her captors.

The park's hotel, May Lodge, offers a choice of rooms, or, for a real escape into nature, one- and two-bedroom secluded cottages. The lodge also houses a restaurant called The Music Highway Grill. The Country Music Highway runs through Prestonsburg, which got its name from a region where so many country stars got their start. I must say the restaurant serves some of the best country cooking I have ever eaten. We unpacked our gear and settled into our room. I told Chuck that I wanted to go down to the lobby to interview some of the employees. I also wanted to start recording for EVPs and take some pictures to see what I might get. It was just before the dinner hour, so the lobby was quiet and free of traffic. I was lucky to meet an employee who had a couple of strange stories, but asked to remain anonymous. I'll call her "Julie." I said, "Tell me what weird things you have experienced while working here." She replied, "I have seen a dark shadow of a man in the lobby. Once I was going into the time-clock room, and when I opened the door, it felt like a cold hand was pushed against my face. I was knocked back out of the doorway. I almost fell down. I opened the door again and asked the lady sitting in the room if she saw what happened, and she said no. She did hear me go back out but didn't realize I was being pushed. It really freaked me out." "Have you ever experienced him again?" I asked. She said, "I don't think so, but one afternoon I was at the front desk, and there was a table across the room with some gift shop items being featured for sale. All of a sudden, I heard a noise and looked up, and, one by one, all the items started to fall off the table. It was as if someone had taken their arm and was sliding it across the table, knocking everything off onto the floor. When the shop clerk came back from lunch, it was very difficult to explain why all of the merchandise was lying on the floor broken or damaged."

"I heard that the kitchen was haunted. Do you know anything about that?" I asked. Julie replied, "Sometimes at night when everyone has gone home, and I am at the desk by myself, I can hear noises coming from the downstairs kitchen." "Wow," I said, "it must be a loud noise for you to hear it all the way up here." "Yes, it was," Julie said. "It sounded like dishes crashing on the floor, and sometimes it sounded like pots and pans being thrown around. The next morning when the kitchen crew came into work, I told them what I heard. They told me that nothing was out of place or on the floor, broken." Then Julie remembered something else that bothered her. She said, "I had to go upstairs to turn on the server to the computer, and when I do that, I go up the spiral stairs on the other side of this office. When I came back down the stairs, I looked at the bottom step and saw a pair of scissors. When I stepped into my office, I asked if anyone had been using the scissors and left them on the steps. Everyone said no."

I thanked Julie for her stories and decided to go downstairs and talk with some of the kitchen staff. Everyone there was so friendly and accommodating, but most of them did not want to talk about the ghosts. When I started to leave, a gentleman standing behind the host's desk caught my attention. Since there were no guests in the restaurant I thought it would be okay to introduce myself. His name was Bill, and I asked him if he had any strange encounters. Bill said, "I have worked here for many years, and during that time I have witnessed many strange or unexplained situations." "Have you ever seen an apparition?" I asked. "Yes, I think that is what I saw," he said. "I was coming into work one day, and as I walked towards the front desk, I saw a man out of the corner of my eye go into Meeting Room #3. I turned and saw the door shut behind him. I asked the desk clerk if the meeting room had been reserved for anyone, and she said no. I turned around and went back to see who had gone into the room. I opened the door to a dark room and turned on the lights. There was no one there."

I told him about Julie's experience with a male ghost and how she had been pushed. Bill told me he had heard about that, and there are others who have seen this strange man. Bill said, "It would make sense that there might be ghosts here, depending on one's belief. There have been many accidental drownings in Dewey Lake. Sometimes people die of heart attacks or commit suicide in their rooms. About fifteen years ago, a man shot his partner and then killed himself while out on one of the trails."

"Randy told me that a man murdered his wife on one of the trails, and there are several cemeteries on the property as well.

After hearing all these stories, I think that this would be a great place for ghosthunters to visit," I said.

I turned to leave and was lucky enough to meet one more employee, Matt Vertrand, who was willing to share some of his experiences. "Randy and some employees were together one night, and they wanted to see who might come through for them. One of the staff members had an uncle who drowned in the lake, so they asked if he was with them. When they listened to the recorder, they heard his uncle's name. They continued the questions and asked him how he died, and the voice on the recorder answered, 'I drowned.' I thought that was pretty weird." "I know this story," I said. "When I talked to Randy he told me that when the employee asked his uncle, 'Who is my gym teacher?' the voice on the recorder said the teacher's name. The last questions was, 'Who is the girl I had a crush on while in high school?' and when they played back the recorder, they also got her name."

Once I had finished my interviews, I returned to the empty lobby where I thought I would continue to take pictures and record a couple of Ovilus sessions. I couldn't believe how lucky I was when I got a shadow of a man standing in a room where there was no one there. I held my camera, and before the shot I asked if there was anyone in the room that could show themselves for me. After about four shots I reviewed my pictures and was thrilled to see the shadow of a man. Most of my interview subjects talked about seeing a man in the lobby area, and now I may have captured his image.

Since the man was seen going into Meeting Room #3, I walked over to the door. I took three pictures, and I got a face in the frosted glass front of the door. For me these were great pieces of evidence.

The afternoon was fast dissolving into the evening, so at 3:00 I decided to go back to my room to see if Serena and Randy

A face in the door of Meeting Room #3 was captured by Patti as she asked the ghost to show himself.

had arrived. As I answered a knock at my door, there stood Serena, Randy, and two friends—Rev. James and Rev. Kelly Collins. Serena has an Internet radio show, "The Awakening," on Z Talk Radio, and she hosts the show with psychic/mediums, James and Kelly Collins. We were headed for the Pine Building where Randy and some other ghosthunters had gotten some good results with EVP sessions.

On our way there, I asked Randy if he could tell me any other stories of staff or guests witnessing ghostly activity. Randy said, "A few months ago, a female guest and her husband were staying in room 244. She woke up during the night when she thought she heard her husband get up to go to the bathroom. She glanced over and saw him come out of the bathroom, but then he did something strange. He went over to the next bed and sat down. She couldn't figure out what he was doing, so she rolled back over to get out of bed and noticed that her husband was still in bed with her. When she looked back over at the other bed, the man was gone. She woke her husband, and they searched the room because she was so sure someone was in the room. Of course, they didn't find anyone." After listening to Randy's story, it reminded me of what happened earlier. "Randy," I said, "you are not going to believe this, but earlier today I captured a picture of a male shadow standing over by the gift section in the lobby." I pulled out my camera and showed him the shot.

When we got to the Pine Building, we set up our infrared camcorder and proceeded with a few EVP sessions. Once the camcorder was running, I turned on my recorder and started an EVP session. I said, "Hello, is there anybody here?" When I reviewed my recordings, I heard a static surge and then a voice come through that said, "I am." During the session I became a bit dizzy, and this is usually an indication that I am about to have an experience with the spirits. Serena has one of the rare Panasonic RRDR60 recorders, and it is the only one that I know of that will do real time EVPs. In other words, when you do an EVP session with this instrument, you get a response with almost all of your questions. It is an amazing instrument, and spirits answer the questions with an intelligent response.

Serena asked, "Can you tell us if you are here?" and the response was, "Yes, I can." Her next question was, "What is your first name?" A voice came through but we couldn't make out what it said. The next question was, "What is your last name?" The response was "Johnson."

It was getting late, so we headed back to the lodge so we could check out Meeting Room #3. Randy has had the best luck in this room, especially using his Panasonic RRDR60 digital recorder, and he thinks that some of his EVPs might relate to Jenny Wiley and her family. Randy said, "During one of my EVP sessions, I asked if there was someone here that would like to speak to us, and I got a female that said, 'My mama is Jenny.' I really liked that one since this is the area in which Jenny Wiley lived. Another time I asked if they could tell me a name, and I got the name Thomas, which was Jenny's husband's name. Another time during my recording, I received a voice that said, 'My three sons need me.'"

We continued to investigate in Meeting Rooms #3 and #4. We had good results and picked up on former employees who had died, along with relatives who were kin to some of the people in our group. The energy was good, and we all had a super time applying our different equipment and getting similar results with words and EVPs that were coming through. Our group was in tune with each other as well as the energy around us, and that was a big factor in our success. I loved staying at Jenny Wiley State Park. I know that Jenny's determination to get back home probably came from the good energy that she felt drawing her back to her home.

CHAPTER 26

Natural Bridge State Resort Park
SLADE, POWELL COUNTY

THE NATURAL BRIDGE STATE PARK RESORT has a very special meaning for me. When Chuck proposed to me in June of 2000, we decided to spend a weekend together at the park to celebrate. We stayed off-site in a little cabin down the road at Torrent Falls but spent most of our time hiking and visiting the Natural Bridge Resort area.

The amazing sandstone archway for which the park is named is seventy-eight feet in length, sixty-five feet high, twelve feet thick, and twenty feet wide. Some geologists believe the bridge to be at least one million years old.

During our nine years of marriage, Chuck and I have returned to the Natural Bridge State Park and stayed at the Hemlock Lodge many times. On one of our most recent visits we decided to research and interview some of the staff to see if any of them had experienced any ghosts while working at Natural Bridge State Park Resort.

We asked the young lady at the front desk if we could meet the park manager. Within minutes, we met Ron Vanover the park manager, a distinguished and rather young, white-haired gentleman. After introductions and an explanation of our mission, I asked Ron if he knew any ghost stories that I could write about in my book. He said that he had not experienced anything himself, but shortly after he relocated to the park, many of the employees told him that there were ghosts at the lodge and in the park.

Ron invited us to sit in on an employee orientation to learn more about the park. He also gave us permission to question the staff to attain more information about the ghosts at the lodge. When the meeting was over, we headed for the gift shop where I was greeted by Kathy Teasley, the gift shop supervisor, who was happy to answer my questions. I explained to her that I was collecting ghost stories for my new book. She was excited to share what she knew about a ghost the staff called the "Purple Lady." Over the years many employees and guests had seen her.

Kathy related a story she had been told by one of the night auditors. It was around three in the morning when the auditor thought she heard someone enter the front door. She looked up and saw a lady wearing a long purple evening gown with her hair pulled into a bun on top of her head. The lady walked by the front desk and proceeded towards the couch in the lounge area across from the front desk. As she sat down on the leather sofa, it softly creaked as the weight of her body sank into the seat. The auditor watched her for a few moments while noticing that this mysterious lady didn't move. The auditor thought it was really strange for someone to be out so late, so she asked her if she could help her. The auditor said the lady turned her head to look at her and smiled. With not a word spoken, she disappeared off the couch. The auditor was shocked. She could even hear the sound of the leather once again as the weight was released.

Kathy also said that late one night the park ranger reported that he was in the lobby doing a walkthrough and thought he heard someone sit down on the leather sofa in the lounge. He turned to look, but there was no one there. When he took a closer look, he could see the indention in the seat of the sofa as if someone were sitting there. He backed off, and as he did, the pressure was released and the seat puffed back up as if someone had just gotten up from the sofa. He commented to others that he believed he had witnessed the ghost of the "Purple Lady."

Kathy told me another story that she had heard from the kitchen staff. It was in the middle of winter, near dusk: two servers were cleaning up the dining room when one of them glanced out the window and saw a figure down below on what is called Hoedown Island, an open-air dance patio. She pointed in the direction of the figure and told the other server to look. They both saw a lady in a long purple dress walking in a circle on the dance floor on the island. It was very cold, and they noticed that the woman was not wearing a coat. Her behavior seemed so odd that the woman called one of the rangers to go and check on her. He went down to the dance floor, and in the snow were footprints in the pattern of a circle, revealing that someone had been walking there. When he came back to the dining room, he told the servers that the woman they saw was gone but that he did, however, see the footsteps. What he really found amazing was that there were no footsteps leading into the circle or walking away from it.

As I was writing down Kathy's tales, another employee came into the shop. Kathy introduced us to Larry Cox, one of the gift shop clerks, who had his own story to tell: "Back in the early 1990s, a new park manager, who was a naturalist, had come onboard. When he started hearing these stories about the Purple Lady, he told everyone that he was a scientist, and he did not believe in ghosts. Until one evening when he had a rather unnerving experience. The manager, his wife, and mother-in-law were closing the lodge and getting ready to leave for their cabin located on the other side of the hill. The manager's wife and mother-in-law were in one car, and the manager followed behind them in his car. Just as they passed the entrance to Whittleton Campgrounds, the manager saw a woman in his wife's car's headlights standing on the side of the road. She was wearing a long purple gown with her shoes in her hand. It was a very cold night, and here she was barefooted and she was not wearing a coat. This caused him concern. So when they got home, he told the wife he might go back out to see if the woman was still on the road. His wife asked him who was he talking about. The manager's wife and mother-in-law did not see this woman he had seen walking on the side of the road. He told me it was at that moment that he realized he had just seen the ghost of the Purple Lady."

I thanked both Kathy and Larry for their stories and walked out into the lobby where I met one of the park's maintenance men. His name was Cecil Tucker and he had been in the orientation with us so he knew who we were. He was a very soft-spoken man, with a slight stoop to his stance. I asked him if he had ever seen the "Purple Lady" and he nodded yes. He said, "I have seen her twice since I've worked here." He said that each time he saw her on the road, just a short distance from the entrance to the Whittleton Campgrounds, walking alongside the road in her long gown. Once she was bending down as if she were picking flowers.

As I was questioning Cecil, Chuck was making a phone call to an old friend he had not seen in years. Al Cornett is an artist and many of his paintings of the Red River Gorge scenery adorn the walls of the lodge. He is also a favorite patron, and all the employees seem to know him. As Chuck explained to Al why we were at the Hemlock Lodge, Al wanted to share his knowledge of the Purple Lady. Al said while painting in the Natural Bridge area he worked closely with the park's naturalist. One day one of the naturalists came to him and said, "I'm almost embarrassed to tell you this." Al asked him, "What could embarrass you?" and the naturalist said, "Being a scientist, I do not believe in ghosts, but yesterday I'm pretty sure I saw the ghost of the Purple Lady."

Al wasn't sure where he had heard the story about a murder that happened on the property that is now Whittleton Campground. Supposedly, a young woman was killed in the cabin, and the murderer was never found. Years later the cabin burned down, and, some time later, the property became the Whittleton Campground.

In one of Larry's stories, he said that a park ranger told him about getting calls in the evening from the campers at the Whittleton Campground. They called to report a woman, who appeared to be lost, walking around the campsite in a long gown. When he would go over to the campground to check it out, there would be no woman there.

While I was standing in the lounge, I saw a picture of a train with a description hanging on the wall. I learned that at one time the only way you could get to the Natural Bridge was by train. In 1895 The Natural Bridge Park was opened by the Lexington and Eastern Railroad. By the 1900s over twenty-five thousand visitors per year were taking excursions on the L&E to spend a day at the Natural Bridge Park. Since there were no roads into the park, the only way in and out was by train.

The original hiking trails were built by the railroad. They also added the picnic shelters, boat docks, gardens, and camp-grounds. Tourists rode the train in from Lexington, Louisville, Hazard, and Cincinnati every weekend. The train excursions to the park continued until 1942. Some of the visitors that come to the park today still remember riding in on the trains.

I went downstairs to check out some other old photos that were displayed in a shadowbox. I saw one of the rock tunnel and train tracks that came down through what is now the huge dance floor called the Hoedown Island and the swimming pool. I went outside and I could see where the old tunnel runs under the Hemlock Lodge. It is fenced off so you cannot get too close because of the falling rocks. It sent chills down my spine when I got permission to go beyond the forbidden area to take a few photos of this dark, wet, deserted tunnel. You can hardly see inside with all the vines, bushes, and fallen rock that keep it hid-den. I pulled out my recorder and pushed my arm through the links in the fence to see if I could get an EVP while I was there. I felt sure that I might hear something from the Purple Lady. The session only lasted a few minutes when a truck drove up with lawnmowers and Weed Eaters that blasted the silence, ending my session.

We walked over to the Nature Store where we found an elderly man working behind the cashier's station. At first he seemed to be too busy to talk to us as he priced the merchandise to be put out on display. After a few questions about the railroad that used to run through the park, he seemed to warm up a little. I asked him about the Purple Lady. He admitted that he had talked to employees who had seen her walking back and forth on the path of the railroad tracks. She seemed to be waiting for someone to arrive. Maybe a lover or friend. He told us that just outside the doors of the store is where the train tracks used to lay. We stepped outside to have a look, and I could see the tunnel in the

Patti standing in front of the entrance to the old train tunnel

distance beyond the Hoedown Island and the pool. I tried to imagine what it must have looked like back in the 1880s.

The mystery of the Purple Lady remains. Some think that she came with one of the railroad excursions, waiting to meet the lover that never came to her. She walks up and down the unseen tracks looking for him. Others think she might be connected to the cabin murder, since she has been seen many times in that area as well. One thing is for sure: wherever she is seen, she always has the purple gown on and her hair up in a bun.

In just one day this heavenly place can bring you peace and happiness. Who knows? Maybe this is one of the reasons the Purple Lady finds it so hard to leave.

CHAPTER 27

Paramount Arts Center
(formerly Paramount Theatre)
ASHLAND, BOYD COUNTY

LIGHTS! CAMERA! ACTION! It's showtime! I can still remember the first time I ever got to watch a movie in a theater. I was six years old, and my mom surprised me and my cousins one Saturday afternoon by taking us to see Walt Disney's *Peter Pan*—and it was in color! All the shows I had seen up to that time had been viewed on my grandparents' black-and-white television set. I knew something was up when Momma told me to put on my frilly pink Sunday dress with my black patent-leather shoes. I just had no idea it was going to be my first movie theater experience. Once we arrived and parked the car, Momma took my hand and led us to the theater. We had to wait in a long line to get our tickets, and when we finally entered the theater, it was like walking into a grand palace—the walls were adorned with delicate tapestries and gold-leaf encrusted wall medallions. I remember how my shoes sank into the rich, plush carpet as I took a seat in the lobby on one of the hand-carved benches upholstered in the finest fabric. Coming from a very modest family, I had no idea that such riches existed.

During the Roaring Twenties, one of the most popular forms of entertainment was going to the movies. The company responsible for providing theaters with films was Paramount Pictures. In 1926 the company built grand movie houses in every major city in the U.S. to help guarantee the maximum in film distribution—and they were all named Paramount Theater.

The Paramount Theatre in Ashland, Kentucky, built in 1931, became one of these splendid theaters. Then the Great Depression hit, and construction on the rest of the theaters slated to be built came to a stop. It is believed that the Paramount Theatre in Ashland, Kentucky, is one of the very few that remain in operation in America today. During the Great Depression, Americans were totally devoted to the movies. The movie playhouses provided a chance to escape the gloom and doom felt during the bad times. At an average price of twenty-seven cents a ticket, the movies offered people an inexpensive way to divert their attention from the harsh realities of the times for a few hours.

Jeff Waldridge called me one afternoon and told me he had

found an article on the Internet about a ghost that was haunting the Paramount Theatre in Ashland. The employees there had lovingly dubbed him "Paramount Joe." He wanted to know if I would be interested in doing a ghost investigation there. Jeff had graduated from my Certified Ghost Hunter Course and had taken on the position of location scout for our ghosthunting group, Ghost Chasers International (GCI). As our location scout, he would find places suspected of ghostly activity and then make arrangements for us to go there. Jeff drove his car to pick us up after he left the jail. Oh, did I mention he was a policeman? Did I tell you that he is also a professional wrestler and is known on the circuit as "Black Rain"? He is a fierce statue of a man with a boy-next-door face. I told him now that he was a ghosthunter as well as a wrestler, he could beat the sheet out of the ghosts. Okay, we thought it was pretty funny at the time.

For this investigation, our ghosthunting group consisted of Chuck, Jeff, Tammy Herring, and me. Tammy was one of our newest students and wanted to get more field experience, so we decided to invite her to join us. During our two-hour drive to the Paramount Theatre, we discussed what procedures we would try first, along with what instruments we would each be responsible for. I wanted to make sure we were filming and using audio devices once we got onstage, since that is where a dark, shadowy figure had been seen. I also wanted to make sure that we used the EMF meters in case we found highly sensitive areas during our walkthrough.

By the time we arrived, we were all pumped and ready to meet this legendary ghost, Paramount Joe. Tyson, the manager of the theater, unlocked the front doors since the building was closed for the day and greeted us with a broad smile and a firm handshake. Even though it was about 8:00 P.M., the staff didn't mind coming back after closing to watch the first official ghost investigation of the theater. Another pleasant surprise was the local TV station sent a reporter and cameraman to record this historic event, along with a newspaper reporter as well. This was a win-win situation since the theater would get some interesting publicity, and we would get recognition for the investigation.

I was awed by the sight of the theater as I passed through the brass entrance doors. The geometric and opulent style of the Art Deco period was evident everywhere, with the original fixtures and furnishings that were in vogue in the 1930s. As we entered the inner lobby I saw something that I had never seen before in a movie theater—a beautiful recessed water fountain. As we went up the steps that led us into the auditorium, I couldn't help but notice the elaborate proscenium arch high above the stage, covered with variegated gold and aluminum leaf with a sprinkle of bronze. My eyes followed the Egyptian theme to the stunning "Lady in an Urn" centered above the stage. The Egyptian design was also popular in the twenties because of the opening of Tutankhamen's tomb. Tyson seemed a little nervous at first, but the more we talked about what we would be doing during the investigation, the calmer he became. He was a little worried that we'd upset or become a threat to Paramount Joe. Once we were all suited up with our equipment, I turned to Tyson and asked, "Before we start with our initial investigation, can you tell us about Paramount Joe?"

Tyson smiled as he turned his head toward the stage and stated, "Shortly after I started to work here I found an interesting report titled 'Paramount Joe—Resident Ghost' as I was going through some of our files." His recollection of the article started with the renovation work on the Paramount Theatre in the early 1940s. It was reported that four construction workers were working on a project inside the auditorium. When lunch time rolled around three of the men left for lunch while the other man, named Joe, for some reason stayed at the theater. When the other three returned from lunch, they found Joe's lifeless body hanging from the curtain rigging. He was cut down and pronounced dead. It seemed that after his death, employees and staff members started to take note of strange sounds coming from the stage area and in the balcony. Items that were in use would go missing and then were found exactly where they were at the beginning. The usual cold spots related to hauntings were felt even when the actual temperature was about twenty degrees warmer. There had even been sightings of a shadowy figure crossing the stage when no one else was in the theater. Even with the weird and unexplained activity, most everyone felt that it was a good-natured spirit and were sure it didn't mean any harm to anyone.

My favorite ghostly account of Paramount Joe came from one of my phone interviews. Once we had finished our investigation, Tyson advised me to call Dale Saunders, one of their maintenance staff. He felt that Dale could tell me some of his experiences while he was working alone in the theater. Dale answered my call in a soft, slow, Southern tone and said he was happy to tell me about his experiences. He said that when he first started working at the theater, he had not heard the stories about it being haunted or even about Paramount Joe. One afternoon as he was working on the seats in the balcony, he glanced down for a moment and thought he saw a man walking around on the stage. Since he was the only one in the theater at that time, he decided to go see if someone had come into the theater. As he approached the stage, he saw a dark shadow of a man quickly cross the width of the stage. Dale stopped and realized that what he saw wasn't natural. This was the first time he thought about the possibility of the theater being haunted. Later on at lunch, he mentioned what he had witnessed to his co-workers, and that's when he heard his first stories about the theater being haunted, as the other employees began to tell him about Paramount Joe.

"Achy
SOME Breaky
GAVE Heart
ALL
Paramount
JOE,
4 Ever
In My
Heart &
My Soul...

The signed poster from Billy Ray Cyrus to Paramount Joe

The country-and-western singer Billy Ray Cyrus is from Flatwoods, Kentucky, which is a suburb of Ashland. He came to the theater in January of 1992 to film his video "Achy Breaky Heart," which later became his number-one hit single, which stayed at the top of the charts for five weeks. Billy Ray learned about the legend of Paramount Joe while he was taking a break from the filming. He thought it was pretty cool to be in the presence of a ghost, so Billy Ray started talking to Joe. He would even laugh and joke with him, and a couple of times he even asked for his help during a few takes. It is customary to get 8 x 10 photographs signed by each performer who appears at the Paramount and then hang the photo on the "Wall of Fame" in the box office. Before Billy Ray left, he autographed large color posters for each of the female employees working there at the time. He insisted on leaving a poster for his new friend, Paramount Joe, upon which he wrote a personal inscription to him. Each woman put her poster near her desk, and Joe's was hung in the box office, near all the other performers. As time passed, the walls in the box office became too crowded with all the signed 8 × 10 photos. The executive director felt that some of the pictures and posters needed to come down, and Paramount Joe's poster signed by Billy Ray Cyrus was selected to be removed. The next day when the staff came to work, to their surprise every single 8 × 10 photo and poster that had been hanging neatly on the wall the night before was now on the floor! Some of the frames had been broken and glass shattered. There was no reasonable explanation to how something like this could have happened. It didn't take long for everyone to agree that maybe Paramount Joe was upset that his poster had been removed. They decided to make other arrangements on the wall and re-hung Joe's poster from Billy Ray. To this day there has not been another framed photo fall off the wall. In his honor, Paramount Joe's poster now hangs in a very special part of The Marquee Room, which is now the site of Paramount Joe's Rising Star Café.

As Tyson was telling us the story of Paramount Joe, the newspaper reporter was jotting down his every word while the TV crew had moved to the stage area to get ready for our investigation. Once Tyson had finished his story about Joe, we moved down to the stage. Jeff and Tammy started taking pictures right away to see if they could capture any anomalies in their photos. I turned on my audio recorder to see if I could capture any EVPs and started to sweep the stage with my EMF meter while Chuck, our videographer, filmed our search for paranormal activity.

The patience of the TV crew paid off because within a few minutes, my EMF meter started to beep and the red light was blinking, indicating a disturbance in the electromagnetic field. I started to ask yes and no questions to see if we could confirm that Joe might be with us. I probed, "Is there a spirit here with us now who would like to communicate with us? Make my meter beep for the answer yes and do nothing for the answer no." We waited a few seconds before the meter started beeping to indicate a yes answer. I continued to ask more questions, and it was revealed to me that we were talking to a male spirit who had died in his thirties, and when I asked if it was Paramount Joe, it expressed a yes response. I didn't get it to admit that he had hung himself, but I did feel like he was happy there.

We left the stage area and walked towards the front entrance of the auditorium. Just above the last row of seats, my meter started beeping again, indicating a disturbance in the electromagnetic field. I stopped and took a couple of pictures while asking the sweet spirits to join us. We got a great example of what we believe to be a spirit in the energy form of a white orb at the top of the first row of seats. As Tyson stood alongside me, I asked him, "Have you ever noticed anything strange in this area before?" He hesitated and then stated, "Once while I was giving a tour to some students something pretty significant happened. As I was telling them the story about Joe, I realized that I had never addressed him before. For the first time I called out and asked, 'Joe, are you here? Is it okay for me to tell your story?' Within a few seconds, in the same row where your EMF meter was beeping, we heard a loud squeak from one of the seats. The next day I got a strange call from a psychic who lives here in Ashland. She asked me if someone in my family or a close friend had died recently. I answered no and then asked why. She told me that she had gotten a message from the other side yesterday, and she was to tell me that Joe said he is here."

I asked Tyson if any of the other employees had experienced anything in other parts of the theater. He thought for a moment and said, "There were two new employees who wanted to go into the basement to check out what was down there in case they had to retrieve some supplies. The manager led them to the top of the stairs and turned on the light. As they started to go down the steps, the manager was called to the phone, so she had to turn and go back up. The new employees didn't see her leave, and they continued their descent to the basement. They thought she was waiting at the top of the stairs, and they yelled for her to please turn on the other lights so they could see ahead of them. In just a few seconds the light came on. After they finished checking out the basement, they started back up the stairs just as the manager returned to the top of the landing. They looked up and said, "Thank you for turning on the light down there. It was really dark." She assured them that she did not turn on any lights. The switch is actually down in the basement, just beyond the area where they were walking. They walked back down, and when they got to that place, the light was out again. So who was turning the light on and off?" I chuckled and said, "Good question."

West

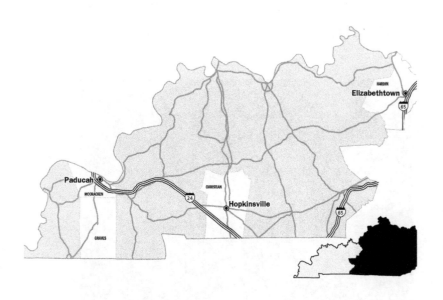

Elizabethtown, Hardin County
Historic State Theater Complex

Hopkinsville, Christian County
Lone Oak House Museum

Paducah, McCracklen County
C.C. Cohen Restaurant & Bar

CHAPTER 28

C.C. Cohen Restaurant & Bar
PADUCAH, McCRACKLEN COUNTY

ONE AFTERNOON, while attending to my Ghost Hunter Shop, my good friend Dotti Kult came in to purchase some sacred white sage for a cleansing she was planning. As we talked about my upcoming visits to haunted places throughout Kentucky, she told me about the haunted restaurant, C.C. Cohen, in Paducah. The restaurant was supposed to be haunted by a female ghost name Stella, along with some of her family members. Dotti told me that she was planning a trip to Paducah in a couple of days to visit her daughter, and she would be glad to make hotel arrangements for us so that she, Chuck, and I could visit the restaurant.

When I returned home from the shop, I immediately got online and searched C.C. Cohen Restaurant & Bar. I was thrilled to see that the restaurant's home page boldly advertised that it was haunted by a woman named Stella Cohen Peine. It boasted that the Travel Channel had produced a special on Stella that aired in 2005 on the series called *Most Haunted Journey*. The description stated that most of the employees, at one time or another, had an experience they believed to be caused by Stella. It was not unusual for an employee to open the restaurant and find the chairs moved away from under the tables or the chairs taken off the tops of the tables and placed back on the floor. They would sometimes find a mess where the salt and pepper shakers had been dumped out onto the table cloths. Others would report the lights turning off and on and the neon signs becoming unplugged when no one else was in the building.

As I continued searching for more information about Stella and her family on the C.C. Cohen's Web site, I decided to call the number provided to see if I could set up an appointment for interviews and a possible ghost investigation. I was surprised to actually get a live person answering the phone instead of a recording. I introduced myself, and the person on the other end introduced himself as Scott Hocker, the kitchen manager. Briefly, I explained to Scott that I wanted to include a chapter in my book about the ghosts that haunt the restaurant. He was receptive to the idea and began to offer stories about some of the current paranormal activity. Scott agreed to set up a time for me to interview the restaurant staff.

I had never visited Paducah before and was curious about its history. During our four-hour drive, Dotti filled me in on the town's history. She told me that in 1827, William Clark, one of the two leaders in the Lewis and Clark Expedition, came to this river town named Pekin located at the junction of the Tennessee and Ohio rivers. The settlers and Indians of this region had lived together in harmony since about 1815. When Clark arrived, he claimed the area as his own and asked the Indians and settlers to move off his land, which they did. Once Clark had developed the land, he decided to change the name to Paducah in honor of the Indian chief, Paduke, who had lived in peace with the settlers before they were required to move off the land.

As we entered the downtown area, I was fascinated by the many art shops and quilting stores. Dotti informed me that Paducah was the home of the American Quilter's Society Museum; the annual Quilt Show draws in lots of quilt enthusiasts and brings large tourist revenues to the town.

Riding down the main street, I saw a large wall ahead of us with a mural of beautiful artwork depicting the historic riverfront. Dotti said the wall was a flood wall, built shortly after the disastrous flood of 1937 in which the waters rose to thirty-seven feet.

We pulled the car into a parking space directly in front of C.C. Cohen Restaurant & Bar. The building was huge and took up most of the corner block and housed other businesses behind the restaurant. The three-story red brick structure had several large, arched windows. A colorful striped awning accented the entire front of the building. Chuck turned to me and said, "This place reminds me of an old upscale saloon that would have been built in the late 1800s." We found out later that the building was constructed around 1865. We pulled open the heavy wooden door then turned left and opened a glass door with the name "C.C. Cohen" written in decorative bold letters across the glass. The first thing we saw as we entered was a wall hung with celebrity photos. It was an impressive collection of famous people who had dined at C.C. Cohen, including Bruce Willis and Demi Moore, B.B. King, Hal Holbrook, Jonathan Winters, and John Prine. We were greeted by a smiling young woman. We followed her to our table, and I told her that we had an appointment to meet with Scott and would she kindly tell him that we were there. She left us our menus and went to retrieve Scott from the kitchen. As I looked around the interior of the dining room, I felt as though I had stepped back into the 1800s. The rich, dark colors of the carved wood surrounded us. Above us was an exposed second floor with a balcony and wooden railing that completed a perfect square opening. The upstairs was supposed to be the most haunted, and I was hoping that Scott would agree to let us go up there. Scott walked towards our table dressed in his white chef's coat. He told us that after we finished our meal he would be more than happy to give us a tour and tell us the ghost stories and history of the restaurant. To our surprise the restaurant became really busy when a tour of teachers and students came through and filled up all the tables. We took advantage of the extra time at our table by enjoying the beautiful surroundings of the restaurant and the delicious food that had been served to us.

When our waitress, Deidra Orer, gave us our check, I asked her if she had any stories or experiences with Stella. She smiled and said, "Of course I have. There are not many of us here who have not, at least once, had an experience believed to be caused by Stella. One evening while attending to a group of people at a wedding reception upstairs, our cash register started to act weird. It would make the sound of a receipt being rung into the register, but when you would go and check it, there was no receipt. There were a lot of people ordering drinks, and I was worried that the register might not record all of them, so I started to write the orders down to keep tabs on everyone ordering drinks. About halfway through the reception, the register calmed down and was not acting out of the ordinary until the priest walked near the register. No sooner did he move there when the register started acting up again. We finally had to turn the register off because it became such a distraction. I looked at the priest and jokingly said that maybe Stella didn't care for a Catholic priest being in her place since she was of the Jewish faith. He laughed and agreed."

"Have you seen anything move or disappear?" I asked. "I was working the night shift and getting ready to close for the evening," she said. "I reached for my keys, and they were gone. I always wear them around my neck or I store them in the Coke bin if I'm working the bar. They were not in either place. I thought Scott might have picked up my keys, so I asked him, but he said he had not used my keys that day. Scott, four other employees, and I started our search for the keys so we could close and go home. We searched everywhere, and finally I went back down to the bar and shouted out, 'Stella, please return my keys; we want to lock up so we can go home.' I thought I heard something that brought my attention back to the Coke bin under the bar. When I looked inside I found the keys. I yelled at Scott and the others that I had found my keys and said, 'Thank you, Stella.' In the next moment, the lights went really bright and then dim again as if she were saying, 'You're welcome.' We all agreed it was time to go."

Once the lunch crowd thinned out, Scott joined our table and we headed upstairs to where most of the ghostly activity has taken place. He told us that the building was built around 1865. In the 1920s, the Cohen family owned this space and ran a successful clothing and dry goods store until 1980. The last member of the Cohen family, Stella Cohen Peine, lived upstairs after her husband was killed in a nearby alley. She remained here until her death in 1980. That is why Scott and the other employees believe that the unexplained happenings are caused by Stella. They believe that Stella is displeased when people go upstairs into what used to be her apartment.

After Scott finished with the history, I asked him, "Can you tell me some of the experiences that you have had while working here?" He answered quickly, "Yes, I have quite a few so I'll tell you the ones that stand out the most for me. One night, after the band stopped performing, I went to lock the front door and proceeded to check and lock up the rest of the building before leaving. I headed toward the reception booth and saw a woman, dressed in a white dress, as she turned to go toward the restroom. I announced that we were closed and she would have to leave. As I got to the corner of the booth and looked toward the restrooms, there was no one there. This freaked me out at first, and then I realized that I might have just seen Stella for the first time."

I asked him if he had seen objects move or anything like that while working here. He continued his explanation and said, "While working in the kitchen late one night, I was cleaning up after everyone had left. I was listening to one of my favorite radio stations when they switched DJs. I wasn't very fond of this DJ, and since my hands were dirty, I didn't want to touch the radio to change the channel. I said to myself that I wish I could change the radio station. Within a few minutes the radio switched on its own, and the new DJ announced their radio station name, and it was not the one I had been listening to. I just said, 'Thank you very much' and kept on working."

"What type of experiences have other employees had with Stella?" I asked. Scott answered, "One of our former employees was a strong disbeliever in ghosts and the stories of Stella. He would even tell people that it was just a marketing tool to get more customers to come to the restaurant. After a big party on Halloween night, this employee started to turn out the lights upstairs. When he got to the men's restroom, he opened the door and reached in to turn off the light. He was startled when he heard a clear voice say, 'Get out of here.' He jerked his hand back and turned to face the other two servers who were standing on the other side of the room. He walked over to the them and asked if they heard a voice say, 'Get out of here,' and they said no. They went back to the restroom and opened the door, turned on the light to check to see if anyone was still in the restroom. When they discovered that no one was there, they all three ran downstairs and left the building immediately. This server was so disturbed by what he had heard that he never came back to work."

"I'm curious. Have you heard of any customers who have witnessed anything related to Stella?" I asked. Scott said, "I was helping the staff wait on a few tables one night when we had gotten very busy. There was a couple sitting at one of the small round tables positioned below the opening of the second floor balcony. When I went to get their order, the lady told me that she saw someone upstairs walking around in the dark. I told her no one was upstairs, but she pointed up at the railing and said that she could see a woman standing right there. I went upstairs and looked around and could not see anyone. I went to the railing and looked down at the table that I was serving to see if the lady was looking up. She was and she saw me looking down so I asked her if she could still see the woman. She said she could and that she was standing right behind me. I turned and could not see a thing. After their meal was finished, the couple left the building and for a while they stood on the sidewalk looking up at the windows upstairs to see if they could see her again."

Scott said that he wanted to tell me a story that involved me. "Me?" I said. "Well let's hear it." Scott said, "The other day, before you called me, I was in the kitchen and I thought I heard an employee call my name. I walked out of the kitchen to see who called me, but there was no one there. Then the phone rang, and it was you. If I had not come out of the kitchen, I would not have heard it ring. It was as if Stella didn't want me to miss your call. I think she is pleased that you are going to write about her in your book."

Before continuing with another story, Scott glanced down from the upstairs balcony and saw the owner, Alan Raidt, sitting at the bar. He said, "The owner is downstairs if you would like to interview him. We can go down now if you are ready." I agreed and we all went down to meet Allen and record his stories of the hauntings. Alan saw me approaching and waved me forward. He was a distinguished-looking gentleman sporting a leather blazer while making some entries into his laptop computer. His silhouette was framed by an artful stained glass window behind him. When I started to speak, I noticed Alan's reaction and could tell that he had great love and respect for Stella. Every time he spoke of her, it was as if she had been his dear friend for years. I asked him how he came to be the owner of C.C. Cohen Restaurant. He told me that he was the general manager of the restaurant from 1985 until 1988. Alan is also a musician and has played with his band at the restaurant for years. In 1988 he decided to buy the business.

I asked him if he would share some of his encounters with Stella. Alan wanted to let me know that everything that had happened to him was positive, and in no way did he believe that Stella would hurt anyone. I told him that in all my years as a ghosthunter, most of my experiences have been very loving and positive, and I understood what he meant. He started with this story: "One evening I was about to close, and I had to unplug the neon sign that used to be above the stained glass window. The long cord to the neon sign was placed around the corner from the window. It was a tricky maneuver that involved bending over and reaching down into a crack to get to the plug. After I finished unplugging it, I went to lock the other doors and check the rest of the building before leaving for the evening. When I went back to the front I noticed that the neon sign was all lit up. I thought, 'No way, I just unplugged that.' I walked back over to where the plug was, bent over to see what had happened, and saw that the cord was not plugged into the outlet. I thought, 'What is going on?,' and walked back over to the neon sign and found that it was now off as it should be. This was one of the most bizarre things I had ever witnessed in more than twenty years of being here. I just couldn't figure out how the sign was on and the cord was unplugged."

I asked Alan if he had witnessed things disappearing and then showing back up again in the same place where he had already looked. He said that he had not observed anything disappearing, but once the items he needed for a construction project appeared on their own. "One evening I had come in to finish up the construction area on the second floor for the band. The platform was completed, but there were a few unfinished projects that needed to be done before the weekend. I had planned to line the stage with a wrought iron fence. To complete the installment, I needed certain hardware to make it work. I also had to install a spotlight and figured that I would go down to the hardware store to buy these and come back the next day to finish up. I had a few employees helping me clean up the area, and one of them said, 'Hey, is this what you need?' He had found an old bucket from one of the closets, and in the bottom was the hardware I needed to connect the wrought iron fence—the exact size and fitting that I needed. I thought this was a coincidence but I was nonetheless happy that I would not have to buy new parts. Then another employee, who had been working around an old, broken Xerox machine, lifted out the glass plate and found this spotlight that looked like it had been stored there for years. He called me over to check it out, and I was amazed that it still worked. I felt that Stella had made it possible for us to find these items to help us get our design of the stage finished so we would leave her apartment. She was believed to be a very private person and didn't like it when things got too busy or hectic up there," Alan said.

As we concluded our visit, Scott advised us to go to the William Clark Market House Museum while we were still in Paducah. He told us that they had a great exhibit about the history of Stella and her family. We took his advice and walked around the corner to the museum. We were delighted to find such a super place to read more about the Cohen business and about the lives of the children of Ike and Anna Cohen.

While reading the history I learned that six family members died on the second floor of the C.C. Cohen Restaurant. Stella had two siblings, Goldie and Carl. They grew up working in the family business. Stella met Ben Peine, a jeweler from Texas, who she later married and moved away with. When Ben retired, he and Stella moved back to Paducah and started to work in the family business again. The story about Stella, on the sign at the restaurant, said that Stella's husband was killed in an alley by thieves, but the history from the museum said that it was Stella's brother, Carl, who was attacked in the alley. He was not killed, but the beating left him mentally challenged, and he was never himself again. Stella's husband, Ben, died in old age and was one of the six people who died upstairs in the apartment.

Stella, Goldie, Carl, and their mother continued to live together in the upstairs apartment. Goldie had an accident and broke her back. She was restricted to places where she could walk, so she sat mostly at her piano. Goldie would play beautiful music: the sound floated out of their open windows into the street below. Stella's brother died, then later her mother, and then later her sister, Goldie. Then Stella was alone, and for six more years she lived upstairs doting on her cats and beloved dog. As Stella grew older, she had less contact with the outside world. Sometimes the cruelty of children would cause her to exhaust herself by opening her doors after hearing knocks that produced no human standing in the entrance. The cruelty of the children didn't stop there. They also liked teasing her dog and making it bark just to hear Stella shout out at her pet to stop barking. Even though Stella had become eccentric in her later years and kept to herself, she did have friends who checked on her daily. In 1974, a friend visiting Stella found her dead, lying on her apartment floor in a position that suggested she was reaching for her door. The coroner noted that she died of a heart attack while suffering from malnutrition. Later in our day in Paducah, we decided to go to Cracker Barrel for our evening meal. Shortly after being seated, our server came over to take our order. Her name was Michelle Rushing. Right away she took notice of my T-shirt with the name "Ghost Chasers" on the front. She asked me if I was doing a ghost investigation in Paducah. I explained to her about our visit to C.C. Cohen, and she lit up with delight. She said, "Oh, I had my wedding there, and we think that Stella made an appearance." I was thrilled and told her I wanted to hear the rest of her story, so after our meal she came back to our table.

"So, Michelle, tell me what happened at your wedding." Michelle said, "My wedding was April 4, 1998, and I planned to have my reception at the C.C. Cohen Restaurant, upstairs where Stella used to have an apartment. I had friends who worked there, and sometimes I would go there to meet them after work. I loved to listen to their stories about Stella and thought this would be a perfect place to have my wedding. It was late in my reception, and most of the guests had left. Only a few of my closest friends remained. One of my girlfriends went over and stood by the fireplace. She placed her drink on the mantle, and as soon as she set her glass down, it slid to the other end without stopping, where it came to a stop. We all witnessed it, and we were delighted to know that Stella had come to my wedding."

My first visit to Paducah was a most rewarding trip. I loved the people I met and how much everyone throughout the town supported the stories about Stella. I would love to return one evening so that I might have the time to spend upstairs to see if Stella would visit with me, as she has with so many others.

CHAPTER 29

Historic State Theater Complex
ELIZABETHTOWN, HARDEN COUNTY

DURING ONE OF MY BARDSTOWN GHOST TREKS,
a young tourist named Anna asked me if I had ever visited the
State Theater in Elizabethtown. Anna said, "I have a friend who
works there, and she knows about the little girl, Lucy, who haunts
the place. I've been there, and I have felt the little girl's presence
as well. If you get a chance you should go there and do a ghost
investigation."

After the ghost walk was finished, I asked Anna to give me
the name and number of her friend so I could call and make an
appointment. I made the call and explained to Dana Beth, the
Executive Director, why I was calling. She was gracious enough

to allow me to come and interview her and the employees while investigating for ghosts at the State Theater. Since Chuck and I arrived at the theater ahead of schedule, the first thing I did was go across the street so I could take a picture of the front of the theater with my new Nikon camera. The clear blue sky made a perfect backdrop for the Art Deco architecture of the theater that was popular back in the 1930s and 1940s. The facade had inlaid geometric designs on either side, which emphasized the grand vertical marquee tower in the center. The theater, which had its grand opening on June 11, 1942, had undergone recent renovation as part of Elizabethtown's Historic Downtown Renaissance program. It made me appreciate how important it was to preserve such a historic building that has been a valuable part in the social life of the community.

After a few shots with my camera, I noticed many students leaving out the side door of the theater, heading for six bright yellow school buses parked in the side parking lot of the theater. I found out later that the theater offers movies to students for educational purposes. This group had just watched *The Swiss Family Robinson* and afterward would return to school to explore all the survival techniques they observed in the movie. Later on in the week, another group of students would be watching *Gone with the Wind* and then discuss different events of the Civil War. The theater also provides concerts, live shows, dancing, and lectures.

I crossed the street to join Chuck, and we went inside the theater. A staff member was cleaning up the spilled popcorn and stopped her chores to take us to the upstairs office to meet Dana Beth, who told me the history of the theater and all about the recent renovations. Two other ladies joined us in the office and were anxious to get started with the ghost investigation. I started to write their names down in my notes, and they asked if they could remain anonymous. I agreed and I will refer to them through their titles as the building supervisor and the receptionist.

As I turned the interview questions to the subject of ghosts, Dana Beth told me that for more than five years there had been sightings of a little girl. She has received reports that the little girl had been seen by both staff and moviegoers. They refer to her as Lucy, and she has been seen running around the concession stand and more often playing in the balcony. Dana Beth recommended that we might want to start our investigation in the balcony since that is the area that seems most active.

While walking up the stairs to the balcony, I asked Dana Beth, "How did you arrive at the name Lucy?" "One day," Dana Beth said, "we had a psychic come visit the theater, and right away she tuned into the little girl's spirit. The psychic told us that the little girl's name was Lucy, and she was an African American. We later had another psychic come to the theater, and, without us telling her anything about Lucy, she picked up on a child named Lucinda. So we had the name validated twice. Anyway, the first psychic said that Lucy had tuberculosis and had died at Waverly Hills Sanatorium in Louisville. When she passed away, she stayed earthbound and came back to her hometown and the place that she enjoyed the most. When she was a little girl, the theater was one of her favorite places to come and watch movies. Since then we have called the little girl spirit Lucy."

I can still remember how much fun I had as a little girl when my mom would take me to the movies. We didn't have a television, so to see a movie on the big screen and get that yummy popcorn was the best treat ever. I could certainly understand the joy the little girl experienced at the movies and why she would want to return to that place of joy.

The receptionist said, "One evening, before closing, I was cleaning up the concession stand and looked up just in time to see a little girl run from one end of the counter to the other end and disappear into the wall on the other side of the room. For a moment I couldn't believe what had just happened until I realized I had seen Lucy. Maybe she was playing a game of hide and seek, but I was too busy cleaning up to play with her."

The building supervisor told me about another common sighting. "He is a tall male who appears in a dark shadow with red eyes, and I call him the Dark One," she said. I asked her, "Do you call him the Dark One because he appears as a dark shadow?" She answered, "No, he has a dark energy around him, and when he appears, several of us are affected by becoming nauseous. He makes you feel uneasy while he is around, as if he is wicked. I just want to leave when I see him." "Where do you see him the most?" I asked. "I've seen him in other places throughout the theater, but mostly I see him in the balcony. We all agree that the balcony is where we experience most of the sightings. We can even see the ghosts in the balcony when we are standing on the stage looking up," she said.

I asked the building supervisor, "Do you see the little girl and the Dark One together, or in the same area at the same time?" She said, "No. Lucy is afraid of the Dark One, and if he is spotted in the balcony, Lucy is usually seen in another part of the stage below. She has been seen with another spirit. He is a slender male, and they have been seen standing together. I know there are more spirits here; I just don't know how many." Chuck had left the group while I was interviewing to work with his pendulum to see if he could get some information about the ghosts. After I had finished the interview with the building supervisor, Chuck shared his dowsing results with us. We were surprised to hear that he had detected the presence of a slender African-American male named Orenthal. He is not the Dark One—he's the one who has been seen with Lucy. We made our way to the balcony for our investigation. When we got to the balcony I suddenly felt nauseated, as did two of the staff members. One of them told me that no theatergoers would sit in the top row in the balcony. She has observed visitors go to the top, but after a few minutes, changed their seats. I wondered if maybe they also got that creepy feeling I now felt.

The longer we stood in the balcony, the dizzier we all became. I thought it was interesting that we were all being physically affected in the same way. I had Chuck walk to the top row of seats and asked him to hold his hands out. He said, "Patti, my hands are tingling, so go ahead and take my picture." I asked the spirits if they were with us to please show themselves above Chuck's hand as I snap my camera. When I checked the viewer on my camera, there was a big orb hovering over his left hand. Taking into account all that was happening, this was a good sign that we were in the presence of a spirit or two.

The building supervisor said, "Maybe it is the Dark One that is present, since we are all being physically affected." I agreed and decided to use the Ovilus to see if we could get a response to the energy we were experiencing. When I turned on the Ovilus, it said, "Up there are people need help." The Ovilus is not programmed to speak in sentences, so I was pleased to hear this good validation from the Ovilus. After that statement, it said the number eight. Then it said, "They are all right." Then it said, "Help us." As I started up the stairs, the Ovilus said, "Be careful there." As I started to probe with other questions, the static started to crack, and the voice of the Ovilus started to get so weak I couldn't make out what was being said; then the battery died. This is a common occurrence if we are in an area with a lot of activity; it seems to drain the batteries.

I turned off the Ovilus and turned to someone who had just joined us in the balcony. She introduced herself as Sandra Sparks and told me that we had met at The Veil, a metaphysical convention in Atlanta. I vaguely remembered her since I met hundreds of people while I was there. She knew Dana Beth, and when she found out I was coming to the theater, she wanted to come see

A spirit orb was captured in the balcony when Patti asked the spirit to go to Chuck's left hand.

me and tell me the things that have happened to her when she has visited the theater.

I asked her, "What type of experiences have you had here?" She said, "Yesterday I came in early to see if I could pick up anything that I could report to you, but nothing happened. I walked into all the places that seem to have the most activity, but still I felt nothing. I sat down and took out my pen and paper for automatic writing. I asked my spirit guides to find someone for me to talk to. Within a few moments a male spirit came through, and I started to write quickly in complete sentences. He was a talker and told me that he had been a mail carrier and his name was Hyrum. He told me that he worked next door. Later that day I went to speak with the ladies at the museum next door about my experience with this ghost. They told me that back in the early 1900s, their building was a post office. I feel there are many different ghosts that come to this theater from different times and for different reasons."

I seem to get good results when I investigate theaters, especially if they have been around for many years. I think the belief in ghosts haunting theaters goes way back in time, even to Shakespeare's day. It was about that time when the theater managers began the custom of leaving a glowing candle (and years later, a lamp) lit in the theaters at night to keep the ghosts away. It was called a ghost light. They felt if there was a light left on the stage, the ghost would not appear.

I asked Sandra, "Do you feel anything here today?" Sandra answered, "Yes, as I entered the balcony, I saw a shadow person sitting in the top row. I guess he is the one you call the Dark One."

I looked over at the receptionist and asked her, "Can you tell me if you have had a ghostly experience while working here?" She answered, "One evening, while I was sitting in the projection room, a section of my hair on the left side started to rise up. I was alone at the time, but I still turned to see who was messing with me, and there was no one there. Again, another section of hair at the back of my head rose up and when I turned to see who it was, there was no one there. Then, for the third time a section of my hair on the right side raised up, and I jumped up and turned quickly, but there was nothing there to explain why I was being touched. I finally told it to stop, and strangely enough it stopped. It still freaks me out a bit, but it has never hurt me."

The receptionist added, "Also, during construction I was sitting in the gallery with Dana Beth, and all of a sudden we heard a crash out where the scaffolding was. It sounded like metal pipes had fallen and hit the floor. We jumped up and went to see what had happened, and there was no evidence that pipes had fallen. We couldn't find any explanation for what we had heard."

I turned to Dana Beth and asked her, "Do you have any experiences that you would like to share?" She said, "One day after leaving my office, I was going down the stairs and it felt like someone was holding on to one of my legs, making it hard for me to move forward down the stairs." I interrupted and said, "That sounds like an action a child would do. They love to wrap their arms around a grownup's legs. I remember when my son was small; he would hold on to my leg while I dragged him across the floor." She replied, "I'm not sure who it was. I just told them to stop, and they didn't bother me any more that day."

Dana Beth continued, "Another experience I had happened one evening just as I was about to go home. I was going to open the door to go into the seating area of the theater, and as I reached for the door handle, something came over me. Every hair on my body stood straight up, and an unknown fear rushed through me. I felt like something was warning me not to go into the room, so I withdrew my hand from the door. I had never felt anything like that before. I decided to heed my feelings and not go into the auditorium. I turned and quickly left the building."

My time with the staff was almost up so we gathered our equipment. I felt that the brief investigation was well worth our time and that the evidence came quickly. The State Theater is a great place to enjoy a movie and see a ghost all at the same time.

CHAPTER 30

Lone Oak House Museum
HOPKINSVILLE, CHRISTIAN COUNTY

IN THE 1980S, I picked up a book titled *The Edgar Cayce Remedies*. I didn't know who Edgar Cayce was until I read this book. I learned that Cayce was considered to be the greatest psychic of the twentieth century and was commonly referred to as the Sleeping Prophet. He got the title from his ability to put himself into a sleep state by lying down, closing his eyes, and folding his hands over his stomach. While in this state of meditation, he could ask many diverse questions and get an intelligent response. These responses became known as readings. They contain valuable insights in addressing problems, sicknesses, challenges, or relationships. Through these states

Cayce claimed to be walking and communicating with God. I began to read as much as I could about Cayce, and since then he has become one of my favorite psychics of all time, with my friend Chip Coffey coming in as a top contender for first place.

When I moved to Kentucky, one of the first places that I wanted to visit was Hopkinsville, where Cayce was born on March 18, 1877. He is also buried in the Riverside Cemetery north of town, where you will find a historical marker that describes Cayce as a psychic counselor and healer. I lived in Kentucky for fifteen years before I made the trip to Hopkinsville. I wanted to check out where Cayce lived and go to the Pennyroyal Area Museum to see his Bible and some artifacts of his on display.

When I visited Hopkinsville with Chuck and my dear friend Dotti Kult, I was charmed by all the ornate, historic architecture and color of the buildings that lined the streets. I could see that Hopkinsville was a true reflection of rural western Kentucky with its scenic vistas and friendly faces. The most friendly of these faces was Cheryl Cook, executive director of the visitor center. She greeted us with a smile that complimented her pretty face and short blond hair. I must say that of all the tourist centers that I have visited over many years, this one had to be the most friendly and most helpful.

The first thing I told Cheryl was that Chuck and I had a dear friend in Lexington with the same name as hers and that she was also a blond. Then I continued by changing the topic to Edgar Cayce and the museum. Cheryl looked at her watch and said, "I'm afraid you are too late for the museum. It closed at 4:30 this afternoon. Do you have any other interest that I might help you with?" I explained to Cheryl that I needed to find a story for a book I was writing and asked her if she knew of any haunted historical places that we might be able to get into before dark. Without hesitation, Cheryl told us about a place called Lone Oak House Museum. I could see her admiration for Jim Coursey as she explained how he had renovated this grande dame of a place, which is the city's first house museum. She thought this would make a perfect place for us to visit.

Cheryl's gracious service didn't stop there. She got out an address book and said to me, "Let me call Jim to see if he can meet with you before dark." Jim agreed to meet us at Lone Oak at 5:00 P.M. I thanked Cheryl and she suggested that while we were in town we might want to check out the Trail of Tears Park. It is one of the sites where the Cherokee people were forced to travel and camp during their removal to Indian Territory. We did drive to the park, but it was too late to walk the trail or visit the areas where they held camp to do an investigation. Because of all the sadness and fear, hardship, and death the Cherokee people suffered on their forced march, I thought there might be some evidence of ghosts and spirits along this path they call The Trail of Tears. I promised Chuck and Dotti that we would come back to this place for a thorough ghost investigation.

It was almost 5:00 so we headed towards 16th street at the corner of Clay. As we drove around the corner there sat a magnificent, antebellum home with four white columns adorning the entry. Built in 1835 by Judge Joseph Crockett, it stands as the oldest home in Hopkinsville. The house was built Transitional in style, between the Federal and Greek Revival periods. Lone Oak was built with six principal rooms in the main house and a separate kitchen. Due to renovations over the years, it now has eight rooms, a balcony, four square columns, a transverse hall, and several Federal and Greek Revival style mantles that have not been altered since it was built.

I called Jim on my cell phone to let him know we were there. My call went straight into voice mail. I told him we were out front and would wait for him to call me back. We got there about five minutes early, so I thought that maybe he had not arrived yet. I grabbed my camera and started to take pictures of the front of the house. I stepped back off the curb to include the arch and fence that protected the property. It was a cold, gray day, but that didn't affect the beauty of this well-preserved mansion. As I was taking pictures, I thought I saw movement on the second floor. This excited me, so I took several more pictures in hopes of capturing a face or something looking back at me from one of the windows. Then, as I walked up to the door to knock, I felt a male presence to the left of me. He was shy and didn't want to be noticed. I felt as if he were hiding. I knocked on the door, hoping that someone would be inside to let us in. No one came to the door, so I started to suspect that the figure I saw upstairs may have been that of a spirit. This was confirmed when I reviewed my pictures later and saw a faint female form in the window. I discovered later that it was the room of the woman who haunts Lone Oak.

I walked back to the car and called Jim again. The voice mail came on, and I left another message. I became a bit worried, knowing that Jim would not agree to meet us and then not show up. I walked around the outside of the fence, and I could see a car in the backyard. I put my hand on the gate to go in, and two guard dogs came running up to the fence, barking at the intrusion. I jumped back and spoke to them sweetly, and they calmed down as their tails began to wag. I probably could have walked into the yard, but I didn't want to take a chance.

By this time it had been about half an hour since we arrived. I called Jim one more time and still it went to voice mail. I was so disappointed that we had come so far and missed the opportunity to investigate this wonderful ancient site. The next day I called Jim and was able to reach him. He said that he didn't retrieve his messages until that day and was shocked that his phone went to voice mail instead of ringing. He said, "Patti, I was there, and while waiting for you, I continued working on a project that I had started before Cheryl called me to make the appointment. I got so busy that I didn't pay any attention to the time until about an hour after our appointment. I wondered why you didn't show up, since Cheryl said it was important that you get to come into the home." I told him that I walked around back, but I'd hesitated because of the dogs. Jim laughed and said, "They would have only licked you to death. They are such sweet animals. I wish you would have knocked on the door; I know I would have heard you." I answered, "I did knock on the front door—really hard—and when there was no one there, we left." Jim responded, "I'm so sorry and can't figure out why I didn't hear you. I was there and you were there—what a shame we missed each other."

I made an appointment with Jim to call him back in a couple of weeks to do an interview so I could find out about the hauntings he had witnessed. He assured me he had some interesting and unexplainable experiences.

During our interview I asked Jim, "Can you tell me how you came to own this house?" "I bought this house from the Winfree family in June of 2006," he said. "The lady who owned it was Nell Winfree. The house once belonged to Nell's aunt, Jemmie Courtney Hickman Thompson. When Jemmie died, she left the house to Nell. From its beginning in 1835, it has served the community in several ways. From the 1970s until the 1990s, it was a couple of different restaurants. Then it sat dormant for about fifteen years. Over the last few years, I've been restoring it and renovating it for improvements."

I consider Jim a modest man because during our interview he did not reveal to me his background. I ran across a site on the Internet that impressed me about Jim's work and his profession. Beginning on Wall Street in the mid-1960s, James B. Coursey (JBC) provided distinguished office design throughout corporate Manhattan for over thirty years. Among the recognizable residential credits in New York City, JBC has designed apartments for Sullivan & Cromwell's Mr. & Mrs. William Ward Foshay, Time Inc.'s Mr. & Mrs. Roy E. Larsen, Dyson Kissner Moran's Mr. & Mrs. Robert P. Dyson, Dr. Anne E. Dyson, CBS's Mr. & Mrs. Thomas H. Wyman, and American Airlines' Mr. & Mrs. Albert V. Casey.

My next question to Jim was, "How soon did you notice strange happenings once you moved into the house?" Jim replied, "The first thing I had to do was add the electrical. It had been vacant so long that there was no meter attached to the house. When the electricians came out to install the meter, I noticed that they had been working for several hours and still no electricity in the house. I asked the foreman if there was a problem, and he said that they had to change out the meter box for six different meters and none of them worked. The electricity was coming to the meter, but it was not going to the electrical panel box. When they left, I went through the house and started to turn on the lights, and some of them worked while others did not. After about three days, most of the electrical switches and outlets worked except for Jemmie's bedroom. There is still no power to the ceiling lights in her room."

"While the house was under renovation, did the workers have any experiences?" I asked. "Yes, they did. The guys used the library as a staging area to keep most of their tools and equipment. This door was always opened so they could easily walk in and out with their hands full and not worry about opening the door. One day, while cutting a piece of wood with a power saw, they heard a loud crying that sounded like a woman. They stopped the saw to listen, and the sound was gone. They started the saw again and heard a woman screaming. They stopped the saw and heard nothing. This time they looked over by the library, and the door was shut. They thought that was almost as strange as the screaming they heard because they never closed that door. About two days later, this same experience happened again, but they didn't have the saw on this time. They were working and heard a woman crying. When they listened, it came from the library room, and when they checked it, the door was closed again."

"Jim," I said, "I noticed that you have dogs, and was wondering if they have acted strangely while in the house?" "They have, indeed," Jim said. "When the dogs follow me upstairs, they will not go near Jemmie's bedroom. Over the last four years, I've had four dogs, not all at once, that have lived here, and every one of them would not go near her room. Once, I took one of them into the room and he started to whimper, and when I let him down, he ran out of her room and down the stairs to the kitchen. Once I came home and couldn't find one of the dogs. I called and searched all the rooms until I heard a bark that sounded like it came from the balcony. I unlocked the door and opened it to find my dog overjoyed at seeing me and getting off the cold balcony. I had not stepped out on that balcony in weeks, and since I live by myself, there was no explanation as to who put my dog out on the balcony."

"I guess by now I've figured out that Jemmie is the lady that haunts this place?" I asked. "Yes," Jim said. "She was one of the previous owners, and I feel that she must have locked the dog out because she does not approve of dogs being in her house. When I first moved into the house, I took the bedroom that once belonged to Jemmie. At night as I lay down to rest, I could sense a presence watching me. It felt female. Then I noticed that the dogs would not come into the room, so that made me suspicious that it might be haunted by Jemmie. I confirmed this suspicion when her tall, thin form appeared to me one night in the door-way to her bedroom as I lay almost asleep. I sat up in my bed and saw her pointing her finger at me, moving her hand back and forth. It was as if she was scolding me for being in her room. I knew then that I was going to have to change my bedroom to another room in the house. I went across the hall where the atmosphere was much better, and now I sleep without feeling she is watching me."

I told Jim that I thought I saw a figure pass by a room upstairs and asked him which one was Jemmie's room. He told me if I was facing the house, it was the windows to the left. I was thrilled when I went back to my pictures and found this faint figure of a woman looking out at me from the window on the left.

I asked Jim, "Has anyone else seen her in the window or had an experience with her." Jim didn't hesitate and said, "I've heard about numerous sightings of a woman in the window. A former neighbor and her son were walking past the house one afternoon, and as they looked up at the house saw a woman standing in her bedroom window. The mother asked her son what he saw, and he described a woman in a long gown looking down at them. It was the same description that the mother was witnessing at the same time. When it was a restaurant, the employees would claim to see a woman standing in the window on their way to work. Some of them reported encounters with an angry spirit lady while working upstairs. I have invited a few of the employees to come and see the improvements I have made on the place, and they refuse to come back. One of them told me that she was going down the stairs and was pushed. She grabbed the railing as she started to fall, and that saved her from having serious injuries. Another one told me that while she was upstairs folding linens, someone grabbed her by the hair and gave her a hard yank."

"Most of the attacks on women are those with blond or red hair," Jim said. really?" I asked. "I promise," he said. "A friend who worked at the bank brought one of her employees for a visit to the house. One woman was a blond and the other was a redhead. As they walked around the house, both of them were in awe of the decor and delighted to see how beautiful it was. When we got upstairs and I took them into Jemmie's bedroom, I felt her presence in my body telling me to get them out of there. She had become very angry that I had taken them into her bedroom."

I was sorry to hear those accounts because I'm a blond. I told Jim that I rarely meet anyone I don't like or who doesn't like me. I have been so blessed throughout my life to be loved by family, friends, students, members, the paranormal community, and celebrities. He laughed and said, "Well, she won't like you, no matter how well you are loved, if you are a blond."

In a flash it came to me why I didn't get to go inside the house when I first came. Jemmie did not want me there. I captured what I believe to be her spirit looking at me through her bedroom window, and when she saw my blond hair the trouble started. Jim was there but didn't hear his phone ring when I called him. He didn't hear me knock on the front door, and when the dogs started to bark a warning that a stranger was near, he didn't hear that either. I made several attempts to get into the house, but Jim did not hear any of them. I think that Jemmie did not want me in her house, and she was the one who kept me out. After explaining my thoughts to Jim, he agreed that it would make sense that she would be the one to keep me from coming into the house.

"I wonder why she seems to be so angry?" I said. "I heard that she and her husband had a troubled relationship," Jim said. "They never had children, but I don't know if that had anything to do with it. Maybe she was jealous of a woman who had blond hair."

"Are there different times of the year when she seems to be more active?" I asked. "Not really," Jim answered, "she is pretty consistent with her activity. Although I do remember what happened during one of my Christmas. I employ a gentleman, Phillip, who helps me with odd jobs, and I bought his six kids Christmas gifts that year. I brought them home, wrapped them, and placed them under the big Christmas tree. About three days before Christmas, Phillip came by to pick up the gifts. We entered the room to go to the Christmas tree and were surprised to find no presents under the tree. Phillip and I searched the house from top to bottom, but those gifts were not to be found. Phillip left empty-handed, and once he was gone, I marched upstairs and went into Jemmie's room. I stood there for a moment getting my thoughts together, and very firmly I said, 'Jemmie, I want you to put those gifts back under the tree. Phillip is a good man, and these gifts are for his children. I want them back under that tree right now!' Nothing happened until the next day. As I passed the Christmas tree that morning, I glanced over and was shocked to see all the gifts back under the tree. Just in time for Christmas."

"Maybe since she didn't have children, she wasn't happy that you bought gifts for someone else's children. And the final insult was putting them under the Christmas tree." Jim said, "I've never thought of that, but it would make sense."

"Do you think Jemmie is the only spirit in the house?" I asked. "When I walked up to the porch I got the feeling that there was a man there." Jim answered, "There might be another spirit here. I had a paranormal group come here several months ago, and it was interesting what they found. Two ladies went down into the basement, and when they came back up asked me a few questions. They wanted to know if the house was ever derelict, and I told them yes. They felt there was a man who broke into the house to live in the basement. He died down there, and they claim that his bones are somewhere in the floor of the basement. They also told me that Jemmie won't allow the male ghost to come upstairs into the inside of the house. She insists that he must stay downstairs." Even though I didn't get to go into Lone Oak, by listening to Jim's details, I feel like I have been there.

Jim seems to think that I might not ever get to come in—or if I do, he says it will be at my own risk. Since many of Jim's experiences of what appear to be paranormal activity have no possible explanations, I would suspect that Lone Oak might be haunted. I would conclude that the activity comes from a troubled female who dislikes other women, especially blonds and redheads, but loves and respects Jim for his talented renovation and design to her home.

Ghosthunting
Travel Guide

Visiting Haunted Sites

Central

Bobby Mackey's Music World   (859) 431-5588

44 Licking Pike, Wilder, KY 41071-2911
www.bobbymackey.com

Bobby boasts that the backbone of Bobby Mackey's Music World is the live
entertainment. Patrons agree as they keep coming back for more good music
and a great place to kick up their heels on the dance floor. For those interested
in the ghosts, check out the haunted basement. The tour includes the
catacombs beneath the infamous night club that is haunted by Johanna.

Open for music every Friday and Saturday, 9:30 P.M.–2:30 A.M. Doors open
at 7:30 P.M. Open for ghost tours every Friday and Saturday; call to schedule
a tour.

Boone Tavern   (859) 985-3700

100 Main Street North, Berea, KY 40403
www.boonetavernhotel.com

During the past century Boone Tavern has provided cozy lodging and fine dining
to many travelers. These features have contributed to the hotel's heritage of
hospitality. Boone Tavern has been visited by many notable guests, such as
Eleanor Roosevelt, Duncan Hines, Archbishop Desmond Tutu, Alex Haley,
Dalai Lama, Jesse Stuart, Robert Frost, and Geena Davis. Now you can be a
distinguished guest by staying at the Boone Tavern. Reserve your room today by
going to the Boone Tavern Web site.

Buffalo Trace Distillery   (502) 696-5926

113 Great Buffalo Trace, Frankfort, KY 40601
www.buffalotrace.com

Learn about the history of Buffalo Trace Distillery while taking tours through the
warehouse and bottling hall. See the spooky, old Riverside house that looks like
a perfect place to be haunted.

Open Monday–Friday, 9 A.M.–3 P.M; Saturday, 10 A.M.–2 P.M., year-round.

Colville Covered Bridge

KY 3118 over Hinkston Creek

When you visit the bridge make sure you bring your audio recorder. The ghosts love to speak and answer your questions. The bridge is located in Bourbon County, just on the other side of Paris, about 4 miles from Millersburg, Kentucky on State Road 3118, also known as Colville Road.

For all the geo-mapping folks: N38° 19476' W84° 12.194'

Hall Place Bed-and-Breakfast   (270) 651-3176

313 South Green Street, Glasgow, KY 42141
www.bbonline.com/ky/hallplace

You will find this antebellum house in the historic downtown district of Glasgow. The dwelling offers four spacious guest rooms with private baths. There is a wonderful parlor and library filled with relics and old books. There's a wonderful Victrola in the corner of the parlor that just might play a song on its own, if the ghosts are active enough. Check out the Web site for weekend specials.

The Haunted Hospital   (270) 239-4334

99 Hill View Drive, Scottsville, KY 42164
www.hauntedhospital.com

Sitting on top of a hill, the forlorn old hospital looks sad and depressed by the overgrown weeds and bushes that surround it. Even before it became deserted, it had ghostly activity reported in almost every station. Now it seems more sinister than ever, with its broken-out windows and barred doors.

Jailers Inn Bed-and-Breakfast   (502) 348-5551

111 West Stephen Foster Avenue, Bardstown, KY 40004-1415
www.jailersinn.com

The Jailers Inn Bed-and-Breakfast is a place to enjoy a bit of history and to "do time" in the old jail. Of course your time will be a short stay as you enjoy their Southern hospitality. They offer a full breakfast, private baths, and a complimentary tour through the historic jail. Please check the Web site for weekend specials.

Kentucky Theatre   (859) 231-6997

214 East Main Street, Lexington, KY 40507-1310
www.kentuckytheater.com

Shows are featured daily. Don't miss the age-old favorite *Rocky Horror Picture Show*. When you go to an event, look carefully in the shadows. You just might see a ghost. To get more information about the concerts and other events, go to the calendar on the Web site for show listings, time, and price.

Lock and Key Café   (502) 867-1972

201 East Main Street, Georgetown, KY 40324
www.lockandkeycafe.com

Not only does the Lock and Key's Café offer delicious, sandwiches, soups, salads, and baked dishes, it also has a boutique that offers beautiful handmade items from local arts and crafts.
  Open Monday–Friday, 7 A.M.–7 P.M.; Saturday and Sunday, 9 A.M.–6 P.M.; closed holidays.

Mammoth Cave National Park   (270) 758-2180

1 Mammoth Cave Parkway, Mammoth Cave, KY 42259
www.nps.gov/maca

There are fifteen different tours ranging from thirty minutes to four hours and traveling from three-quarters of a mile to four miles. A bit of trivia: Mammoth Cave is so long that if you took the second- and third-longest caves and joined them together, Mammoth Cave would still be the longest by almost one hundred miles. With so many trails to explore, it would not be surprising to see a shadowy figure from the past.

The Mansion at Griffin Gate Resort   (859) 231-5100

1800 Newtown Pike, Lexington, KY 40511-1330
www.mansionatgriffingate.com

The Mansion at Griffin Gate Resort provides wonderful cuisine in a pristine, historic Southern setting. This exquisite setting in all its beauty makes a perfect home for the ghosts that haunt this place. Open only for private parties. To book your event, call (859) 288-6142.

Maple Hill Manor Bed-and-Breakfast   (859) 336-3075

2941 Perryville Road, US 150 East, Springfield, KY 40069
www.maplehillmanor.com

Voted "Most Historic Charm in the US" and "Best B&B in Kentucky" and "Best Breakfast in the Southeast." You will find lots of amenities, which include a full country gourmet breakfast, homemade desserts and refreshments during the day with hot and cold beverages available. Check out the Web site for a variety of weekend specials.

Mud Meeting House and Cemetery   (859) 734-5985

Harrodsburg, KY 40330
www.harrodsburghistorical.org/html/hhs_oldmud.htm

Approximately two-and-one-half miles south of Harrodsburg on Route 127, then two miles west off Route 127. To find out more about the history of the Mud Meeting House, go to the Harrodsburg historical Web site.

Mullins Log Cabin   (859) 322-3082

305 Scaffold Lick Creek Road, Berry, KY 41003
www.mullinslogcabin.net

You get closer to nature at the Mullins Log Cabin. Judy Mullins offers workshops in basketweaving and herb picking if you want more to do. There's so much to enjoy while staying at the cabin, and telling ghost stories by the fireplace at night might conjure up a ghost or two. Call Judy for reservations.

The Old Talbott Tavern   (502) 348-3494

107 West Stephen Foster Avenue, Bardstown, KY 40004
www.talbotts.com

The Old Talbott Tavern has provided shelter and nourishment to Kentucky travelers since the late 1700s. It is said that the Tavern is the oldest western stagecoach stop in America. It continues to serve good home-cooked meals and furnish comfort and rest for the weary traveler.

Serving times: Monday–Friday, 11 A.M.–4 P.M. (lunch) and 4–8 P.M. (dinner); Saturday, 11 A.M.–4 P.M. (lunch) and 4–9 P.M. (dinner); Sunday brunch, 10 A.M.–2 P.M.

Perryville Battlefield State Historic Site   (859) 332-8631

1825 Battlefield Road, Perryville, KY 40468-0296
www.perryvillebattlefield.org

The museum at Perryville State Historic Site is a must-see for Civil War buffs. The history depicted on the walls of the museum is a learning experience for all. While walking on the battlefield, beware of the galloping ghost horse.

Open April 1–October 31; Monday–Saturday, 9 A.M.–5 P.M.; Sunday, 1–5 P.M. For winter hours call (859) 332-8631.

Planters' Row Golf Course Clubhouse   (859) 885-1254

2080 Lexington Road, Nicholasville, KY 40356
www.plantersrowgolflinks.com

Planters Row features 18 holes for a 56 par course. Doug Thornberry manages
the course. Who knows what ghosts you might see on the course or in the
clubhouse? To reserve a tee time, please phone or go to the Web site.

Rohs Opera House   (859) 234-9803

133 East Pike Street, Cynthiana KY 41031
www.rohsoperahouse.com/ghostwalk.shtml

The Rohs Opera House "rocks" literally, from the rocking sounds of the Classic
Country Band every Saturday night. The show is hosted by Carl Hollingsworth,
who sets the stage for what is about to happen. Audience reviews have been
fantastic. The fun continues at the Rohs Opera House with other events, movies,
and tours. Show up in September through October for one of the biggest hits of
the season, the Cynthiana Ghost Walk, which starts and ends at the opera house.
Please check out the Web site for what they have scheduled next.

Springhill Winery and Plantation Bed-and-Breakfast   (502) 252-9463

3205 Springfield Road, Bloomfield KY 40008
www.springhillwinery.com

Springhill, the stately and historic 1857 plantation, is a destination to discover
both the historic past and ghostly activity. After a delightful day, what better way
to end it than to have a glass of wine from the vineyard. Check out the Web site
for weekend packages and special events.

Tent Girl—Georgetown Cemetery   (502) 863-1173

710 South Broadway Street, Georgetown, KY 40324-1165
www.tentgirl.com

Todd Matthews continues to investigate the lost identities of the John and
Jane Does. When he learns about an anonymous corpse that is found on
the roadside, in the woods, in an alley, or floating in a river, his passion to
find out its identity is relentless. Todd is featured in a documentary called
Resurrection, which includes more details about the Tent Girl. He is also a
consultant for the TV show on the ABC Network called *The Forgotten,* staring
Christian Slater. If you need help finding a missing loved one, please call Todd at
(931) 397-3893.

For all you geo-mapping folks, here are the coordinates for the Georgetown Cemetery: N 38° 11.857 W 084° 33.657; 16S E 713581 N 4230553.

Thoroughbred Community Theater   (859) 846-9827

127 East Main Street, Midway, KY 40347
www.thoroughbredtheatre.com

The Thoroughbred Community Theater's motto is to entertain, enrich, and educate through the arts. The theater's doors are open to the public for special rental, to host particular events, to hold concerts, and for performances. Please check out the Web site for all current programs being offered.

The Waverly Hills Sanatorium   (502) 933-2142

4400 Paralee Lane, Louisville, KY 40272
www.therealwaverlyhills.com

By now everyone has heard of the infamous Waverly Hills. People from all over the world come to Waverly in hopes to see and interact with the ghosts. You can sign up for a two-hour tour, but if that is not enough time, you can opt to stay the night. There are half-night stays for four hours or a full-night stay for eight hours, the choice is yours. Check out the Web site for a listing of all the tours and special events.

White Hall Historic House   (859) 623-9178

500 White Hall Shrine Road, Richmond, KY 40475-9159
parks.ky.gov/findparks/histparks/wh

While visiting White Hall, you may think you have returned to the 1860s as you are surrounded by antiques and original furnishings that belonged to the Clay family. This feeling is reinforced by costumed tour guides that will tell tales of the wealthy and historical past of White Hall. In October, you can join a tour that will take you through the mansion and introduce you to the spirits of those that used to live there.

Open daily April 1–Labor Day, 9 A.M.–4 P.M.; after Labor Day–October 31, Wednesday–Sunday, 9 A.M.–4 P.M.; November 1–March 31, group reservations only.

East

Coals Miners' Museum   (606) 789-8540

78 Miller's Creek Road, Van Lear, KY 41265-0369
www.vanlear.org

Through the mountains and in the hollers are tales of ghosts and things that go bump in the night. That is certainly the case at the Coal Miners' Museum in the mountains of Van Lear. It's full of haints. Call for information on when the museum is open.

Jenny Wiley State Resort Park   (606) 889-1790

75 Theatre Court, Prestonsburg, KY 41653-9799
parks.ky.gov/findparks/resortparks/jw

A secluded and tranquil retreat surrounded by peaceful and beautiful mountains is what you'll find when you stay at Jenny Wiley Park. The land is filled with the rich history of settlers, Indians, and war. These make good elements in finding a haunted place to stay. You can make your reservations online or call.

Natural Bridge State Resort Park   (606) 663-0849

Highway 11, Slade KY 40376
parks.ky.gov/findparks/resortparks/nb

The Hemlock Lodge at the Natural Bridge State Park was built into the mountainside overlooking a beautiful lake. Every room has its own balcony from which you can see the lake. It is invigorating to sit out in the fresh air and hear the sounds of nature so close by. The history of the railroad ties in with some of the ghost stories that are told about the "Lady in Purple." You can book a room online or call.

Paramount Arts Center (formerly Paramount Theatre)   (606) 324-3175

1300 Winchester Avenue, Ashland, KY 41101
www.paramountartscenter.com

There's not too much out there that can beat an evening at the theater with family and friends. Pick a hit movie and off you go; don't forget your popcorn and soda. When you go to Paramount, you might get more than a good seat and a great show. If you are lucky, you might see Paramount Joe as he haunts the aisle and balcony of the old theater. Check out the show times and events online.

West

C.C. Cohen Restaurant & Bar   (270) 442-6391

103 Market House Square, Paducah, KY 42001
www.cccohen.com

Along with excellent food and a cozy ambience, C.C. Cohen also offers live
music. While you are there be sure to look up towards the upstairs railing. The
resident ghost, Stella, might be watching you, just as she has so many others.
  Open Monday–Thursday, 11 A.M.–8 P.M.; Friday and Saturday, 11 A.M.–10 P.M.;
closed Sunday.

Historic State Theater Complex   (270) 234-8258

209 West Dixie Highway, Elizabethtown, KY 42701
www.historicstatetheater.org

Do you remember what it was like to go to the movies when you were a kid? The
best part was to see how much popcorn and candy you could eat during the
show. The State Theater will wake up those memories as you enter the doors to
the auditorium, but don't let the nostalgia fool you. The theater has state-of-the-
art digital entertainment for big-screen enjoyment. Who knows, you might even
see Lucy while you are there. She is the cute little girl ghost that keeps the staff
on their toes. Check the Web site for showtimes and a listing of other events.

Lone Oak House Museum   (270) 707-7056

317 East 16th Street, Hopkinsville, KY 42240
www.visithopkinsville.com

As you walk up to the wrought iron fence, the ivy that grows around the arch
will reach out to touch you, a little reminder of what you might feel once you go
inside the very haunted Lone Oak. The mistress of the house is a domineering
specter that will not put up with any shenanigans. It would be wise to rethink
what you have in mind when you visit her home.
  To find out more about Lone Oak, go to the Web site and click on "Things
to Do," then click on "Historic Places" and scroll down to "Lone Oak House
Museum."
  Contact Jim Coursey. By appointment only.

Other Haunted Sites to Visit in Kentucky

Following are more haunted sites to visit within the state of Kentucky that are not covered elsewhere in this book.

Barbourville

Warfield Cemetery is haunted by a walking ghost who will follow you.

Bardstown

Chapeze House has a little boy ghost who likes to tease those who visit.

Wickland Mansion is haunted by a woman who walks the halls.

Rosemark Haven is haunted by laughing children.

Heaven Hill Distillery has ghosts who have been heard talking.

Pioneer Cemetery has many ghosts who have been seen near the headstones.

Oscar Getz Museum of Whiskey History is haunted by a little girl looking for her daddy.

Many ghosts reveal themselves on the Bardstown Ghost Trek.

Bloomfield

Maple Grove Cemetery has a ghost named Anna Beauchamp.

Bowling Green

Greenwood Mall is haunted by a man who died in a car.

Campbellsville

Spurlington Tunnel is cursed by a witch who haunts the tunnel.

Corbin

Cumberland Falls State Park is haunted by a bride who fell off a cliff.

Closplint

Child's Creek Bridge has a ghost who appears to drivers, causing them to crash.

Covington

Madison Theater is haunted by a murdered woman and her killer.

Cumberland

The ghost of giggling schoolchildren haunt the Benham School House Inn.

East Bernstadt

Alomont No. 9 Tunnel is haunted by a man who was murdered there.

Elsmere

Allendale Train Tunnel is haunted by a man who hanged himself in the tunnel.

Foster

Meldahl Dam is haunted by those who died accidentally and those who committed suicide.

Franklin

A Civil War ghost stalks the rooms of Octagon Hall.

Harrodsburg

Harrodsburg Spring Park is haunted by a dancing lady who died at a dance.

Hopkinsville

Bart's Grill and Racket Room Pub has ghosts who throw objects across the room.

Independence

The ghost of a man struck by a train haunts Twin Tunnels.

Jackson

Frozen Creek is haunted by those who died when swept away in the 1939 flood.

Combs Cemetery is haunted by dark shadows and strange noises.

Lake Barkley

Hawkins Cemetery is haunted by a slave who died near the cemetery.

Lexington

Highland Cemetery is loaded with ghosts.

Bell House has a man and a nude woman haunting the building.

Waveland State Historic Site is haunted by a former owner and slaves.

Gratz Park Inn is haunted by a little girl dressed in 1800s clothing.

Campbell House Inn is haunted by people who died there.

Hunt-Morgan House is haunted by nursemaid Aunt Betty.

Louisville

The DuPont Mansion is still inhabited by Albert DuPont, even though he has been dead for a long time.

The Seelbach Hilton is haunted by a bride who died after jumping out a window.

Louisville Theater is haunted by a noisy, former lighting technician.

Phoenix Hill Tavern is haunted by a ghost who moves things.

Speed Art Museum is haunted by a woman who used to live there.

Elmwood Mansion has had sightings of ghosts dressed in 1800s clothing.

Marion County

Baker Hollow Road Cemetery is haunted by ghosts of human and animal form.

Maysville

Hayswood Hospital—former patients haunt its halls.

Washington Opera House is haunted by Loretta, who died during a show. It was a really bad show.

Mt. Olivet

Blue Licks Battlefield State Park is haunted by Native Americans, settlers, and soldiers.

Mt. Sterling

The Patten-Everett House is filled with strange noises and apparitions.

Muhlenberg

Skipworth Cemetery is haunted by a Civil War soldier.

Murray

Bull Pen Steaks & Spirits has ghosts of patients from the days when it used to be a hospital.

Nicholasville

Camp Nelson is haunted by Civil War soldiers that have been seen on the walking tours.

Owensboro

Theatre Workshop was once a church and is haunted by a priest and his daughter, who both committed suicide.

Paducah

Oak Grove Cemetery is haunted by Della, who was murdered by her boyfriend there.

Paintsville

Old Town Cemetery is haunted by an old woman who protects the place.

West Point

Applegate Landing Bed-and-Breakfast is haunted by ghosts who throw things.

Winchester

Walmart is haunted by both a murder victim and a suicide victim.

ABOUT THE AUTHOR

PATTI STARR, Certified Ghost Hunter, is a ghost researcher, author, lecturer, consultant, dowser, and teacher with over thirty years of ghost investigation experience. Her first book, *Ghost Hunting in Kentucky and Beyond,* was published in 2002. Patti Starr is also the owner of Ghost Chasers International, Inc., and the Ghost Hunter Shop in Lexington, Kentucky, and she runs the Bardstown Ghost Trek. She taught ghosthunting courses at the Bluegrass Community and Technical College for seven years. Her Ghost Hunter Certification Home Study Course enrolls students from all over the world.

Patti's work has been documented in numerous newspapers and magazines including the *Atlanta Journal-Constitution,* the *Philadelphia Inquirer, Oracle 20/20, Ghost Magazine,* and *Southern Distinction.* She is also a frequent guest on television and radio programs, including A&E Airline and the Food Network's *The Best of Fright Food,* which was filmed at the haunted Old Talbott Tavern in Bardstown, Kentucky.

Haunted America Tours voted Patti one of the Top Ten Ghost Hunter Paranormal Investigators in America from 2007–2010. Patti also produces the annual ScareFest Horror and Paranormal Convention in Lexington, Kentucky, the largest of its kind in America.